Arab Women

Arab Women

Between Defiance and Restraint

EDITED BY SUHA SABBAGH

OLIVE
BRANCH
PRESS

An imprint of Interlink Publishing Group, Inc.
New York

First published in 1996 by

Olive Branch Press
An imprint of Interlink Publishing Group, Inc.
99 Seventh Avenue, Brooklyn, New York 11215

Copyright © Suha Sabbagh 1996

Library of Congress Cataloging-in-Publication Data

Arab women : between defiance and restraint / edited by Suha Sabbagh.
p. cm.
Includes bibliographical references and index.
1. Women — Arab countries — Social conditions. 2. Feminism — Arab
countries. 3. Muslim women — Arab countries. 4. Women in Islam —
Arab countries. I. Sabbagh, Suha.
HQ1170.A73 1996
305.42'0917'4927 — dc20

96-5136
CIP

Printed and bound in the United States of America
10 9 8 7 6 5 4 3 2 1

Contents

PART FOUR ■ Women and Education

PART FIVE ■ Women and the Civil War in Lebanon

PART SIX ■ Palestinian Feminism and Nationalism

PART SEVEN ■ Women in Political Islam

Contributors

Julinda Abu Nassr is the head of the Arab Women's Institute in Beirut, Lebanon. She writes extensively on women and development in the Arab world.

Taghreed Alqudsi-Ghabra teaches library and information science at the College of Graduate Studies, Kuwait University, Kuwait. She writes on women and children's literature in Kuwait.

Abla Amawi heads the Department of Publications at the Queen Noor al-Hussein Foundation in Amman, Jordan. She writes on gender issues and Islam.

Sheila Carapico teaches international relations at the University of Richmond, Virginia. She visits and writes on Yemen regularly.

Mounira Charrad teaches sociology at the University of California, San Diego. She writes on women's rights in the Maghreb.

Richard Curtiss is the editor of the *Washington Report on Middle East Affairs*. He writes on U.S.-Arab relations and has interviewed many personalities from the Arab world.

Fadwa El Guindi teaches anthropology at the University of Southern California and is a Fellow at the Center for Near Eastern Studies at UCLA. Her field of research includes Arab, Nubian, and Zapotec cultures and Arab-Americans. She has written extensively on women in the Islamic movement.

Nagat el-Sanabary teaches a course in women's studies at the University of California, Berkeley. She is a consultant on gender and education and writes on women and education in the Arab world.

Rita Giacaman teaches social health and women's studies at Bir Zeit University on the West Bank. She has written extensively on women and public health policy in Palestine.

Sarah Graham-Brown is the author of several books on women in the Arab world.

Yvonne Yazbeck Haddad is Professor of Islamic History at the University of Massachusetts in Amherst. She is the author of many books on Islam.

Samira Harfoush-Strickland is the director of the Middle East and North African Programs at the Educational Development Center in Washington,

D.C. She was previously on the faculty of King Saud University in Riyadh, Saudi Arabia.

Mervat Hatem teaches political science at Howard University in Washington, D.C. She writes on women and gender in Egyptian society.

Nadia Hijab is Regional Programme Officer with the United Nations Development Programme. She writes on women and development, including women in the workforce.

Suad Joseph teaches anthropology at the University of California, Davis. She has published extensively on sectarianism, gender, and the family in the Middle East.

Ramla Khalidi lives in London, where she works on human rights issues.

Eileen Kuttab is a member of the Women's Document Committee. She is a coordinator of the women's studies program at Bir Zeit University on the West Bank and head of the women's unit at Bisan Center in Ramallah.

Jean Makdisi teaches at Beirut University College and writes on the impact of the Lebanese civil war on the individual and society.

Hala Maksoud teaches Middle East history and politics at George Mason University, Virginia. She was the founder and president of the Arab Women's Union, Washington, D.C. She writes on politics in Lebanon.

Fatima Mernissi is a Moroccan sociologist who holds a research appointment at Morocco's Institut Universitaire de Recherche Scientifique. She is the author of numerous books on women in the Muslim world.

Samer Reno is a freelance writer and journalist whose articles have appeared in many Middle Eastern journals.

Suha Sabbagh currently teaches at Bir Zeit University on the West Bank. She was the director of the Institute for Arab Women's Studies in Washington, D.C.

Bouthaina Sha'aban is Professor of Literature at Damascus University and the author of several books on the plight of women in Middle Eastern countries.

Susan Slyomovics teaches comparative literature at Brown University. She is a contributing editor of *Middle East Report*.

Jane I. Smith teaches at the Hartford Seminary where she is the co-director of the MacDonald Center for the Study of Christian-Muslim Relations.

Joe Stork is the former editor of the *Middle East Report*, published in Washington, D.C.

Judith Tucker teaches history at Georgetown University and writes on women in Arab culture. She is the author of several books on women in Palestine and Egypt.

Introduction

The Debate on Arab Women

Suha Sabbagh

Through Western eyes, Arab women are perceived in popular culture as docile, male dominated, speechless, veiled, secluded, subdued, and unidentifiable beings. This situation has been slowly changing in academic studies, where the tendency was to focus on what one academic woman has defined as the "hot spots" of anthropological research on Arab women, the exaggerated emphasis on all that makes Arab women different: honor killings, female circumcision, cousin marriage, the harem, and the renewed obsession with the veil. The image that most Westerners have of Arab women is a stereotypical image that has little to do with the lives of real Arab women; no Arab woman I know recognizes herself in it.

Leila Ahmed, a professor of Women's Studies at Amherst College and a well-known intellectual who has written extensively on Arab women, has argued that, "American women 'know' that Muslim women are overwhelmingly oppressed without being able to define the specific content of that oppression." She goes on to say, "These are 'facts' manufactured in Western culture, by the same men who have also littered the culture with 'facts' about Western women and how inferior and irrational they are."[1] Leila Ahmed is making a reference here to the roots of the stereotype of Arab women in the visions of male Orientalists who visited the Arab world in the early nineteenth century. Indeed, for these early male travelers, the Orient *is* its women. There is a general consensus among Arab-American women in academia that there is something fundamentally wrong with the logic of those American writers who see no conflict between perpetrating these oppressive views of Arab women produced by the dominant male culture while simultaneously fighting against the dominant culture's biased perception of women in general. Marnia Lazreg, a university professor and writer, points out that feminism, which purports to insure liberation for Western women from an epistemological and political domination, must do the same for Third World women. All Arab women writing on this subject agree that the perception of Arab women as an "Otherness" must be revised. Like the internationally renowned Columbia University Professor Edward Said, Marnia Lazreg proposes that greater emphasis be placed on a humanistic tradition in the field of Arab studies, including Arab women's studies, which stresses the common experience of individuals, in this case women, in the East and West.[2]

THE CURRENT STEREOTYPE OF ARAB WOMEN

Popular novels about Arabs in the United States may be divided roughly into two categories. The first, representing by far the greater majority, consists of so-called thrillers: spy stories, international political intrigues, and war or nuclear disasters. The term "thriller" inscribed on the cover communicates to the reader a fast-moving plot coupled with scenes of sex and violence. The second category consists of what are described as "historical accounts," such as the bestselling novel *The Haj*, and similar adventure novels. The plots of both categories deal with three main topics: the Palestine Liberation Organization (PLO) within the context of the Arab-Israeli conflict; global atomic or financial disasters originating in the Middle East; and the excesses of Islamic fundamentalism. This last category accounts for a substantial amount of current literary offerings.[3] Occasionally, a mass market novel about Arab women is published, and almost invariably it purports to tell the whole story of Arab women's oppression and to remove the shroud of silence from what is generally considered as a wasted life, lived in total suffering and isolation.

Images of Arab women in Western novels are few and leave a comparatively less powerful impression than images of Arab men or the images of their European counterparts. Yet, it is important to note that here, as also in the abundant magazine and newspaper articles about Arab women, a certain reversal takes place over the early seductive, alluring, feminine stereotype. The contemporary stereotype casts Arab women as quintessential victims of the beastliness and backwardness of Arab men. Whereas in past stereotypes Arab women lived only for sensual pleasure and were condemned for their wantonness, Arab women's lives are now described as being devoid of the most simple pleasures or achievements. They are depicted as existing on the margins of society, victimized to such an extent that it defies credibility that such individuals could continue to wage the heroic daily battle that many Arab women in real life undertake to survive.

The stereotype of Arab women is presented even more forcefully in press and magazine accounts posing as facts. Whereas in the past the mere mention of Arab women evoked images of sensuality and physical pleasure, the same mention now evokes images of women as the victims of Islamic tradition, presented as an unmitigated fountain of oppression against women. This analysis suffers from the naiveté of perceiving another culture through the prism of Western consciousness. That women in different cultures might have a somewhat different agenda or methods of achieving their objectives is rarely considered. The titles of articles that purport to analyze the oppression of women under Islam stress sensationalism and show that when it comes to writing about Arab women stereotypical, distorted imaging has continued unabated since the early days of Orientalist writings. The press continues to show irresponsibility through its tantalizing titles and subtitles. A recent article, "Women of the Veil," written by two overnight American experts, Deborah Scroggins and Jean Shifrin, contains all the following sensational headings: "Women of the Veil: Islamic militants pushing women back to an age of official servitude"; "Male Honor Costs Women's Lives: It's dangerous to be born female in the Islamic world"; "A Mother's Glory Is Her Sons: Daughters barely count"; "Women: Political Islam brands them as inferior"; "Using Rape to Settle Scores: Women are pawns in men's game of revenge"; "Rapes Are Rarely Investigated"; "Honor and Shame: A life spent locked away."

None of these titles reflects the resistance or strength of Arab women or their cultural institutions; rather they reflect a greater degree of domination than that actually exercised by men over women within Muslim culture. The unmistakable interest in focusing on what I call a "culture of misery" serves only to establish the positional superiority of the writers and, through them by proxy, Western women. The result of such articles is not to form bonds of sisterhood across cultures, nor to depict the happy and unhappy realities of women's lives, nor to liberate Arab women, but rather to establish the superiority of Western women's lives and, through them, Western culture. This body of literature is clearly about establishing Western domination and not about liberating Muslim women.

During the Gulf crisis, misinterpretations of the role of Arab women reached their seasonal peak. The National Organization of Women (NOW) issued a statement by Molly Yard, president of NOW at that time, in which she stated that her organization was opposed to the involvement of the United States in the Gulf War because the countries of the Gulf (Saudi Arabia and Kuwait) practiced apartheid against their own women and denied them basic human rights. Her reasoning and that of her group maintained that since the U.S. is opposed to apartheid it must refuse to come to the aid of countries in which a social system evolved where men and women lead somewhat segregated lives. What is wrong with this statement is that it is ethnically insensitive and it also perpetrates a double standard in foreign policy. All countries of the world still practice some form of discrimination against women. But U.S. foreign relations are not always based on how its allies treat their female population, although one might wish that this were indeed the case. The NOW statement went on to say that the Arab world treats it women like "chattel." Well intentioned as it might have been, NOW's statement, which purports to support Arab women, denies Arab women recognition for the serious daily battles that each wages to meet her needs in the field of education, work, and family. Molly Yard and members of NOW met with members of the Arab-American community over the wording of this statement, and NOW has since shown greater sensitivity to the concerns of Arab women. My point is that if the largest women's organization in the U.S. can make such a mistake it is because the stereotypical view of Arab women as non-entities has permeated the culture to the point where even a women's group failed to see the misrepresentation of Arab women's reality.

Ancient cultures cannot always be judged by the same yardstick we employ to judge progress on women's issues in the industrialized world. The Arab world is the cradle of civilization; the oldest continually inhabited town in the world, of Jericho, is located in the West Bank. Early on, Arab culture evolved a social system in which the extended family offered each individual all the amenities that the state currently offers its citizens in the West. The similarity between these two systems prompted one intellectual to name the Arab world the "republic of cousins," since the patriarchal extended family system operated like a mini-republic.[4] Unemployment benefits, health insurance, and protection against all forms of disaster were and continue to be offered to women through the extended family. The social system that evolved in the Arab world based on segregation of the sexes maintained the extended family, which in turn protected the individual, including women. Before we ask women to give up this system we must insure their survival from a social and an economic standpoint.

Like a modern-day corporation, in order for the extended family to survive as a social unit men and women are assigned different roles.

For women these roles have come to be labeled as "traditional," referring generally to the fact that women's responsibilities are within the home while men are the providers. At one point Arab women's traditional lifestyle offered them a very viable system that protected them, and one can only hope that any new system that evolves will be equally viable for women. But, as with all ancient cultures, the deep historical and traditional roots have proved to be a mixed blessing for women today. The extended family is slowly breaking down under the impact of greater mobility and added financial pressures. Fathers or husbands can no longer protect women against premature entry into the workforce or unemployment or sweatshop exploitation as they once could in a less chaotic, more primitive society, while the state is ill-equipped to provide the same amenities to the individual as in Western countries.

When Western women ask the implied question, "Why can't Arab women be more like us?", they mean why can't Arab women be individuals as opposed to being part of an extended family system which is patriarchal and where the family is the social unit. Figuratively, the question also implies the recommendation that Arab women should jump out of an airplane without the benefit of a parachute. Worn down and ill-equipped to deal with women's growing needs, the extended family nevertheless remains the best insurance system around. In fact, many women have returned to the principles of Islam based on the traditional role of women within the family, because of their disappointments with the alternatives.

Until such time as the Arab world reaches a state of development that can offer women education, guaranteed employment, benefits, and all the protections offered by the state to its citizens in the West, women will have to accommodate as best they can to the patriarchal rules of the extended family, while fighting for a greater compliance with their needs. But even in a developed world, few Arab women will be willing to give up the social relations, warmth, and sense of security afforded by family ties, and the family will remain at the center of Arab society for a long time to come.

Also during the Gulf War, *Time* magazine published an article on Arab women in a special issue on women around the world, which carried the headline "Life Behind the Veil: Muhammad Boosted Women's Rights, But Today Islam Often Means Oppression." There are one billion Muslims in the world today and the Arabo-Islamic world alone exceeds two hundred million people living in 22 Arab countries. Each country interprets women's rights under Islam somewhat differently, and within each country social class is a determining factor in the way in which women's personal rights are treated. We must ask ourselves how is it possible to discuss women and Islam in such sweeping generalizations as this one-page article purports to do? Would it be possible to speak of women's rights in Christianity in the same way, without arousing scorn for such vulgar journalistic methods of reporting?

The attack on the Arab world under the guise of supporting the rights of women was also reflected during the Gulf War in many cartoons. One such cartoon by Jeff Macnelly for the *Chicago Tribune* juxtaposes two short Arab women covered with a black *abaya* (cloak) showing only their perplexed eyes with a tall and clearly emancipated American woman soldier dressed in fatigues and looking down on the two creatures. The caption underneath reads "When Mideast Meets Midwest."[5] Just because there is a stringent patriarchal system in the Arab world does not mean that women are docile non-entities. In fact, strong patriarchies often breed the opposite: strong women who work very hard to insure the compliance of the system with their needs. What such an attitude reflects is the ignorance about cultural differences on the part of Western writers, cartoonists, and readers of the press.

Letters to the editor often reflected the impact that these stereotypical views have on readers who have not been exposed to the Arab world. On August 23, 1991, the style section of the *Washington Post* published an article by Molly Moore and Amy Goldstein that included comments on the life of Saudi women. In a letter to the editor, Margaret M. Basheer, a Chevy Chase resident whose last name suggests a relation to the Arab world, commented on the responses of some of the *Post's* female readers through their letters to the editor regarding the above article. She wrote, "The letter writers were quick to describe the rules governing female conduct as 'humiliating,' 'disgusting' and 'sexist' while labeling the Saudi government as one 'that treats its women like cattle.'" She argues that difference should not be automatically understood in this culture as "wrong" or "disgusting." However, her most poignant argument was that undressing a woman's body for material exploitation, to sell commodities, is perhaps less forgivable than excessively covering a woman's body. She writes, "Perhaps it is better to veil a woman than to exploit her body across the pages of tasteless magazines." It is important to remember that all cultures are sensitized to internal forms of oppression, but it is essential not to judge other cultures through the norms of the culture that we live in. Viewed in this way, all cultures seem wanting and the exercise only serves to establish the positional superiority of the culture of the speaker rather than reveal any serious information about the culture described.

Championing Arab women's rights as a means of attacking Arab culture has not subsided very much since the Gulf War. A recent novel, *Princess: A True Story of Life Behind the Veil in Saudi Arabia,* by Jean Sasson, the purported autobiography of a Saudi princess which made the bestseller list, contains preposterous lies about Arab values. The book gives the impression that honor killings occur in the Arab world as often as afternoon teas and that families discuss together the premeditated killings of their daughters who get in the way of family honor. The back cover reads as follows: "Because she is a woman she is considered worthless — a slave to the whims of her male masters. She has watched her sisters, cousins, and friends ... brutally murdered for the slightest transgression, in accordance with cruel and ancient religious laws." There are no statistics about how many honor killings occur in the Arab world because they are an aberration, occurring far less often than random murders in this country. Yet, few critics seemed to mind this twist between fact and fantasy, and the magazines and papers which have formed a chorus hailing this book for revealing the truth about the Arabs include *People*, the *San Francisco Chronicle*, *Entertainment Weekly,* and *USA Today*.

Sandra Mackey, author of *The Saudis: Inside the Desert Kingdom*, who reviewed the book for the *Washington Post*, is critical of some of the misconceptions on which the book is based. She writes, "Statements such as 'Young men of Saudi Arabia could not afford to purchase a wife' make it sound as though women are bought. The 'bride price' is not a purchase price, but rather is the financial settlement bestowed on a woman at the time of her marriage; it remains solely her property whether the marriage survives or not." However, Mackey's contribution lies less in her analysis of *Princess* than with her description of a culture which has evolved in a way where the family, rather than the individual, is the social unit. She writes, "Before the mid-1920s, there was no government to control the desert tribes. An individual's only security lay with his family. A family's security in turn depended on its size and the alliances it could make with other kinship groups. Consequently, every member drew an assigned role in keeping the family strong. The men were the protectors, the women the producers of children. Marriages were arranged for the benefit of the family, not the happiness of the individual. The system worked because without it the individual could not survive." Mackey does not refute all the preposterous statements of Sasson, yet she provides a context in which to view the role of women in Saudi society, while explaining that change is being introduced in this system. Mackey continues, "A half-century later, a Saudi still regards the family as his or her guarantee of security. Major changes in the role of either sex within the family threaten the stability of the linchpin of the entire society. Yet the Saudi family has not escaped the pressures of change. The middle and upper classes are educating women if for no other reason than to make them better mothers. But this education is pushing women on beyond their traditional roles."

The status of women under Islam is probably one of the least understood subjects in the Western world. But the intentionality of the writer needs to be questioned when a nine-page article entitled "Tearing off the Veil" (*Vanity Fair,* August 1993) dedicates the first several pages to the issue of female circumcision — not an Islamic but a traditional African practice — while reserving to the last page conversations with Fatima Mernissi, the renowned Moroccan feminist who has published a large number of books and articles on women's roles and has a virtual army of women doing research for her on issues touching women's lives. Mernissi is mentioned only briefly in connection with her statements on Islam. One might ask, why doesn't the article discuss some achievements of women, such as the ambitious research projects that Mernissi heads and which deal with nearly every aspect of the role and image of women? Why are there virtually no positive articles in the popular press that describe how much Arab women are doing to change their world?

On the first page of the same *Vanity Fair* article a caption reads: "As the influence of Islamic fundamentalism spreads, more and more women are fleeing its repressive laws — compelling Western nations to deal with such cruel traditions as forced marriages, honor killings, and female circumcision." One 22-year-old Saudi woman requested asylum in Canada in April 1991 based on gender discrimination, and that is reason enough to ponder such a hypothetical question as "what to do if half of all Muslim women, who number roughly 500 million, were to seek refuge in the West?" The question is absurd because women living in Muslim culture do not see themselves in the same way as the authors of this article see them. Through non-formal education and through traditions, all cultures inculcate into the deepest recesses of every individual in young adulthood the role that he or she must perform in society. The result is that the individual becomes sensitized to the forms of oppression in which he or she lives, whether it is in Arab or Western culture. Consequently, the majority of women in the Arab world do not see their oppression as overwhelming and might indeed view women in other cultures as being less fortunate than themselves. Women do not regard their own world with the same degree of "disgust" and of "otherness" expressed toward them as the writers of this *Vanity Fair* article. In place of wasting space pondering an absurd question, why is it that there are not more articles about the problems that really concern Arab women, such as education, work, and problems involving personal rights. Why is it that we don't see articles written by Arab or Arab-American women who understand the issues instead of the overnight experts who don't even speak or understand the Arabic language.

Arab women appear less often in television soaps and thrillers than Arab men, yet their image does not fair much better. Also during the Gulf War, NBC aired a soap called *Santa Barbara*. The plot of this soap focused on two feuding Arab rulers: the Sheikh, ruler of Kabir, and the Pasha, ruler of Khareef. The Sheikh is interested in stealing the Pasha's oil, and toward this end he is about to invade Khareef. In the process the viewer is treated to a full range of misconceptions about Arabs in general and Arab women in particular. In his vibrant analysis of this soap, Jack Shaheen said, "The Pasha has 'sacred ways' that include 'a harem.' None of his wives pleases him. To him, Arab women are chattel. He believes 'the kind of love' Eden shares with Cruz (two Americans) is rarely seen in Khareef."[6] Shaheen implies that *Santa Barbara* posits love between men and women in the West on a higher plane than love between men and women in the Arab world. Love, which is a universal human trait, is here given a hierarchical structure, whereby love between the American couple is on a higher level while love in the Arab world belongs to a lower order.

In fact, perhaps no culture has produced as much poetry or prose on love as Arab culture has. Volumes of classical poetry on the same subject are still recited in schools and in poetry readings that constitute a national preoccupation in much of the Arab world that rivals the place occupied by football in this country. Nearly all songs heard daily on the radio in every Arab country are about the beauty of love or the longing for the beloved. In Arab culture, love between men and women is held in the highest esteem, although perhaps it is not practiced with the same degree of sexual freedom as it is currently in North America. When Spanish culture first came in contact with Arab culture in twelfth-century Spain, European culture adopted from Arab culture the courtly love tradition reflected in poetry. It is quite ironic, then, that in the twentieth-century, when the media has turned the world into a global village, that such important information is dropped.

Arabs are also portrayed in *Santa Barbara* as willing to exploit their wives sexually in order to achieve political goals and to increase their wealth. The Pasha orders his wife Shaila to sleep with Cruz in order to obtain from him a talisman. Anyone who knows Arab culture is aware of the strict sexual restrictions placed on the conduct of women. Even the story line of *Santa Barbara* emphasizes this point. How is it, then, that a husband is likely to make such a dumbfounding request from his wife in such a cultural context? One must assume that when it comes to defaming Arabs all contradictions are permissible. The plot, which posits Western women in a superior role, has some clear objectives which Jack Shaheen describes as follows: "*Santa Barbara* depicts Eden as the Ann Landers of Arabia. She teaches the Pasha to eliminate his 'prejudice' against women. Eden convinces the potentate to free Shaila, to grant other women freedom and equal rights."[7] Not only are Western women portrayed as superior to Arab women, but they are also their saviors. This kind of propaganda, which purports to support the rights of Arab women, is in fact intended to demonstrate the positional superiority of Western women and through them the Western world. It is a discourse that legitimizes racist views of the "Other" and anyone who subscribes to this view is missing the point of the feminist motto "sisterhood is global."

After the show had aired, NBC conceded that the *Santa Barbara* story line described Arabs in a negative way and offered an apology, following a letter of objection from the Arab-American Anti-Discrimination Committee (ADC). In its response to the ADC letter, NBC acknowledged "unfortunate and misleading stereotypical portrayals" and said the offending story line had ended. However, this did not erase the damage, since the negative image of Arab women was viewed by millions of viewers and no alternative image was provided to form an unlearning process. To date, there are no positive roles for Arab women to counteract the prevailing negative stereotypes on television.

Like women everywhere, Arab women lead full lives that include moments of happiness and a degree of struggle. In some Arab countries, women pursue their daily lives in especially difficult conditions. Whether in remote and spartan rural areas, in refugee camps, in shanty towns, or under stringent patriarchal institutions, all have had to develop strong and self-protective methods of coping with a heavy-handed patriarchal system. Their strengths, rather than their purported weaknesses, or their marginalization, should be recognized in articles that seek to define them or to champion their rights. Precisely because of their difficult living conditions they are forced to develop strong methods of resistance, fighting for their rights within a difficult environment. To a certain degree, the difference between Arab and Western women writing about Arab women is the difference between seeing the glass half full or half empty: Arab women focus on the strength and resistance shown by their illiterate and disenfranchised sisters, while Western reporters interpret such oppression as an unchallenged aspect of "Muslim" culture.

The stereotypes of Arab women will have disappeared on the day that the titles and the text of articles about Arab women stress their strength, their resistance, and the commonality of their experience with women in the West. Since the current stereotypes are inextricably bound to the power struggle between the West and the Arab world, Western women writing about Arab women need first to consciously disengage themselves from the dominant male discourse and ideology toward the Arab world.

WESTERN VISIONS OF THE HAREM

Today's stereotype of Arab women has its roots in the writings of the early European travelers to the Middle East — the Orientalists, as they are generally referred to. But this stereotype has undergone some drastic changes since then. The Orient, as the Arab world was called in Orientalist texts, was important to European writers of the late nineteenth century as a place where women languished sensually in the harem and where the veiling of women was a symbol of female sexuality. In brief, the Orient was for these writers the locale for polygamy, veiling, and unrestricted sexual license. And in this respect women were the focal point of this male vision of the East. Edward Said, who has analyzed Orientalist writings as a system of "knowledge" about Arabs, argues that the feminization of the Orient reflects the desired relationship of power sought over the Orient as woman. In this context the Orient-woman serves to establish Western domination in writings about the Arab as an "Other." In time, the same relation of domination came to be established in the outside world in the form of Western hegemony or colonization over most of the Arab world.[8] Several critics have analyzed the "feminization" of the Orient, where women lurking in harems seem almost to invite male domination. Yet the image of women in the Orientalist texts has not been fully researched to this date. Fedwa Malti-Douglas argues that, "The image of women languishing under the yoke of Islam titillates the Western observer and permits him to place himself in the superior position. Women and their role become a stick with which the West can beat the East."[9] An unfortunate modern-day consequence of employing the role of women to settle scores is that this discourse has exacerbated the situation for Arabs who decide to raise the issue of the rights of women in the Arab world. Malti-Douglas writes, "Since the debate on women's liberation is tied to Westernization in the modern Middle East, the subject of women's rights becomes enmeshed in a civilizational debate that often impacts on the lives of women in the Middle East." Arab women who seek greater rights are incorrectly accused of having internalized Western perceptions of the Arab world, when in fact gender and women's roles are issues that have occupied Arab male writers in every century.

The images of Arab women brought back to Europe by the Orientalists served to titillate the imagination of European men but were not founded on the real behavior or circumstances of Arab women. It is doubtful whether European male travelers had any contact with Arab women other than entertainers and prostitutes. It would not have been possible for a European male to enter the female quarters of a harem since the very formal Arab culture institutionalized the segregation of the sexes. And the word "harem," derived from *haram*, means "forbidden," and refers to that section of the house from which women excluded the men.[10] The "harem institution," which has come to mean in the West all the wives and concubines that one man can own, simply means in Arabic the womenfolk of one household. According to Said, European male travelers, barred from entering harems, resorted to scenes from the *Thousand and One Nights*, thus improvising on what harems might contain in terms of seduction and mystery to stimulate the interest of male readers back home.

Although some European women travelers were permitted access to the female quarters of the Arab house and published alternative views of the harem, yet it is the European male image of that harem that triumphed and made its way into the silent movies of the earlier part of this century. Some European female tourists, such as Lady Mary Wortley Montagu, wrote about life within the harem of a household in Constantinople. Other women travelers, following her example, attempted to revise the image of the harem as a place of sexual license, focusing instead on the activities of daily life and the beautiful costumes, jewelry, and extravagant meal preparations. Yet their narratives remained marginalized, and were unsuccessful in providing an unlearning process to the distortions of Oriental life offered by male writers.

How Should Western Women Concerned with Women's Issues Relate to Arab Women?

This question is raised time and again by Arab-American women, following their polite objections to an unduly rosy presentation of the

role of women in Muslim-Arab culture or, more often, following stri-
dent objections to a lecture fraught with Orientalist misconceptions.
For this dialectical opposition dominates all that can be publicly said
on this subject. So forceful are these currents that any speaker on
Arab women fears that her comments will be misinterpreted either as
belonging to the Arab-bashing camp (when stating critical views on
the role of Arab women) or, more often, as being complacent about
the conditions for Arab women, presenting them as totally satisfied
with their status. Arab women's reality, their daily battle against occupation, war, an entrenched and stringent patriarchal system, their
fight to control their bodies and their destiny, their small victories,
and their empowerment, all fall outside the parameters of this dialectical opposition. Furthermore, the current debate risks becoming a
contest in positioning the greater victimization of Arab women,
which, once established, automatically translates into a victory of the
West over a regressive and violent Arab East. Cultural biases toward
Arab women have forced Arab-American women like myself, who
hold feminist views, into a defensive position. Those of us who were
vocal in our critique of traditions that hamper the development of
women find it difficult to voice that same criticism in an atmosphere
that is charged with negative misconceptions about Arab women in
the context of the Islamic traditions. And, as most Arab-Americans
know, the negative images of Arabs have some serious repercussions:
they condone aggressive behavior toward Arabs both in this country
and in the Arab world.

Can one actually begin a serious debate on Arab women in this climate? Unless current conditions change, such a debate distorts the
experience of Arab women and risks becoming an oppressive rather
than a liberating tool. Before we can address women's liberation in
the Arab world we must liberate this culture's views about the Arab
"Other," especially women.

Leading feminists have often noted the need to both acknowledge
and overcome the differences facing women across the globe. Underlying those statements is the assumption that despite the different
forms that female oppression takes in different cultures, despite the
fact that the current historical reality has imposed on some women
the double burden of fighting both a war of liberation and a struggle
against patriarchy, despite all the different experiences of women
across cultures, women are still very much the same. Some American
and Arab feminists can, if they so choose, transcend the relations of
domination and subordination that characterize the relations between
their two worlds.

Listening to the "Other" is essential when speaking across cultures, even if that voice speaks from beneath a veil. Arab women's reasons for donning the *hijab* (head-dress) are as numerous as the different forms that it takes. In some cases the *hijab* has become a symbol of defiance against Western policies in the region, and cannot be considered outside this context. To see the *hijab*, in such cases, only as a sign of conformity to Islamic principles, and therefore a form of oppression of women, is to miss the point. If the relation between an ideological struggle and control over women's bodies is reminiscent of the plight of women in other cultures, this is because control over women's bodies often reflects an ideological battlefield. While Arab and Western women's agendas may differ, yet methods of control over women's bodies are often similar. All societies become sensitized to the oppressive measures within, and only a self-conscious and critical consciousness is capable of distancing itself in order to see oppression of women in global terms.

DIFFERENT SYSTEMS IMPACT ON WOMEN IN DIFFERENT WAYS

In the West most view discrimination against women as the product of a culture of male domination. In the Third World, women say their struggle cannot be considered outside the regional political and developmental issues. Women are doubly oppressed during periods of colonization: they are oppressed by the system as a whole, and each woman is also the first victim of her husband when the latter is under excessive stress due to political factors. Periods of decolonization are also the moment when Arab women emerge into the political sphere and assume leadership roles outside the home. All these factors must be taken into consideration in order not to impose a myopic view of the role and the oppression of women in the Arab world. To use the same yardstick by which we measure the role of Western women on Arab women will produce a myopic view of the latter; we will be measuring some aspects of male domination but not the essential ones, and such an analysis risks reducing the drama of women's emancipation to the domestic sphere.

Western feminism, of course, is grounded in Western thought, ideology, and values. Arab women's struggle is equally grounded in the religious, cultural, and political norms of the Arab world. According to some Arab women, it is a difficult if not impossible task to write about Islamic feminism in a climate that assumes the universal supremacy of Western feminism. They believe that Western feminism is rejected by Muslim women because it calls for a form of cultural conversion at a time when the West is seen by them to be a dominating force. For example, although Eastern women are donning the *hijab* in greater numbers, some believe that unlike their predecessors they are fighting to maintain their place in the workforce and to maintain leadership roles in their segregated communities.

Arab women are also challenging the Western feminist paradigm from a secular nationalist point of view. In a recent annual conference of the National Organization of Women (NOW), Hanan Mikhail Ashrawi was honored for her work as a spokeswoman of the Palestinian people at the Middle East peace negotiations; there she was heckled by a listener from the audience saying, "We came here to hear Arab women talk about their oppression by Arab men." Ashrawi was being asked, from this perspective, to address only her oppression as a female in Arab culture while blindfolding herself to the world of work. Such a view is a capitulation to the patriarchal traditionalist paradigm which requires that women stay away from the political sphere. Feminist theory can bring about retrogressive results if it is applied without consideration to the wide range of conditions of women in the Third World.

I argue that in many countries of the Arab world the fate of the women's movement and the nationalist movement are often intertwined. This was the case in the Egyptian struggle for national independence; in the Algerian struggle for independence this was also true, although there were many disappointments for women after the new state was formed. Currently, it is Palestinian women who are making strong strides in the process of rebuilding their country and it is to be hoped that the coming five years will not bring about the same fate faced by their Algerian counterparts.

THE OBJECTIVE OF THIS BOOK

I have lived in the United States much longer than I have lived in the Arab world and I consider the U.S. to be my home. But neither I nor any of my female Arab-American friends recognize ourselves in the images of Arab women propagated in the media blitz targeting Islam and Arabs, which have their roots in the Islamo-phobia of some early Orientalist writings. For a long period of my life I have fought for the rights of Arab women to lead full and emancipated lives. But I have come to the realization that the stereotypical views of Arab women perpetrated in this country constitute a worse injustice against Arab women than the patriarchal oppression that they must face in their own countries. The extended Arab family based on the patriarchal system at least once served to protect the individual, especially women. But popular stereotypes of Arab women only serve to establish the positional superiority of Western women, hardly a true expression of sisterhood.

This book is the work of a group of women writers who set out to write their articles because, like myself, they feel that it is their duty to reveal the misconceptions regarding the role of Arab women. Arab women have led serious struggles to develop their world and they cannot be dismissed either as "chattel" or as "cattle." At the same time, I never intended this book to be an apology for the denial of women's rights in certain areas of the Arab world. Mine is a double critical position: while I disagree with the images propagated in the West of Arab women as docile and male dominated entities, I also disagree with the notion that women have achieved their rights in the Arab world. Not a single country has given women full equality in every domain, and the Arab world lags far behind in this respect. Nevertheless, to use Arab women as a stick with which to beat the Arab world is dehumanizing first and foremost to the women of the Arab world. Such an attitude cannot be mistaken for feminism; rather, it is a degradation of this term.

The women who contributed to this book are from a number of Arab countries, all are professionals, and all seek to make a serious contribution in their respective fields. Most of the contributors received their education in Western institutions, and they understand the complexity of communicating across cultural borders. Many have survived wars in their countries and they speak about its impact on women from a personal as well as a professional standpoint. The majority are educators and understand the importance of providing an unlearning process to the images of Arab women inculcated in the deep recesses of most media viewers in this country. The politicians among them are aware that these images impact on the interaction between the United States and the Arab countries, and that these images can easily influence public opinion in the West. The book is intended for a young readership, because the young are more willing to experiment with new realities and new ideas, and perhaps some will be encouraged to travel to the Arab world and explore the role of women with less preconceived notions about the answers they are seeking.

Finally, the analysis in this book takes place through a dialectical relation between regional and international political conflicts on the one hand and the internal psychosocial dynamics of culture on the other. The intent is to analyze the conditions that affect the changing role of Arab women and the dynamics that influence their participation in national development, while avoiding the pitfalls of an analysis that views women in resistance struggles as mythic heroines placed beyond time, a metaphor that has in the past earned women very few rights after liberation. Given the constraints imposed by the use of a foreign language and paradigms developed through Western thought, the work as a whole attempts to define the experience of Arab women from a point of view which is internal to the culture, and which accurately portrays both their feminist and nationalist aspirations.

The objective of this collection of essays is to carve out a space for discourse on Arab women within the tradition of writing on Third World women that can accommodate both their nationalist and their feminist aspirations, without selectively stressing one form of victimization over the other.

Notes

1. Leila Ahmad, "Western Ethnocentrism and Perceptions of the Harem," *Feminist Studies* vol. 8, no. 3 (Fall 1982).

2. Marnia Lazreg, "Feminism and Difference: The Perils of Writing as a Woman on Women in Algeria," *Feminist Studies* vol. 14, no. 1 (Spring 1988).

3. For further information on the stereotype of the Arab, see Suha Sabbagh, *Sex, Lies and Stereotypes: Images of Arabs in American Popular Fiction,* ADC paper no. 23 (Washington, D.C., 1989).

4. Germaine Tillon, *The Republic of Cousins: Women's Oppression in Mediterranean Society* (London: Saqi Books, 1986).

5. Published in the *Washington Post,* September 8, 1990.

6. Television Commentary, *Christian Science Monitor,* September 17, 1990, p. 11.

7. Ibid.

8. Edward W. Said, *Orientalism* (New York: Pantheon Books, 1978) p. 5.

9. Fedwa Malti-Douglas, *Women's Body, Women's World: Gender and Discourse in Arabo-Islamic Writing* (Princeton: Princeton University Press, 1992).

10. Leila Ahmad, "Western Ethnocentrism."

PART ONE

Feminist Consciousness and Leadership Roles

1

Women and Politics in the Middle East

Sarah Graham-Brown[*]

In the 1990s, the Western image of the Middle Eastern woman's role in politics is contradictory. On the one hand, Hanan Ashrawi appears as the sophisticataed, articulate spokesperson for the Palestinian delegation to the peace talks; on the other, male politicians of the Islamic Salvation Front (FIS) in Algeria speak of women as subordinates who should not be allowed to work outside the home, let alone participate in politics.

This contradictory image reflects broad conflicts and debates in the Middle East over the nature of society and the status of women. These conflicts arise in part from the cumulative impact of a century of intense economic change and social dislocation, generating crises that have become particularly acute over the last decade. Women have been active political players throughout this process. They have not always won their battles, but there is no doubt that they have fought them.

As early as 1911, Egyptian writer Malek Hifni Nasif stood up in an all-male nationalist congress and demanded that women have the right to be educated to whatever level they desire. Eighty years later, women have much greater access to education and opportunities to work; in many Middle Eastern countries they have the vote, and some positive changes have been made in the laws governing family and personal status.

---

* This essay first appeared, in expanded form, as number 2 in the MERIP Special Publications series Women in the Middle East. Reprinted with the permission of MERIP/Middle East Report, 1500 Massachusetts Avenue, N.W. #119, Washington, D.C. 20005.

Yet there has been no simple, linear "progress." Economic changes have altered expectations and patterns of family life, but not always to women's advantage. The extent and impact of economic, social, and legal changes vary greatly according to social class, geographical location, and ethnic or national group. Today, struggles continue unabated over who should control women's lives, in the family and in the nation.

Most "secular nationalist" states — for example, Egypt, Syria, Iraq, and Algeria — initiated changes affecting women's opportunities for education, health care, and improved access to employment. In these states women's organizations have usually been closely linked with or part of the ruling political party structures. Their main role has been to mobilize women around the goals and tasks set by the party and the state. In Iraq, Suad Joseph argues, the official women's organization pursues goals set by the state; increasing women's participation in the workforce when, as during the Iran-Iraq war, there were labor shortages, or attempting to loosen the bonds of tribe and family in favor of loyalty to the state and the party.

Today there are more individual women's voices to be heard in the political and artistic arenas (art in the Middle East is seldom separate from politics). Yet collectively, women still have little political influence.

In contrast to Western feminist movements, political enfranchisement has not been a major priority of women's struggles in the Middle East. Turkey has been a partial exception to this rule, but it is notable that there are fewer women parliamentarians there today than there were after women first got the vote in 1934. In general, the struggle for democratic rights for men as well as women has yet to be won in most Middle Eastern countries. In this respect, access to the right to vote is less significant than the right to organize without state direction and heavy censorship of unwelcome opinions.

One of the few women's groups to make enfranchisement its main demand was the Egyptian group Bint al-Nil (Daughters of the Nile), led by Duriyya Shafiq, in the early 1950s. Women did gain the vote in Egypt under Nasser in 1956, and subsequently the right to stand for election. Until the introduction of a multi-party system in 1979, only a handful of women were elected or appointed to parliament. Three women have held ministerial posts, all in the Ministry of Social Affairs. Since 1979, more women have been elected or appointed under a quota system of women-only seats. Almost all of these women belong to the government party. Women in parliament have tended to pursue issues important to their party rather than to all women. The only occasion on which both independent opposition women and some women parliament members joined forces was to campaign against the rescinding of Egypt's liberalized personal status law at the beginning of the 1980s.

In the Gulf states, women do not have the vote. Women were not able to vote in Kuwaiti elections in late 1992, despite renewed demands from some Kuwaiti women, emphasizing the role which women played in the resistance to Iraqi occupation.

The increasing importance of Islamic politics has not always prevented women from exercising the vote. Some Islamist groups have recognized the potential of women's votes to boost their own support. For example, women have not been deprived of the vote in Iran under the Islamic Republic, despite the regime's highly misogynistic attitudes which have pushed women out of public life and limited employment in mixed work places.

In Algeria, the Front Islamique du Salut (Islamic Salvation Front, or FIS) has not objected to women voting but does want to limit their employment outside the home. This policy may be motivated as much by high levels of male unemployment as by a moral or religious objection to women working.

The vote alone does not guarantee improvements in the overall status of women. Women can easily become ballot fodder for political parties, whether Islamists or secular. Where they have little liberty in other respects, they can be pressured into voting for the candidates chosen by husbands or male relatives.

Socio-Economic Change

In urban societies, a large percentage of women now pass through the state education system and a larger proportion than in the past are employed outside the home, though the ratio is still low by international standards. Access to education, and housing shortages in many urban areas, have raised the average age of marriage. These changes, however, have not inevitably led to more freedom or autonomy for women. In some cases, patriarchal controls have grown even stricter as women's new roles have threatened to erode traditional male prerogatives.

Among rural peoples, perhaps the most socially disruptive factor has been land hunger, and the consequent mass migrations to cities and abroad. Turkey, Lebanon, Jordan, the Israeli-occupied West Bank and Gaza Strip, Egypt, and the countries of North Africa have all experienced very high levels of male migration. In regions experiencing war and civil conflict, families may also lose males through imprisonment, exile, or death.

Whatever the cause, prolonged absences of husbands and fathers undermine many of the assumptions of the "classic" patriarchal household, with its head as the provider. Women are left with day-to-day responsibility for the household, unless close male relatives are nearby. Does this increase women's autonomy and power? In practice the outcomes are often ambiguous. Women's responsibilities may increase, but in the long term their status may be unaltered, particularly after husbands or fathers return.

Male unemployment in both rural and urban areas may result in more stringent controls on women. When a man cannot fulfill his side of the "patriarchal bargain" by providing economically for the family, his response may be to assert lost authority through other means — physical violence, greater monitoring of women's behavior and dress, confining them to the home, or responding negatively to their demands for education and employment.

These socio-economic changes, and their ambiguous outcomes, form the context for ongoing debates on "the woman question." While the majority of women in the Middle East are not involved in formal organizations — women's groups, trade unions, or community associations — many resort to time-honored methods of resisting or evading male control, mostly with support from kin and neighborhood networks. These methods have long provided a sense of solidarity and strength to individual women, yet they also perpetuate the overall divisions of power and authority between men and women.

There has been a growing awareness among activist women in the Middle East that even where women enjoy greater legal rights (for example, in Turkey or Tunisia) or improved rights to education and employment (as in Egypt, Syria, and Iraq), male control of women's personal lives and sexual behavior is little changed. This is highly controversial terrain. Women who challenge the patriarchal norms of virginity at marriage, male sexual freedom compared with control of women's sexuality, and in some regions, genital mutilation, risk accusations of betraying their culture, their religion, and even their own sex. In the view of many, to challenge these norms is to accept Western norms of sexual and personal behavior. This is despite the fact that many women who are critical of their own culture are also critical of the West and its attitudes toward the Middle East.

While some of the ideas advanced on the politics of personal life may have been "seeded" from the West, their expression is shaped by the region's specific political and social context. Most women who regard themselves as feminists or campaigners for women's rights are acutely aware that they may be regarded as promoting ideas associated with cultures which have challenged and tried to subvert their own.

The Egyptian doctor and writer Nawal el-Saadawi argues that women suffer severe damage from sexual repression and oppression by men, and that this internalized repression is passed from one generation of women to another. While she is highly critical of genital mutilation, she points out that this practice is not in any sense Islamic and is prevalent in many non-Islamic cultures in Africa.

El-Saadawi regards Islam as having progressive potential for women, and objects to conservative interpretations which cast women only in subordinated roles. She also argues that the problems facing Middle Eastern women are compounded by the encroachments of Western cultural and economic imperialism. Women are therefore caught in the repressive social controls of their own society, while they are also prey to some of the worst aspects of Western "commodification" of women. She also points to the impact of poverty and social inequality in determining women's status and opportunities, and contends that the overall lack of democratic rights has limited women's ability to organize.

Moroccan sociologist Fatima Mernissi is an outspoken critic of sexual double standards. She is critical of the role of religion, particularly Islam, in creating or legitimizing patriarchal power. She has argued that Islam regards female sexuality as active, but therefore potent and dangerous — capable of disturbing the social order and male morality. She also asserts that "Arab identity" has been conceived in a way which regards change as threatening to the moral order, and thus impedes the development both of democracy and the emancipation of women.

A prominent trend in the 1980s was the revival or creation of Islamist movements in most countries of the region. These have gained numerous women adherents, including many college graduates. These groups are far from homogenous in their political stances, but have fairly similar views on the "woman question." They have played an influential role in setting the tone of debate in the 1980s, often putting their critics on the defensive. Their strong condemnations, not only of the encroachment of Western values in the Middle East but also of the "corruption of indigenous moral values" have challenged exponents of women's rights in a more secular tradition.

Most Islamist groups stress the importance of male authority and emphasize the primacy of women's roles as wife and mother. They stress sexual purity and control, and the danger of losing it, as a justification for increased male supervision of women and for insisting on self-control by women themselves.

Women activists working within Islamist groups clearly have to tread a fine line between political commitment and the pressure to prioritize the roles of wife and mother. The tension is not always resolved. For example, Zaynab al-Ghazali, who broke with the Egyptian Feminist Union to form the Muslim Women's Association, a group closely linked to the Muslim Brotherhood, left her first husband over her devotion to political work. She included a clause in the contract for her second marriage that she would be free to do political work. Nonetheless, she frequently emphasized that a woman's first duty is to her family.

While some feminists view Islam, and indeed all major monotheistic religions, as incompatible with women's emancipation or liberation, the majority of Middle Eastern women activists seek some kind of accommodation with religious belief, because of its critical role in indigenous culture. Some women have sought in the earliest days of Islam a model of women's role in society which differs from those which have evolved since. This has been a largely speculative and even polemical exercise, although historical research has helped to revise ideas about women's roles in Middle Eastern societies. Stereotypes of the passivity of Middle Eastern women in the face of oppression are embedded in most histories of the region written by Western and Middle Eastern male historians. Women and their concerns frequently have been omitted entirely from the historical record. Recently, efforts to recoup this hidden history of women have challenged these assumptions and revealed a far more complex picture. Recent historical work has shown that women often played active roles and on occasion resisted oppression, both by the state and by their own menfolk. Some studies also suggest a considerable difference between the way women actually behaved and the prescriptive writings on "proper" female behavior which have come down to us from religious scholars and other male writers. Some recent films, novels, and plays have also challenged this assumption that men monopolized history.

At the present time many Middle Eastern societies are going through particularly intense political and cultural identity crises, generally coupled with severe economic dislocation. In these circumstances, women's symbolic roles tend to take on added significance, and to the detriment of women themselves.

Women themselves, as activists and participants in political and social movements in the Middle East, continue to struggle as they negotiate and renegotiate the way they present themselves at home, in the workplace, and in the larger political arenas of the neighborhood and nation.

2

Women's Rights
in the Arab World

Ramla Khalidi and Judith Tucker[*]

For many Westerners, the issue of Arab women's rights and the broader problematic of gender and power in the region can be neatly summed up in one word: "Islam." The image of Islam as the fount of unmitigated oppression of women, as the foundation of a gender system that categorically denies women equal rights and subjugates them to men, recurs in the movies, magazines, and books of our popular culture as well as in much academic discourse.

The difficulties of coming to terms with the question of women and Islam are compounded by the tendency, both outside and within the Arab world, to label any pervasive social practice "Islamic." But the role of religion must be kept in perspective. One must confront the complexities, not only of the situation of women in the Arab world, but also of the historical and political forces that have shaped our own views of the issue.

In the nineteenth century and the first half of the twentieth century, colonial powers repeatedly used the issue of gender to advance their own agendas in the region. They argued that the oppression of women justified colonial intervention, and that the imperial project would elevate women to the standard of equality putatively present in northern Europe. The debatable sincerity and validity of these claims aside, the linking of gender issues to Western intervention and the invocation of Western standards to which all must aspire left a bitter legacy of mistrust.

---

[*] This article first appeared as the fourth in a series of special publications on Human Rights in the Middle East. Reprinted with the permission of MERIP/Middle East Report, 1500 Massachusetts Avenue, N.W. #119, Washington, D.C. 20005.

This legacy continues to cloud relations between women in the West and women in the Arab world. Many Westerners assume that the symbols and content of women's oppression are constant across cultures, that how women look and act has a similar meaning everywhere, and that the issues of women's liberation as they developed historically in the West should prove to be the same in the Arab world. In fact, the specifics of Western historical experiences and the particularities of gender oppression in the dominant culture incubated in northern Europe have shaped our basic beliefs about gender and our reading of the meaning of gender in other societies. Westerners tend to search out certain benchmark aspects of society as a measure of the position of women. Legal equity, reproductive freedom, and the opportunity to express and fulfill the individual self through work, through art, or through sexuality recur as central topics of feminist inquiry.

Are these the natural universals of feminism, the absolute measure of women's condition? Increasingly, people who study the Arab world are taking their cue from the concerns actually expressed by many women within the region. Legal reform, political participation, education and health, and employment: these have been among the principal concerns. They are part of the ongoing discussion in the Arab world today, and, as we shall see, there has been more progress on some issues than others.

WOMEN AND ISLAM

Islam has not been a neutral force in the definition of gender in the Arab world. Identifying a single essence or "spirit" of Islam, a single blueprint for gender roles, however, immediately proves difficult. Islam is not one thing, but rather is a set of beliefs and values that has evolved over time, in rhythm with changing historical conditions and the local customs and practices with which it came into contact.

The formal Islamic view of gender is based first upon the Quran, the uncontested bedrock of Islam, which does prescribe gender difference. Sura IV, for example, states that "Men are the protectors and providers (qawamun) of women." Nonetheless, many of the verses treating gender are vague and subject to varying interpretation. There is, for example, the famous injunction that women "cover their adornments," a phrase understood by some to legislate veiling for the good Muslim woman and by others as simply reasonably modest dress. The question of equality arises in a number of other places with equally mixed results. Before God, man and woman enjoy basic equality — they have the same religious duties and the same potential to receive divine reward or punishment. In certain very specific matters, however, femaleness suggests disability or at least inequality: women's legal testimony is worth one half that of men's, and their shares in the inheritance of relatives are usually fixed at one half of the corresponding male share. Still, as a basic document, the Quran contains material that can be used to support the arguments both of those who wish to argue for the equality of women under Islam as well as the arguments of those who wish to restrict women's rights.

Another set of Islamic texts which addresses the question of gender is the *hadith*, the collections of stories about the works and deeds of the Prophet Muhammad. Many of these stories contain material on relations between men and women and their relative positions in society which can be employed to construct a restrictive vision of the Islamic view of women. As some Arab women point out, however, the *hadith* were collected and compiled by male Muslim scholars nearly 200 years after the death of the Prophet. The process of selection and editing may well have favored those stories which tended to support the scholars' own restrictive views and deleted those stories which highlighted the active public role many feel women played in the early days of Islam. And just as the original compilation of the material was the result of historical development, the selection and reading of *hadith* can vary enormously with any subsequent interpreter's times and purposes.

A third and final point of reference for the formal Islamic view of gender is the *shari'a*, the body of Islamic law based primarily on the Quran and the *hadith*. Developed in the early centuries of Islam, the four main schools of Sunni Islam do agree on many of the rules and principles governing gender relations. Certain aspects of the *shari'a* institutionalize women's oppression and have been a central concern of women's movements in the Arab world. The ability of men to divorce their wives without cause and with little penalty, the vesting of ultimate child custody in the father and his family, and the permitting of polygyny are all stipulations of the *shari'a* still in force in most Arab countries.

On the other hand, some provisions of the *shari'a*, notably its affirmation of a woman's legal independence and absolute rights to her own property, compared very favorably with most legal codes in the West until very recently. Nor were women's rights to property and familial support, if needed, mere legal fiction: all studies we have of specific historical settings, including Aleppo in the eighteenth century, affirm that the Islamic courts upheld women's claims to property, to shares in inheritance, and to control of capital. Indeed, these legal rights enabled women to become important holders of urban real estate prior to the twentieth century in all Arab cities for which we have solid information.

The *shari'a* does, of course, make distinctions between men and women, assigning men the role of protectors of the family. The implications of these distinctions remain a source of concern for many Arab women today. For while the *shari'a* has been reformed to some degree in most Arab countries, women's personal lives are still governed by its underlying vision of gender difference.

The Quran, *hadith*, and *shari'a*, then, provide a textual basis for understanding the Islamic view of gender. Yet they are historically produced documents, subject to ongoing interpretation. There is no one orthodox version of gender in Islam, a reality well reflected in the debates of the Arab world today about what, exactly, Islam prescribes as far as gender difference is concerned.

Further complicating the discourse about gender in recent years has been the emergence of Islamist movements in the political scene of the region. Adherents of these movements generally have well developed ideas about the question of Islam and gender: they tend, on the whole, to subscribe to a restrictive view of women's activities. Critics of the movements focus on their overall conservative orientation, including their emphasis on distinct gender roles, and their insistence on female veiling, for example, as both a religious and a political statement. Other observers argue that these movements, by virtue of their inclusion of women as participants in religious classes and other movement-sanctioned gatherings, have the unintended consequence of bringing women more into public life. Where self-identified Islamic parties have come to power or won elections, such as in Sudan and Algeria, many Arab women are concerned about the new governments' agenda with regard to women. It remains to be seen whether and to what extent these political victories will roll back some of the hard-won achievements of Arab women.

CULTURE AND SOCIETY

Cultural traditions and social practices are often labeled — whether accurately or otherwise — as "Islamic." Yet many of the traditions and social constraints placed on women in the region apply as much to Christian as to Muslim women. The preservation of "honor," in the sense of being able to control a woman's sexual behavior by prohibiting sexual contact before marriage and limiting sexual activity thereafter to the marriage bed, is a widespread concern of families. There is nothing particularly Islamic about the weight placed upon premarital virginity and marital fidelity. We are dealing here with an aspect of a social system in which family alliance played and still plays a major role in political, economic, and social life: families needed to be able to arrange marriages and guarantee paternity in order for the system to operate. The fear of an independent female (or male) sexuality arises out of certain social conditions that have nothing to do with Islam as such, even if restrictions on women find justification, at least at the popular level, in Islam and are viewed as the direct consequence of an "Islamic social system" in the West.

For example, many Westerners see the practice of clitoridectomy in some parts of the Arab world as a highly explosive women's rights issue. Yet this is a practice specific to East Africa, with no prescription or sanction in Islamic scripture. In the Arab world, clitoridectomy is practiced in the region of the Red Sea, mostly in Sudan, Somalia, and Egypt. According to a study in Sudan in the early 1980s, most men and women there do think that the practice should continue, citing tradition (including the belief that it is religiously prescribed), physiological myths (including the belief that women are infertile until they undergo clitoridectomy, and sexual control (by making intercourse impossible or less pleasurable). There are obviously health problems, both physiological and psychological, associated with the practice. Arab women who have taken a stand against the practice argue that a tradition with such negative health consequences for women and children should not be preserved, and some go further to focus on the harm done to women's sexual fulfillment. The practice has indeed been the object of sporadic government attempts to ban it, and more sustained campaigns by indigenous women's groups. Many Arab women do argue, however, that Westerners present the problem in a sensationalist fashion that obscures the complex historical and social background of the practice and helps little in its eradication.

Four sets of issues that have been of greatest concern to Arab women in the modern period include their legal status, political rights, education and health-care, and employment opportunities. It is around these issues that most women and women's movements have organized, though there is no unanimity on the relative weight of these issues. Nor do most Arab women construe progress in these areas as movement toward a Western model.

PERSONAL STATUS

Reform of the *shari'a* has been a goal of feminist movements in the region since it was first raised by the Egyptian feminist movement at the turn of the century. Then the Egyptian Feminist Union, led by Huda Sha'rawi, lobbied for changes in the personal status laws, advocated restrictions on marriage age, polygyny, and divorce, and called for the reform of laws governing child custody and inheritance. Some relatively minor reforms have been forthcoming: a minimum marriage age, some conditions on a man's right to unilateral divorce, and limits on polygyny have been instituted in states as diverse as Egypt, Syria, Iraq, Tunisia, and Algeria. In general, however, reform has been piecemeal, based on the modernist Islamic framework designed to preserve the intent of the law and remove provisions not in keeping with the needs and demands of modern times.

Nor is the history of reform one of steady progress toward a liberalization of the *shari'a*. On the contrary, the 1980s were a decade of "re-Islamization" of the legal structure: in Egypt, Sudan, and Algeria, reaffirmations of the centrality and immutability of the *shari'a* have eroded the basis of legal reform. Thus, despite a great deal of attention paid to the issue of legal status, most Arab women still live under laws which allow the ex-husband broad powers of divorce, give custody of children to the father once they reach a certain age, permit polygyny, and assign women half the inheritance share of men.

POLITICAL RIGHTS

Arab women have been rather more successful in gaining formal political rights. In the early part of the century, despite active female participation in the various nationalist movements against foreign rule, the newly independent states of the region did not enfranchise women. Political reforms in the 1950s, 60s, and 70s, however, included the extension of the franchise to women in most Arab countries, with the notable exceptions of the Persian Gulf states (including Kuwait, Saudi Arabia, and the United Arab Emirates).

Women's voting rights have not translated, however, into female access to ruling circles. Women have, at best, only a token presence in elected parliaments (often as holders of seats designated for women) and very little representation at the ministerial level, with the exception of the occasional appointment to head up social affairs or education ministries. Egypt is often cited as a country in which women are most politically active, yet women in 1987 were only four percent of the deputies in parliament. It took until 1979 for the first woman to be appointed an ambassador, and there has never been a female judge. Only three women have held cabinet-level positions — in all cases that of minister of social affairs. Overall, the situation in the Arab world appears like that in the United States, where the female franchise likewise did not give women access to political power.

Women have played active roles in various mass-based political movements in the modern period, from the nationalist movements against colonial rule in Egypt and Algeria to the Sudanese Communist Party or the Palestinian resistance movement. In these settings, women have moved into the political arena as organizers and activists whose talents and skills are recognized and valued. In the process, many of the constraints on women's mobility and contact with unrelated men have been relaxed, and women certainly play a more active role in these movements than they do in establishment politics.

Still, the various nationalist and revolutionary movements have not actively confronted the issue of women's power and place in society. Arab women activists are divided on the question as to when and how the issue of gender should be raised, and they remain vulnerable to the charge that the interjection of women's issues can be divisive and harmful to nationalist or revolutionary goals. This problematic relationship between women's issues and nationalist aims is far more central a concern to Arab women than access to formal politics.

EDUCATION AND HEALTH

Since the turn of the century, most women's groups have stressed a third area, that of female education and health-care. With respect to education, the statistics show some striking results. All countries now have educational institutions open to females at all levels, and elementary education is mandatory for both sexes. At the secondary and higher levels, the percentage of young women in higher education has grown steadily over the last two decades and approaches 50 percent in many countries. In some countries, notably Saudi Arabia, higher education is sex-segregated, and the difficulties of providing a teaching staff prejudices female education. In most other countries, however, young women are admitted to the universities alongside men on the basis of merit-based examination systems.

One result has been, of course, a dramatic decline in, although not eradication of, female illiteracy, at least among the younger age groups. For the women of the upper and middle classes, professional education is also available, especially in the fields of education and health-care, in part because of a perceived need to train women to minister to members of their own sex. Women also pursue professional training in other fields: in Egypt, the numbers of women in engineering programs swelled in the 1970s and 1980s as male migration abroad opened new job opportunities at home. In some Gulf countries, where indigenous professional training for either men or women is a relatively new phenomenon, women have been able to enter medical programs, for example, in numbers equal to or greater than those of men.

Arab women's organizations have also concentrated on extending health-care to women and children. Since women are the primary health-care providers in the family, taking care of both young and aged, their own health and knowledge of simple cures are seen as crucial elements for a healthy society. Women organizers have augmented government services and proved invaluable in the delivery of services and information concerning basic health-care, prenatal care, and child-care. They also continue to struggle to provide information on family planning and birth control in environments where the access to such knowledge may be strictly controlled or forbidden.

Recent interest in grassroots preventative health-care and mother and child health (exemplified by "women in development" programs in most development agencies) have combined with an improved infrastructure to vastly improve both the quality of care and, consequently, the health of women and children. The infant mortality rate (deaths per one thousand live births) in Jordan, for example, dropped from 114 in 1965 to 43 in 1988, while life expectancy at birth increased from 52 to 68 years.

Despite these marked improvements, many women and children, particularly in rural areas and poor urban districts, remain without adequate health-care and lack the knowledge to treat simple illnesses. Thus, women's groups remain active in providing health-care to women and children not reached by government health services.

EMPLOYMENT

Seemingly more intractable problems arise in the field of employment, the fourth area of concern. For professional women, issues of equal pay and family support do not arise with much frequency. Women are close to a third of the technical-professional workforce in a number of countries, including Bahrain, Egypt, Kuwait, Lebanon, and Syria. On the whole, pay scales appear to be standard. Women also benefit from a greater official commitment, in most countries, to family support in the form of day-care facilities, allowances for dependents, and liberal leave policies for maternity and family crises.

Despite such considerable achievements, professional women appear vulnerable to changes in the regional economy. Slowing economic growth in the oil-producing states has reduced demands for professionals and led to underemployment in some countries such as Egypt. As the labor market has tightened, a "back-to-the-home" movement has surfaced in the popular press which portrays women as supplemental workers whose primary role should be that of wife and mother.

Non-professional women face a very different set of problems. Prior to the oil boom of the 1970s, women rarely worked in the industrial sector, where women come into contact with unrelated men in a situation of powerlessness and without the good salaries and prestige enjoyed by professional women. Women did not receive training for the more skilled industrial or agricultural jobs (despite the high level of their participation in agriculture) on the basis that they are not interested: they were severely disadvantaged in the wage-labor force as a consequence.

Male labor migration as a result of the oil boom did change this situation insofar as women began to enter factories as replacement labor in countries like Egypt and Jordan, but these higher levels of female participation may well prove transitory. The highest levels of female labor in production are found in Morocco and Tunisia, where women are employed in large numbers in the sweatshops that produce "traditional" crafts and in European-owned textile plants which take advantage of cheaper and more flexible female labor.

CONCLUSION

All these issues — legal reform, political participation, education and health, and employment — form part of an ongoing discussion in the Arab world today. Opinion is severely divided among both men and women on the issue of further reforming the *shari'a*. The issue of political participation is a complex one because of the limits of most formal political systems in the region; access to meaningful political power can only come, one suspects, through participation in mass-based movements that are contesting the status quo. A woman's right to education is probably the least heated issue at present. Access to education is close to equal, and the major obstacle for women lies in the reluctance of some families to invest time and money in the education of a female who may not "use" that education outside the home. Likewise, provision of adequate health-care is not a controversial issue, although family planning information is far from readily available. The issues of the differential treatment of male and female children, in terms of access to medical care and adequate nutrition, as well as the harm bred by domestic violence, however, have recently been finding their way onto the agenda of women's groups. These groups continue to work and lobby actively for improvements in the health-care delivery system and in the quality of care for women and children. In the area of female employment, equality is perhaps less of an issue than the vulnerability of female gains to dramatic shifts in the region's economy.

There is no one "Arab woman," of course, and no one set of issues that resonates equally across the multiplicity of Arab communities. These appear to be the concerns, however, that Arab women past and present have most frequently identified as critical to the future of the women of the region.

PART TWO

Women Political Leaders

3

Palestine's Hanan Mikhail Ashrawi: An Interview

Suha Sabbagh

Dr. Hanan Mikhail Ashrawi became known to the world through her numerous appearances on television as the spokeswoman of the Palestinian delegation to the peace process, which culminated in September 1993 in the signing of a peace agreement between Israel and the Palestine Liberation Organization. Before that, she was the head of the English Department at Bir Zeit University on the West Bank. In the following interview, which took place in the summer of 1995, she discusses her recently published book, *This Side of Peace*, her relation with her husband Emile, and her future plans.

In your book This Side of Peace, *you describe your husband Emile as a strong supporter of women's rights both in theory and in practice. What is your formula for obtaining this kind of unqualified support?*

Emile's narrative is a separate narrative. I can tell you that he was brought up in a very traditional home with several sisters who waited on him as is the custom in this part of the world. Before we got married I visited him and was surprised to hear his mother ask one of his sisters to get Emile his slippers as he was coming out of the shower. I had no brothers and was brought up in a home with four sisters. I was not used to the prerogatives of males in our culture. Around this time Emile began to reflect on the preferential treatment that he received as a male in our culture and was unhappy with it. It became important to him to try and change the definition of gender roles.

Emile and other male members of his family are musicians and their sensitivity to music and lyrics has also added to their interest in issues of equality. He is particularly sensitive to some of our progressive and radical male friends who say all the right things about women's equal status but see absolutely no relation between what they practice and what they preach. Consequently, their views become clichés and slogans. And he is, therefore, suspicious of men who preach too much on this subject. Emile has always maintained that the process of inequality has also robbed men of their ability to fully experience the pleasures of fatherhood. By excluding themselves from participating more fully in the process of bringing up their children, men have cheated themselves out of a very important and meaningful experience. Of course, housework can often be drudgery; it is uninteresting work and we have agreed that no one person alone should be saddled with it. It was really his decision to participate fully with raising the children and with the housework.

Your book is written from a feminine or a feminist point of view in that you always address the dailiness of life surrounding major political events and including your feelings as a mother about leaving your children to participate in the negotiations. However, in your political role it has been said that you do not address yourself enough to feminist issues. What is your reaction?

I don't describe myself as a feminist, but I am a person who believes in women's rights and it is very difficult to suppress this view. However, when I am asked about issues that have to do with negotiations I have to address this issue and not women's rights. Yet, the way in which I dealt with the issues in the period when I was the spokesperson for the Palestinian delegation was very much through a woman's approach: honest, straightforward, direct, and never self-serving. I sought the moral approach to politics; I addressed issues from the humanist point of view; and I always dealt with the truth.

There were times when as a speaker I was asked to forget about the occupation and to deal with women's oppression only. This is not possible, of course, and women who asked this of me had their own political agenda. We women do not live in a vacuum: how can I not speak of women who abort as a result of teargas? If women are to address only women's issues then our lives will be very short-sighted and narrow. This is reminiscent of arguments that were used against the emancipation of women out of the kitchen—it serves to oppress women rather than increase their participation in all walks of life. It is not in any way a liberating stance.

To what degree did Oslo perhaps open up the gates for Palestinians to appear on the theater of world events? And did this lead in any way to their inclusion in the space from which we were previously excluded?

I think that some individuals like Edward Said reclaimed this space strictly on the basis of individual excellence and merit. But there were also some political events in our history, the Sabra and Shatilla massacre in the Lebanon camps and the intifada, for example, that forced the Palestine question on the consciousness of the world. Oslo was a non-creative event. This includes the text of Chairman Arafat's speech in Washington, D.C. The language of that speech was a regressive language in that it did not mark any transformations in vision or consciousness. By "Oslo," I mean to include not only the negotiations which took place there but also the last several rounds of [Madrid-initiated] talks in Washington, D.C., which seemed to be going in circles. The agreement in Oslo is ambivalent; it could lead to statehood or to disaster; as such it reflects the imbalance in power between the two parties.

How would you describe the consciousness or the mood on the West Bank these days?

Some people feel extremely disappointed and let down and have lost their hope. Others feel a sense of disempowerment: this feeling is predominant among those who were the active agents in the past. Going to Madrid met with controversy but it was a willful act. After Madrid the feelings of let-down started to take over slowly. The long-term consequences could be very bad. Madrid built expectations and hopes, and when people have their hopes dashed and crushed they will react. We must roll up our sleeves and work with the current situation to change this sense of disempowerment. There is no savior and no scapegoat, as I have said many times before. We are responsible for reactivating these forces through institution building; addressing the legal aspects and forming mechanisms of election. We cannot be prisoners of the here and now. Many seem to confuse the transitional stage which consists of autonomy for Gaza and Jericho for the final stage. We should force ourselves to project our thoughts into the future. The moment you lose your will and become trapped in reality you lose your freedom. I always believed that we can transform the present and that the process is irreversible. I don't believe in relinquishing our voice. There will be a Palestinian state in the end, although there might have been a better way of going about it.

A number of factors have led to the current mood in the territories. Intifada fatigue is one; also, the return of the exiles whose consciousness has been formed through a totally different experience from those in the territories. Both have been trapped in their objective realities, and communication is sometimes difficult between the two. Israel is exercising undue power and defining the parameters of the discourse of both sides. The current leadership is being called upon to deliver within the framework of Israeli discourse. If security is the most urgent issue for Israel it becomes the issue that receives priority. Consequently, the current leadership have weakened themselves in the eyes of their own constituency.

In spite of all the factors delineated above I don't think that we should abandon hope. Such a situation can still lead to positive transformations. We have yet to use all the resources available to us. Part of the problem is that people here have been active agents and now they feel that they are disempowered.

Can you elaborate perhaps on the role that you foresee for the Palestinian Independent Commission for Citizens Rights which you headed until recently, and to what extent would you say that this organization has a special agenda for women?

The situation for women has not changed drastically since Oslo. I have said earlier that during the intifada women were often asked to relegate their struggle for equal rights to a secondary place, giving the national struggle priority so as to not to "weaken ourselves." The same rhetoric is now used again to exclude women from positions of power on all levels. The same argument of "we cannot fragment the struggle" is now a tool to keep women out of the economic arena and from obtaining future positions in new institutions. The role of the commission is to safeguard against any form of discrimination against women. We have established a system of accountability safeguarding the basic freedoms of all individuals, and the gender issue is a basic component. We review all complaints with an eye toward non-discrimination against women. We insure that there is no exclusion of women from all levels of positions. We conduct an investigation of all complaints filed by women and have obtained some positive results. This organization can be an avenue for dealing collectively with gender empowerment, since one of its objectives is to rectify the unequal status of women.

The legal department, in particular, and the field research department can best serve the interests of women. I feel, however, that above all the interests of women will be served if this institution is run in a democratic way and as such can serve as an example to other institutions. In other words, we have to practice democracy within this institution if we are to implement democratic principles in the community. We have to practice what we preach. And this is why I sought to remove myself from the position of General Commissioner, since our bylaws call for rotating the position among the board members each year. I, therefore, did not accept to run again this year.

4

Jordan's Leila Sharaf:
An Interview

Abla Amawi

The honorable Leila Sharaf, Jordanian member of the Senate and former minister of information, was interviewed by Dr. Abla Amawi, Jordanian writer and women in development expert currently associated with the Queen Noor al-Hussein Foundation for women in development. Sharaf was asked about her views and opinions regarding Jordanian women's role in the democratization process and about their role in the November 1993 elections. Jordanian women have achieved many basic political rights within the past twenty years. They have earned the right to vote in national elections since 1974 and in municipal elections since 1982.[1] In Jordan's new and pioneering experiment in free multi-party elections, women's votes are increasingly important in determining the final outcomes of elections. Women constituted about 50% of voters in the 1989 elections,[2] and twelve women candidates ran for elections, mostly in urban centers. However, the women candidates did not win. In the November 1993 elections, one woman, Tujan al-Faisal, won a seat in parliament.

In your opinion, why did Jordanian women candidates fail to be elected in the 1989 parliamentary elections?

Jordanian women have failed for several reasons. The 1989 elections were their first try as voters and candidates. Women's presence was perceived as strange by the Jordanian public. Jordanian women were not used to seeing other women as part of the political process. Men for the first time felt the equality in the political fields that was not there before and they had to share it with another party. Second, women were not part of any organization. They ran on personal bases and the elections required a huge organization structurally and procedurally. They were not trained for this and did not have the staff-power to carry that role. Third, since women gained the right to vote, society has started to move to the political conservative right. The effect of this move to the right on the women's issue is exemplified in the reaction to Tujan al-Faisal case: she is an outspoken political candidate who first ran in the 1987 elections and was sued for apostasy by certain fundamentalist Islamic groups in the court system; and she later lost the case. Although this act had affected women's candidacy negatively, nevertheless, Tujan al-Faisal was elected to parliament in 1993. Fourth, the women who ran for elections did not have a wide range of experience in society at large. Lastly, women have not joined the main leadership in political parties, they still did not have the political framework to promote them, and they had no structure in which they could prove their political value as leaders.

Much has been said of the role of women in the November 1993 elections. What is your opinion on this?

It did not change very much since the 1989 elections, although as stated earlier one woman, Tujan al-Faisal, did win this time. Women have barely started to organize within the political structure. Emerging political parties are still young. Since parties have to fight hard to prove themselves as a political force, I believe women's chances are slimmer than men's. Parties are simply not going to sacrifice possible seats in the legislative branch for women.

The establishment of political parties will help the role of women in the political arena if they join in big numbers. Parties provide a framework and a structure in which women can move and act. Parties can also promote women's capabilities, whereas now women are turning around in circles without a political structure to assist them. Within parties women's role is more structured. In a democratic system, disenfranchised groups like women will have the means to work together and to assemble without restrictions.

Many are calling for an imposition of a "quota" system which would guarantee a number of seats in the parliament for women. What do you think of this idea?

The quota system, currently being discussed, is intended to help women emerge and employ their capabilities in the legislative branch of society. Society still perceives women as lacking in experience and they have little confidence that if they send a woman to the legislative branch she will be able to participate and make a contribution. In the Jordanian National Consultative Council, women participated very successfully and on an equal basis with men; their performance was respected by their male colleagues and women contributed in a very mature way. But the times have changed; in this new democracy, people forgot the role played by women in the previous National Council and have started again to doubt women's capabilities. Although there are many prominent examples of women's success in the professional field where women are doctors, architects, lawyers, and so forth, society still does not readily accept a political role for women. On this subject the credit goes to the leadership of the country, which gave women the opportunity to participate in high posts. However, this benefited the individual women who were involved and not women as a group.

I believe in the quota system for the advancement of women, not in terms of assigned seats but in terms of a specific percentage of parliamentary seats. Many European countries have this system and it is a good system to introduce Jordanian women into the new political process. Since there are no provisions in the current electoral law for the quota, a new formulation should be found. However, the quota system should not become a permanent feature, it should not last for more than two or three rounds of elections. The purpose is mainly to prepare the society to accept women and by then we would have women who excelled and became known.

Men say that giving women a quota is an undemocratic method. What do you think?

I do not believe in disenfranchising a group of people. The argument used by men against a quota for women is the same argument used by men who say that a woman should not work since the husband works and is able to provide for his wife. Women in Jordan have been disenfranchised because of similar thinking. This situation should not continue in a pluralistic society.

What is your opinion of the suggestions that the present election law (which assigns parliamentary seats on ethnic and religious lines and which allows a person to cast more than one vote) should be changed?

The electoral law should be changed, but this requires a restudy of the whole law in view of our new circumstances. We are now a pluralistic, modern society that needs a new pluralistic, modern law. Everyone is currently generalizing and jumping to hasty conclusions. We must, however, consider the ethnic and religious composition of society along with women's issues. So we need a comprehensive, serious study of the electoral law.

What problems or issues do Jordanian women share with women in other developing countries, and what issues are particular to Jordanian women?

The role of women and its scope is a predicament for women around the world. Society's perception of women, of what a woman should be doing, is the same all over the world. This perception of women is changing in the Western world because the women's movement there is addressing this issue. In the Third World, poverty and lack of economic independence leaves its impact on the role of women and on women's behavior.

In a strange way the protection of the family in our part of the world is a plus and a minus for women. It is a plus since it provides a psychological support for women and it is a minus because it is over-powering, overwhelming and prevents women from assuming the de-cision-making role even regarding her own future. A situation which is shared by women in many developing countries. These are not spe-cific Jordanian women's issues. Rather, what Jordanian women face is the heritage of the entire region — a burden that all women share and carry on their shoulders. In Jordan, women are facing new difficulties because of the period that we are passing through, manifested in the rise or reintroduction of the conservative right-wing forces, which had ebbed from the 1950s to the mid 1970s and re-emerged with a politi-cal arm in the 1980s and 1990s.

Many Western societies judge the progress made by women in the socio-economic and political realms by "head counting," looking at how many women are found in executive positions, in the government, etc. Should this same standard be applied for determining the progress of Jordanian women, and particu-larly rural women, or can we look to other indices to reflect gains made here?

The existence of women in the executive branch or governmental structure is not the sole criterion by which we could measure the pro-gress of women in Jordan. The absence of a democratic life in Jordan and the special political, military, and historical circumstances that the country witnessed meant that women sought to excel in areas other than the political arena. Their absence from the political arena meant greater emphasis on participation in the labor force, a greater per-centage of professional women, an increase in the number of women in universities and in the different professional fields of specialization. It can also be measured in women's own development initiatives, which have become a characteristic of educated women in Jordan, whether in launching private businesses or in choosing their educational preferences. When these criteria are measured, Jordanian women rank quite high on the scale.

Can you evaluate your personal experience as one of only two women ever to become a minister and as one of two woman to sit in parliament?

Neither I nor any other woman alone can make a difference, especially in a conservative society in transition, like ours. In my personal experience as a minster of information, as a member in the National Consultative Council, and as a senator, I never felt any different from my male counterparts. They respected my presence and contributions to many issues like environment, communication, human rights, and foreign affairs, even more so than those of certain male members. However, whenever women's issues were raised, the male members used to revert to the old mentality of arguing that "yes, you are capable, but that does not mean other women are," which is stereotyping by exclusion. This thinking creates a vicious cycle, whereby it becomes impossible to point to examples of women who are active in the political process. No woman on her own will be able to effect any change with the present stereotyping of women. We need at least six or seven women in parliament who can influence legislation as well as the male mentality, which assumes that the political realm is a male domain and that women are invading it.

What has been the role played by women's organizations so far in advancing women's political role?

Women's organizations have been effective in causes other than those of advancing women's political participation. They have borne the burden of the parallel responsibility with the government for social development, care for the elderly, for orphans, for the handicapped, and for the poor. As for advancing women's political causes like suffrage, participation and voting, these same organizations are still finding their way. Moreover, many women who have participated in political parties, legal or underground, never made women's issues their cause. They adopted the causes of society as a whole. It is only now that women's organizations are realizing that society is passing them by and they did not take their own cause seriously.

Some argue that for the new democratization stage to succeed, organizations in civil society need to be strengthened. What has been the role of Jordanian women's non-governmental organizations (NGOs) in this regard?

There are three types of NGOs dealing with women issues in Jordan. The traditional NGOs function as charitable societies and deal with women's issues in a remote way, as a support charity organization, and make no connection between their work and changing the image of women in society.

The general Federation of Jordanian Women is supposed to be the politicizing organization of women. It has failed miserably because it has suffered from the same image problem which women themselves are experiencing and has not gone beyond the traditional role of women. They reinforced the traditional image of women and failed to politicize women or educate them in the effectiveness of their role and the impact of their political votes on changing society. The Federation, however, is only now trying to redirect its effort and its role.

Then there is the modern outlook toward women presented by organizations such as the Queen Alia Fund and the Noor al-Hussein Foundation (NHF). The NHF attacks the problem of women on economic and social levels by giving women the chance to own their own income-producing projects. They also help women change their image and role not only in society but also within themselves.

Deep down, most women have not been able to change the image implanted in their childhood regarding their female role or their image and its scope in society. So NHF is trying to help women in an indirect way by shaking off the old image of women and showing them the new images of themselves as producers and by teaching them new skills

The crisis of women in Jordan is the crisis of political organizations. In a few years, the women's movement, I believe, will achieve maturity and hopefully become a real women's movement. The individual woman in Jordan is extremely advanced in the sense that chances are open to her for educational and career advancement, but as a group Jordanian women still suffer from many obstructions.

How do you judge the previous (1989-1993) parliament's record on women's issues?

The parliament's record on women showed that the mentality in both houses of the parliament was conservative, not progressive. Unless there is a strong women's lobby outside the parliament that can lobby and threaten parliamentarians with their votes, women's issues will not be advanced. Women need a political force which can be very effective outside the parliament. In this regard, women have failed to form such a lobby.

Notes

1. This statistic was derived from UNICEF, *Situation Analysis of Jordanian Children and Women* (Internal Draft Report, 1992), p. 70.
2. See Kamel S. Abu Jaber and Schirin H. Fathi, "The 1989 Jordanian Parliamentary elections," *Orient*, 31 (1990), p. 80.

5

Women's Rights: An Affair of State for Tunisia

Richard H. Curtiss*

The total equality of women and men in civil rights, education, and employment is a legal reality that affects all aspects of life in Tunisia, and Dr. Nebiha Gueddana, secretary of state to the prime minister in charge of women's and family affairs, helps to keep enforcing it at the top of her government's list of priorities.

She is proud but not surprised that Tunisia's legislation puts the country in the forefront of the struggle for women's rights in the Arab world. Among Islamic countries, she acknowledges a Tunisian debt in the field only to Turkey, where the late President Kemal Ataturk adopted a civil code mandating equality of the sexes in the course of forcibly converting his country to a democratic secular state in the 1920s and 1930s.

Mrs. Gueddana's present concerns, however, do not center on the rights already guaranteed by Tunisian law, but rather on encouraging women to seize the opportunities mandated not only in the professions and industry, but in government and politics as well.

---

* Editor's Note: Dr. Nebiha Gueddana, former Tunisian secretary of state for women's and family affairs, is currently the head of the Department of Family Planning in Tunis. She was interviewed in Washington, D.C., in March 1993, by Richard Curtiss (editor of the *Washington Report on Middle East Affairs*) when Dr. Gueddana held her position as minister of women's affairs. During her career she undertook in her newly-created position in 1992 the task of establishing the proper structures to insure the implementation of the national policy for the promotion of women and family; the establishment of communication and information strategies to prevent any form of discrimination against women; and the promotion of women's programs, particularly in education, health, and professional training. Reprinted by permission.

An Early Reformer

The roots of Tunisia's pioneering role in women's affairs reach back to the beginning of the twentieth century. It was then that a modernizing Islamic reformer, Tahar Haddad, a scholar of Tunisia's Great Mosque of the Zitouna, called for freeing women from all of their traditional bonds. In a book entitled *Our Women in the Shari'a and Society*, published in 1930, he advocated formal education for women and maintained that over many years Islam had been distorted and misinterpreted to such an extent that women no longer were "aware of their duties in life and the legitimate advantages they could expect."

In the name of Islam, Tahar Haddad denounced such abuses against women as "repudiation," whereby a husband could divorce his wife without grounds or explanation, sending her back to her family or leaving her for another wife. Refuting assertions that such conduct is permissible for Muslims, the reformer declared: "Islam is innocent of the oft-made accusations that it is an obstacle in the way of progress. Rather it is the religion of progress par excellence, an endless source of progress. Our decadence is the consequence of the chimera with which we have filled our minds and the scandalous paralyzing customs within which we have locked ourselves."

Building upon the positive atmosphere created by Tahar Haddad's writing, Tunisian women advanced their own cause significantly by playing active roles in their country's struggle for independence, which broke into the open in 1938 when leaders of the Destour Party, and women who joined in a party demonstration, were arrested. On the eve of World War II, when Tunisians informally suspended their agitation for independence from France in order to support the allied cause, members of one group of women were arrested and jailed for 15 days for unfurling the party's banner in the presence of the visiting French president.

In 1950, as post-war agitation for independence resumed, the Neo-Destour Party founded its first official women's section. A large number of women members were arrested in subsequent demonstrations that preceded French withdrawal and the attainment of Tunisia's independence on March 20, 1956. One woman who was prominent in the women's movement then, and who remained so until her recent death at age 87, was Bchira Ben Mrad, who translated Tahar Haddad's teachings into action. As a result of local practices, the prominent role of women in the new nation's politics, and — perhaps most of all — the remarkable foresight demonstrated by Habib Bourguiba, leader of the Neo-Destour Party and Tunisia's first president, women benefited almost immediately from the country's independence.

Having negotiated that independence almost bloodlessly, less than five months later President Bourguiba, in a speech on August 13, 1956, paid special tribute to the role of women in the independence struggle and issued a Code of Personal Status (CPS) to "remove all injustices" and promulgate laws "rehabilitating women and conferring upon them their full rights."

From that time on, polygyny became a crime punishable by a fine and imprisonment, a unique development in the Arab world, but one patterned upon a similar prohibition previously adopted by Turkey. That and other reforms incorporated in the CPS were based upon the Islamic practice of *ijtihad*, making legal judgments reached by consensus by applying the underlying principles of Islamic jurisprudence to changing modern conditions.

Other reforms incorporated in the 1956 CPS abolished the right of a father to force his daughter to marry against her will. Now marriage in Tunisia can only take place with the consent of both parties to the marriage. The code also set the legal age for marriage of a man at 20, and for a woman at 17, with marriage below those ages permitted only with the consent of both parents and the decision of a judge. Also abolished was unilateral repudiation, the custom mentioned above whereby a husband could simply terminate his marriage without explanation.

Now in Tunisia either a husband or a wife can initiate divorce proceedings. A divorce can be granted only by a judge who has exhausted all efforts to reconcile the two parties. Women also may be granted a financial settlement under the law, and the government has set up a fund to pay the divorced husband's obligations to his former wife if he fails to do so himself. Also abolished was the custom of awarding custody of children from the age of seven in the case of boys and nine in the case of girls automatically to the father. Custody arrangements now are worked out on a case-by-case basis by the court as a part of civil divorce procedure.

Similarly, where previously widows did not automatically retain custody of their children, the CPS provides that a surviving parent, regardless of sex, remains the principal guardian of minor children. Inheritance laws, too, were overhauled to improve protection of the rights of women.

Tunisian law also protects the rights of women to decide whether or not to have an abortion. "The right to decide whether to give life and decide the number of children she would like to have is the essential element in woman's emancipation," says Nebiha Gueddana, who was a Sorbonne-educated medical doctor before entering government service.

The fact that Tunisian women are exercising their legally protected right to choose is manifested by the reduction in the size of the average Tunisian family from eight persons (including the parents) at mid-century to 4.5 persons at present. This means Tunisia has virtually stabilized its population growth, another pioneering development in the Arab world.

The change from tradition to the Code of Personal Status has shattered some other stereotypes. Formerly a woman was treated by the law as a minor until two years after her marriage. Now, under Tunisian law, men and women alike gain full adult rights at age 20. After that, men and women have exactly the same rights to vote, enter into contracts, and buy and sell property and goods.

Penal law also applies equally to men and women. The penal code, as amended on March 8, 1968, stipulates that adultery is a crime and lays down equal sanctions for a wife or husband judged guilty of adultery. These are up to five years imprisonment and a fine of 500 Tunisian dinars, roughly equivalent to U.S. $500.

Penalties for rape also have become increasingly severe. A March 1985 law allows the death penalty in cases of rape where violence and armed threat were used, or where the victim is under 10 years old. The penalty for all other kinds of rape is imprisonment and hard labor.

Another inequity was ended very recently when Tunisian women married to foreigners were granted permission to pass on Tunisian nationality to their children, just as can Tunisian men.

In the workplace, women also can serve in any government, political, or party capacity, and are guaranteed the same rights to work as men. At present, Dr. Gueddana is concentrating her efforts in this field.

She points out that women already are serving in all professions and industries, even in some jobs traditionally reserved for men such as airline pilots, judgeships, and uniformed police and military positions. Although women now occupy some 28 percent of civil service positions, the secretary of state for women's and family affairs would like to see more women in public office. She feels that only when women hold a significant share of political power will everyone feel certain that the progress of Tunisian women is irreversible.

At present, fewer that five percent of members of the national Chamber of Deputies are women. On the municipal councils, however, which are training grounds for future national parliament members, participation of women had risen from less than two percent in 1959 to some 14 percent in 1990.

In Tunisia and, in fact, throughout the Arab world, a high percentage of medical doctors are women, like Dr. Gueddana, a pediatrician.

Her 1981 medical dissertation at the University of Paris was on the *Immune System of the Underweight Newborn*. Subsequently she earned her certificate of specialization in pediatrics from the Université Réné Descartes in Paris and an asistanceship diploma from the University of Tunis Medical School.

While practicing medicine at women's care centers in working-class neighborhoods in Tunis, she continued her research and writing. Her published study on *The Tunisian Adolescent, Health and Environment* earned an award from the Paris-based International Children's Center. Another publication in French, *Un Enfant et Deux Tunisies,* analyzing causes of infant mortality in Tunisia, won an award from the Maghreb Societies of Medicine and Tunisian President Zein El Abidine Ben Ali's award for medicine in July 1990.

Although she is the mother of two boys, now aged 17 and 14, and a girl, aged 10, her husband, also a medical doctor whom she met at the University of Tunis, always has supported her increasing role in women's organizations and in the Democratic Constitutional Rally, Tunisia's incumbent political party. Initially she served as secretary of state to the minister of social affairs from 1989 to 1991, and then as secretary of state to the minister of social affairs in charge of social welfare from 1991 to 1992. Her present appointment was made by President Ben Ali in August 1992, emphasizing his own strong personal dedication to women's rights.

Dr. Gueddana devotes much of her time to strengthening Tunisian women's organizations, which have grown from one, the Girl Scouts, in 1947, to a network of diverse women's groups capable of wielding real political power. In her determination to further insure the irreversibility of women's gains in Tunisia, she is completely in tune with the president.

Not long after assuming office, he stated on March 31, 1989: "On more than one occasion, we have reaffirmed our commitment to defending women's rights and gains. We will devote ourselves to firmly entrenching the latter and to sanctioning them. Better still, we will work to expand them in order to guarantee women an effective role in our struggle for progress."

Since then, Secretary of State Gueddana points out, the president has matched his words with deeds. Today, in her opinion, the remarkable combination of laws and social achievements that has made Tunisia a model of true equality for all citizens constitutes a strong and irreversible foundation for Tunisia's continued economic, social, and political evolution.

PART THREE

Women and Work

6

Women and Work in the Arab World

Nadia Hijab*

When a labor force participation survey in Syria asked men whether their wives worked, a large proportion replied that they did not. But when the question was rephrased as, "If your wife did not assist you in your work, would you be forced to hire a replacement for her?" the overwhelming majority answered yes.[1]

Research on women in developing counties since the 1970s has uncovered a vast army of "invisible women" whose work may neither be reflected in national statistics nor compensated in monetary terms, yet who work, on average, longer hours than men. Most of these "invisible" women work in agriculture or other family-run businesses, in the domestic economy, and elsewhere in the informal sector. The consequences of invisibility are serious: if these women are not even recognized as workers, they are certainly not given access to the training, credit, and technology of modernizing society.

Of all the world's regions, women in the Arab world perhaps suffer from the worst case of invisibility.[2] Even as recently as 1990, figures of women's recorded participation were below 10 percent of the total labor force in seven Arab countries. As in other parts of the world, however, statistics do not always reflect reality. In India, for example, when the International Labor Organization's (ILO) revised definition of economic activity was applied, initial estimates that only 13 percent of all women were economically active had to be revised upwards to 88 percent.[3] Similarly, in Egypt, where 1990 figures show women com-

* This essay was first published in *Middle East Report,* November-December 1991. Reprinted with the permission of MERIP/Middle East Report, 1500 Massachusetts Avenue, #119, Washington, D.C. 20005.

prising 11 percent of the total labor force, samples of rural households in Lower Egypt revealed that half the wives plowed and leveled the land, and between 55 and 70 percent were involved in agricultural production. In upper Egypt between 34 and 41 percent were involved in agricultural production and 75 percent were engaged in animal husbandry.[4] If one expands the definition of economic activity, as the ILO has done, to include rural Egyptian women's very arduous home-

Arab Women in the Labor Force, 1990

	Pop. in millions (1991)	Labor force as % of pop.	Women as % of labor force
Algeria	25.6	24	4
Bahrain	0.5	27	10
Egypt	53.6	28	11
Iraq	18.7	24	6
Jordan	4.1	23	10
Kuwait	2.1	39	14
Lebanon	2.8	30	27
Libya	4.7	24	9
Mauritania	2.1	33	22
Morocco	25.7	31	20
Oman	1.6	28	8
Qatar	0.4	42	7
Saudi Arabia	15.4	29	7
Somalia	8.9	29	39
Sudan	25.9	35	29
Syria	12.8	26	15
Tunisia	8.2	30	13
UAE	1.6	50	6
Yemen	12.1	25	13

Source: UNDP Human Development Report, Oxford University Press, 1993.

based work, the figures would be much higher. Faced with mounting evidence that women's economic activity is not well-reported, data collectors have begun to revise their approach.

Yet the figures reported from the Arab region are so low compared to other regions that we must ask whether women in this region face specific constraints over and above the ones that women face worldwide. The 1993 *Human Development Report* of the UN Development Program (UNDP) shows that, on average, women account for 29 percent of the labor force in the countries it identifies as enjoying high human development, 39 percent in countries scoring medium human development, and 26 percent in countries with low human development. Yet the majority of Arab countries are well below these averages — more than two-thirds of the Arab states report that women account for less than 20 percent of their workforces.

THE SOCIO-CULTURAL FRAMEWORK

Do Arab women face greater cultural or social constraints as they seek entry into the modern workforce? There are no definitive answers to this question, but it is clear that this part of the world does formally attach greater importance to its cultural identity, and to the role of women in the family in preserving this heritage. The report presented by the Economic and Social Commission for Western Asia (ESCWA) to the United Nations Conference on Women in Nairobi in 1985, for example, begins with a cultural definition of the region that no other area felt necessary to emphasize: "The Strategy for Arab Women in Western Asia to the Year 2000 is based on the heritage of Arab-Islamic civilization and the religious and spiritual values of this region, the cradle of the messages of God which affirm the dignity and freedom of all human beings in this universe."[5]

In the Arab debate on women and work, there are frequent references to the region's "Arab-Islamic identity." This reveals a fear that what constitutes "Arabness" is not well-defined enough to resist erosion by the process of modernization. The effort to define and construct Arab identities in the area of nation-states has been made more complex by the many ethnic and religious groups in the region. The majority of Arabs are Muslims, but some countries include large Christian and other religious communities that are among the oldest in the world. While the majority of the region's inhabitants believe in a shared ethnicity, there are large groups of non-Arabs who live in the Arab region, including Kurds and Berbers.

Post-independence efforts to define Arab identities in ways that would encompass the diversity in the region — for example, Arab nationalism or socialism — foundered because of, among other things, autocratic rule and incompetent economic policies. More recently, weak state systems have been unable or unwilling to challenge Islamist forces who seek to impose their own definition of identity on society at large.

For women, the implications of this phase of the continuing search for identity are perhaps most stark in Algeria, where both Islamist militias and their opponents have attacked women simply because of their dress. During the 1970s and 1980s, the Algerian debate on personal status (family) law was heavily influenced by the concern to preserve an "Arab-Islamic" heritage. Throughout the Arab region, patriarchy has been a factor in prescribing interpretations of Islamic law that circumscribe women's roles. As Egyptian columnist Ahmad Bahaeddin observed, "Those who interpret the rulings of *shari'a* are men, and those who pass laws of all description are men."[6]

The struggles in Arab society over the construction of identities and heritage are tied to efforts to preserve the family and community. As in other parts of the world, such as southern Europe or Asia, where strong family ties predominate, many Arabs tend to view the family as the linchpin of society, and women as the core of the family. Many family functions have not been, and cannot be, replaced by state institutions. Besides warmth, companionship, and moral support, the family provides material benefits such as social security and employment — by caring for the infirm and the unemployed, and promoting family-run businesses or family contacts in the private and public sector.

The ESCWA report mentioned above dedicated an entire section to the family, giving it more prominence than did reports from other regions: "Constitutions, charters and legislation in the region have asserted the role of the family as the nucleus of social organization in Arab society. It is necessary, therefore, to make available to the family the economic, social, cultural and psychological conditions that would ensure its stability and satisfy its needs." The determination to support the Arab family is not, in theory, supposed to be at the expense of women's other roles. The document explicitly endorses "the right of women to choose their roles in and out of the family." Elsewhere, however, it accords "priority to the work of women who devote their time to family and home affairs and hence ensure the continuity of generations, the cultivation of values and the transmittal of knowledge and expertise from one generation to another."

How are these conflicting textual messages reflected in actual lives? Throughout the Arab world, people both see the need for social change and feel threatened by it. Libya, for example, sought to integrate women into that country's modern workforce by promoting education and employment (Muammar Qaddafi used to create a stir with his flamboyant use of female guards when he traveled abroad). Libya is also one of the few Arab countries to have ratified the International Convention on the Elimination of All Forms of Discrimination Against Women.[7] But when Qaddafi spoke to a conference on the Arab and African family in Benghazi in 1990, he focused at length on family problems in the West, the importance of having a stable home environment for children, and the role of mothers. He repeatedly attacked the use of day-care centers as places to dump children, calling on Libyans to march against them and to bring up their children themselves. The requisites of modern society, however, are such that Libyan women continue to make use of such facilities. The day after Qaddafi's speech, one could visit a center run by the Libyan Women and Family Department and see what looked and sounded much like a day-care center, a place teeming with children and a line of mothers pulling up their cars in front of the door to drop off their offspring before going to work. "This is not a kindergarten," one women manager carefully explained. "It's a children's 'club.' Children can spend an hour or two here, or all day if they like."

ALTERNATIVE FRAMEWORK

Heritage, identity, religion, patriarchy, the family and community, women's central role within the family — are these issues so unique to the Arab region? Documents from the 1985 UN World Conference on Women identified the obstacles that continued to block the advancement of women everywhere as: deeply-rooted traditions, poor understanding of the significance of women's issues, and lack of financial resources to reform the position of women. Both the language and the issues in the debate on women's role in the Arab region should be familiar to students of nineteenth- and early twentieth-century Europe and North America, when rapid industrialization also spawned debate about women's roles within the family and society. Current controversies in the U.S. under the rubric of "family values" indicate the persistence of this debate in the West.

Are these socio-cultural factors crucially affecting the rate of Arab women's entry into the modern workforce? Certainly, writers about the Arab world tend to give predominance to these factors over others in reporting on the status of women. A more careful examination, however, shows that wherever there has been a need for women's work — by society or by the family — there have been no serious socio-cultural obstacles to Arab women's participation.

As elsewhere, Arab economies have shifted rapidly from a subsistence basis, where work is done primarily at home, to one where labor or skills are exchanged for wages in the marketplace. This has meant that both men and women, rural and urban, have had to seek work outside the home or neighborhood, often moving from the countryside to the city, or even from one country to another, to do so. As a result of rapid population growth and urbanization, governments have found it hard to generate employment and maintain health, education, and welfare services. Unlike other parts of the world, however, modernizing Arab economies had not yet created a pressing demand for women's work by the mid-1980s. Since then, worldwide recession has brought serious unemployment to all but a few oil-rich Arab states with small populations.

As economies modernize, and, for example, subsistence agriculture gives way to cash crops, women's traditional productivity is frequently undermined, without other income-generating avenues opening up. General ignorance of women's traditional productivity has repercussions not just for women but for the region at large. The region's imports of foodstuffs have tripled over the past decade. By the year 2000, per capita food imports are expected to rise from $100 to $300 annually. Arab states, with just four percent of the world's population, import around 13 percent of the world's food output, and 20 percent of the world's cereals, using up hard currency that could be productively invested. This situation can be partly attributed to economic mismanagement and to environmental factors. But the belief that Arab women have marginal roles in agriculture is also a contributing factor.

The slow growth of women's participation in the modern workforce could reflect not socio-cultural obstacles but the absence of new opportunities for women and poor understanding of their traditional productivity. An accurate picture of the situation requires that we examine three interlinked factors: the need for women's work, whether as a result of national economic development or the need for more family income; the opportunities for women's work that are created through legislation and the removal of socio-cultural barriers; and the investment in women's abilities through education and training.[8] Using this framework, one finds that wherever there are pressing needs and opportunities for Arab women's work, socio-cultural obstacles do not intrude.

Jordan, for example, had made substantial investment in women's education and training by the 1970s. When the country faced labor shortages because of extensive male labor migration to the Gulf, there was a pool of skilled female labor from which to draw. The government actively promoted women's participation in the modern workforce through consciousness-raising seminars and legislation. At the same time, as inflation cut into family incomes, families also actively encouraged participation of women in the labor force. The trend toward more female participation in Jordan's modern workforce slowed by the mid-1980s due to recession, and later as a result of the return of many male labor migrants. The government's interest in women's labor has waned, as has happened in other societies in similar circumstances (for example, in Britain and the U.S. after the two world wars). Yet family need for women's income has remained high. Jordan's Business and Professional Women's Club drew attention to women's pressing need for wage employment. "At one point," the legal counseling staff explained, "600 graduates came to us wanting work. We organized a conference on female unemployment in 1985, which we followed up in early 1989 with a conference on women and work."[9] This concern is shared by women in other Arab countries. "The economic pressures are so strong that any woman, veiled or otherwise, who lands a job tries to keep it in the face of growing unemployment," Egyptian writer Farida Nakkash pointed out back in 1983, when recession began to hit the region.[10]

By contrast, in the Arab Gulf states, although there is a pressing need for labor power and there have been substantial investments in education, women's labor force participation remains low. This is because, among other things, oil wealth has allowed governments to import foreign labor. The need for women's income at the family level, moreover, is not as pressing as it is in other countries. Here again, economic factors are important to an accurate understanding of women's labor force participation.

ENABLING ENVIRONMENT

In addition to the economic need for women's work, we need to ask whether an enabling environment has been created by legislation and by attempts to overcome socio-cultural obstacles. Arab women have increased access to formal education, although there is still a long way to go in poorer countries. Those countries with resources have almost achieved parity in education between girls and boys, up to and including the secondary level.[11]

Arab Women's School Enrollment	
	Combined primary/ secondary enrollment per 100 pop.
Algeria	61
Bahrain	95
Egypt	60
Iraq	71
Jordan	90
Kuwait	88
Lebanon	81
Mauritania	19
Morocco	41
Oman	49
Qatar	98
Saudi Arabia	46
Somalia	16
Sudan	30
Syria	76
Tunisia	66
UAE	85
North Yemen	13
South Yemen	28

Source: UN 1989 World Survey on the Role of Women in Development; data 1986 or latest available.

Education is increasingly seen as not just an opportunity but a right for women. A study by Hind Khattab and Syada al-Daeif of more than 1,000 female students from the lower and lower-middle classes in Cairo in the early 1980s showed that the vast majority of parents expected their daughters to continue their education, and the vast majority of daughters shared this expectation. No less than 93 percent of the girls believed women should work outside the home after completing their education.[12]

A problem facing women and men alike is that the content of education is often unrelated to the needs of the labor market — so much so that some rural families prefer not to send their children to schools where they will lose useful agricultural skills and emerge with unmarketable "knowledge." Schools, furthermore, often foster dismissive attitudes toward manual labor, which has exacerbated productivity problems in the region. An innovative approach to this problem was recently adopted at a project in Jordan.[13] The director of a center for social services in the village of Husban saw that many of her center's income-generating projects (e.g. knitting, dressmaking, traditional handicrafts, medicinal herbs) were not as successful as anticipated, mainly because of problems with quality control and marketing. She also noted the relatively high net profits which cash-crop farmers secured. So she set about encouraging village women to return to agricultural production, leasing land in the area. She convinced male household heads to allow their wives to participate in lentil production — not for wages but for a share in the net profits. Since the women were able to avoid being perceived as wage laborers, and were able to choose working hours which fit their domestic duties, husbands were not threatened.

Regarding the enabling environment created by legislation, Arab labor laws in reference to women are generally fair by international standards. Legislation in areas such as maternity leave, time off for child-care, and protection from dismissal because of pregnancy is adequate. However, as in countries elsewhere, application of the law is easier in the public sector than in the private sector. For example, in Egypt, where the law requires companies to have on-site child-care facilities when they employ over 100 women, many stop just short of employing that number.

Laws Governing Maternity Protection, 1984

	Maternity leave	% wages paid during leave
Int'l Labor Org.	12 weeks	66
Algeria	12 weeks	50
Bahrain	45 days	100
Egypt	50 days	100
Iraq	10 weeks	100
Jordan	6 weeks	50
Kuwait	70 days	100
Lebanon	40 days	100
Libya	3 months	100
Morocco	12 weeks	50 for 10 weeks
Oman	45 days	100
Saudi Arabia	10 weeks	50 to 100
Sudan	8 weeks	100
Syria	50 to 60 days	50 to 70
Tunisia	30 days	2/3 salary
UAE	45 days	50 to 100
Source: Hijab, Womanpower		

The public sector generally offers the most trouble-free and re-spected employment for Arab women. For women in such jobs, how-ever, the problems and benefits are similar the world over. Anton Rahmeh's survey of 119 Syrian women working in the public sector underscores this reality: 45 percent of married women and 42 percent of single women said they found the double work load (at home and on the job) exhausting and would welcome low-priced restaurant and ready-made foods. An overwhelming majority (81 percent of married and 88 percent of single women) said that male members of the family did not help with the household chores. Most of the women owned and relied on labor-saving devices and electrical appliances. Most of the married women considered the child-care situation unsatisfactory: 51 percent left their preschool children with relatives, 18 percent placed them in nurseries, and 18 percent had no fixed place to leave them. In spite of the difficulties, 75 percent of the working women surveyed favored women's work outside the home. The great majority (84 percent) said they felt self-confident as working women, and that they were doing work equal to that of men. The majority also said they enjoyed the respect of their husbands and families, as well as of their colleagues and society at large.[14]

Arab women also account for a small but visible share of the professional class in the region. The achievements of these professional Arab women are broadcast widely through the media: the first Jordanian women pilot, the first Qatari broadcaster, the first Egyptian woman film director, a Sudanese marine biologist.

The situation of women holding low-paid jobs in factories is quite different from those in the professions. According to a recent study by Nadia Ramses Farah, over a million Arab women work in the industrial sector. They are concentrated in Egypt, Morocco, and Tunisia, particularly in textiles, weaving, and ready-made clothing, and, to a lesser extent, in chemical industries, food-processing, and metallurgy. They are also concentrated in low-level jobs, and often receive lower pay than men in the same job.[15]

Mona Hammam's survey of 148 women factory workers at a textile plant outside Cairo showed a working mother's day beginning at 4 a.m.: she prepared breakfast for her husband and children, then she left for the factory. If she had no male relatives to accompany her to the bus stop, she might be harassed. After a full day on the job, she would shop — 80 percent did not own a refrigerator — and return home to cook and care for her children. Few women liked to use the factory's day-care center, which they viewed as a last resort. Although these workers took pride in the fact that they were contributing members of society, they did not see factory work as a suitable occupation for women. All the single women planned to leave their jobs when they married, but many women who had left the factory to get married had returned because of economic pressures.[16]

When Arab women cannot find wage employment in the modern workforce, they, as women elsewhere, do what they can in the informal sector — food production, domestic service, needlework, or child-care, for cash or in-kind services. They are also active in family-run businesses as paid or unpaid partners. The extent of women's activity in the informal sector, which is poorly reported and where workers enjoy few rights, has been documented in micro-studies in Lebanon.[17]

POWER FOR CHANGE

Clearly, Arab women have less access to the modern workforce than men do, although prevailing economic conditions have made full employment a distant dream in Arab and other societies. Economic and socio-cultural factors are critical to an understanding of Arab women's status. To what extent do Arab women have the power to address their socio-economic position? The number of women in formal power structures is low in the Arab region, as elsewhere. Women's influence in society is primarily expressed through traditional structures, such as in family ties where women's power and status increase with age and the number of children they bear, and through women's organizations.

There has been a change in the approach of women's organizations in recent years, moving from an agenda of nationalism, development, and feminism to one stressing the gender dimensions of socio-economic change at the policy level. In the occupied West Bank and Gaza, the grassroots Palestinian women's committees that emerged in the late 1970s, for example, brought in a new, politicized generation of women and new organizational techniques. The committees have spread social as well as nationalist consciousness from urban to rural areas, while offering services in health and education, along with a range of income-generating activities.

Recently Palestinian women have moved to set up some five independent women's research centers that articulate a frankly feminist agenda and seek to keep a distance from the factional differences that have affected the Palestinian women's committees. The centers see their role as advocates for policy reform so as to create an enabling environment for women's socio-economic and political rights. They plan to lobby the new Palestinian authority for services rather than provide services themselves, and to train women in political and other skills to enable them to argue their case. They are tackling hitherto undiscussed issues related to women's legal and economic status, such as violence in the family, inheritance, school drop-out rates, and women's economic activities in the informal sector.

Organizations with a sharper feminist focus have also emerged elsewhere in the Arab world. There are well-established women's research networks in North Africa, for instance, and a regional Arab Women's Training and Research Center in Tunisia was set up in 1992 with UN support. An independent Arab women's publishing house, Nour, was established in Cairo in 1993.

Social and cultural traditions certainly bear on women's status, but it is misleading to see only these as the predominant factors affecting women's entry into the workforce. In the Arab region, tradition has often served as the ready answer for those in search of simple explanations to complex phenomena, or as the excuse of policy-makers unable to generate enough employment for men and women.

The emerging feminist understanding in different parts of the Arab region is a sign that women are preparing to fight for their social, economic, and political rights on their own terms. They will not be alone. The enormous gathering of women from around the world at the United Nations-sponsored World Conference on Women in Beijing in September 1995 provided convincing evidence of the shared problems that women face worldwide, and of their determination to keep organizing until these problems are resolved.

Notes:

1. M. Chamie, "Labour Force Participation of Lebanese Women," in Julinda Abu Nasr et al, eds., *Women, Employment and Development in the Arab World* (Berlin: Mouton Publishers, 1985), p. 99.

2. In this essay, the Arab world comprises the members of the League of Arab States: Algeria, Bahrain, Djibouti, Egypt, Iraq, Jordan, Kuwait, Lebanon, Libya, Mauritania, Morocco, Oman, Palestine, Qatar, Saudi Arabia, Somalia, Sudan, Syria, Tunisia, United Arab Emirates, and Yemen.

3. The ILO redefined the economically active population to include "all persons of either sex who provide labour for the production of economic goods and services. All work for pay or in anticipation of profit is included. In addition, the standard specifies that the production of economic goods and services includes all production and processing of primary products, whether for the market, for barter or for home consumption." See *Women: Challenges to the Year 2000* (New York: United Nations, 1991), p. 39.

4. Nadia Hijab, *Womanpower: The Arab Debate on Women at Work* (Cambridge: Cambridge University Press, 1980), p. 73.

5. The UN defines Western Asia as Bahrain, Egypt, Iraq, Jordan, Kuwait, Lebanon, Oman, the occupied Palestinian territories, Qatar, Saudi Arabia, Syria, the United Arab Emirates, and Yemen.

6. *Al-Ahram*, May 12, 1985.

7. In addition to Libya, the Arab countries that have ratified the Convention are Egypt, Iraq, Jordan, and Morocco.

8. For a detailed expositiion of this argument, see Hijab, *Womanpower*, pp. 63-93.

9. "Jordanian Women: A Programme with a Difference," United Nations Population Fund, November 1989.

10. Hijab, *Womanpower*, p. 82.

11. In Algeria, Bahrain, Iraq, Jordan, Kuwait, Lebanon, Libya, Qatar, Syria, Tunisia, and the United Arab Emirates girls account for over 40 percent of the student body up to the secondary level.

12. Hijab, *Womanpower,* pp. 65-68.

13. Camillia Fawzi el-Solh and Nabiha Masmoudi Chaalala, "Women's Role in Arab Food Security: A Gender Analysis of Selected Agricultural Projects," United Nations Development Program, Regional Bureau for Arab States, 1992; unpublished papers.

14. Hijab, *Womanpower,* pp. 86-87.

15. See the Final Report of the United Nations Development Program's conference "Socio-Economic Challenges for the 1990s: Arab Women's Contribution to Development" (1990).

16. See Mona Hammam, "Egypt's Working Women: Textile Workers of Chubra el-Kheima," *MERIP Reports* no. 82 (November 1979), pp. 3-7.

17. During the civil war in Lebanon, for example, Chamie (op. cit.) found that women tried to survive by doing sewing and handwork at home, house-sitting for absentee owners, and house cleaning. See also the filed survey on Lebanon undertaken in 1989-90 by Omar Halablab for the Amman-based United Nations Economic and Social Commission for Western Asia. For an excellent study in a non-Arab Middle Eastern setting, see Jenny B. White, *Money Makes Us Relatives: Women's Labor in Urban Turkey* (Austin: University of Texas Press, 1994).

7

The Status of Women in Syria

Bouthaina Sha'aban

The status of Arab women in the Western media is so simplified and unilateral that it is daunting to start to draw the complex and perhaps inconsistent picture of the real status of these women. In my desperate search for an easy to digest, easy to comprehend reality of Syrian women to present to Western readers in my book *Both Right and Left Handed,* I had to acknowledge the fact that my country is composed of divergent and discordant islands as far as women's issues are concerned. These islands are shaped by class, region, traditions, religion, and education. I had my first shock when I was interviewing a pioneer Syrian teacher, fighter, and feminist, Thoraya al-Hafez in 1986 and I happened to ask her about her opinion on women's right to choose their husbands. After frowning at me and twisting her eyes in utter amazement at such an unnecessary question, she answered me categorically: "There is no woman in Syria who can't choose her own husband." Of course, there are thousands of women in Syria, including university graduates who, for one reason or another, cannot choose their husbands, but this has to be understood in its cultural and historical context.

Halim Barakat, a Syrian-Arab sociologist at Georgetown University, defines the family as the central socio-economic unit of society: "The traditional Arab family constitutes an economic and social unit in the sense that all members cooperate to secure its livelihood and improve its standing in the community."[1] Within this context, Barakat explains that marriage is a family and communal or societal rather than an individual affair: "Officially it [marriage] has been perceived as a mechanism of reproduction, human survival, reinforcement of family ties and interests, perpetuation of private property though inheritance, socialization, and achievement of other goals that transcend the happiness of the individual to guarantee community interests."[2] It is important to note that the family which offers all kinds of amenities to the individual also offers women a form of unwritten contract stipulating that they will take responsibility for the recommendations that they make. If a woman who has complied with the recommendation of her family regarding the choice of her husband finds herself in a situation whereby her marriage is failing, the parents will see to it that their daughter and her children are provided for. Often this means that the woman moves back to live with her family while the husband offers some form of financial support. If parents are unsure of the economic standing or of the character of a potential suitor for their daughter, they may tell their daughter that she is free to marry him, if she insists, but that they will not guarantee or take responsibility for the consequences of such a decision on her part, meaning that they cannot guarantee the success of the marriage. The responsibility of the parents in arranged marriages is often overlooked in literature on the Middle East.

Syria is an agricultural country with just over 50 percent of its population living in the countryside. It is a well-established fact by now that women in rural areas throughout Third World countries do most of the work in the field and get nothing of the harvest. Syria is no exception. Muslim and Christian women alike succumb to the same rules and are governed by the same traditions. In the countryside, in particular, they dress in the same way and, similarly, shoulder the responsibility both at home and in the field. Folk stories are still being told by our grandmothers and mothers of that lovely, happy, and loving woman in a distant village who was working with her husband in the field when she suddenly said to him "my cousin [women in the Middle East call their husbands cousin], would you rest for an hour or two while I go home to run an urgent errand." After about three hours she was back in the field, gently waking him up in order to resume their work together. He looked at her surprised and noticed that she was no longer pregnant. "What happened to you?" he asked her. "I gave birth to a lovely baby boy," she answered, "and I breast-fed him. Let's do some more work before darkness falls." This folkloric legend, which may or may not have taken place, projects the image of the perfect woman according to rural social norms: she is able to handle childbirth, breastfeeding, and work in the field with a smile on her face.

During the last twenty years Syrian women have made their presence felt in the workplace, particularly in areas related to education. Elementary school teaching is almost exclusively a female domain by now. In 1989 there were 253,890 female students in the preparatory schools in Syria, against 369,923 male students. In the same year there were 105,399 female students in secondary schools in Syria, against 140,169 male students. The female student population in four universities in the country was 50,182 in 1989, while the male population at the same universities and for the same year was 102,240. Female students outnumber male students in pharmacy colleges and in colleges of fine arts and human sciences. In dentistry and architecture colleges female students constitute about 40 percent of the student population, whereas in all other branches their percentage stands at more or less 50 percent of the male student population.

In the four universities in Syria there are women heads of departments and many full professors. There has been one woman dean, Dr. Saleha Sonkor, who was the dean of the College of Pedagogy at Damascus University from 1978-1985. There is now one woman deputy dean at Tashrin University. It is safe to say that women face no particular difficulties related to their gender in becoming lecturers or full professors at universities in Syria. In the French and English departments at Damascus University at least 60 percent of the professors are women. Yet, according to 1984 statistics, the ratio of working women in Syria still stands at one-seventh of the workforce in the country. Illiteracy is still higher among women, although the number of women enrolling in anti-illiteracy classes is almost equal to that of men. (In 1989, the number of women who enrolled in anti-illiteracy classes was 25,020, whereas the number of men was 28,241.) In 1984, there were over 2 million illiterate people in Syria (about 20 percent of the population); almost a million and a half of them were women. Hence, illiteracy among women during that same year could be estimated at about 36 percent. Of course, one major factor for the remarkable increase of female population at both schools and universities is the introduction of the obligatory schooling law. Parents have to send their children, both boys and girls, to school until the age of 12. Anyone who does not abide by this law is liable to penalties, including imprisonment.

Besides the noticeable female presence in the field of education and teaching, which have traditionally been acceptable domains for women, the number of women graduating from engineering, medical, and law colleges has been on the rise for the last 20 years. The true spirit of Arabic culture supports a healthy attitude toward women working in different and uncustomary professions. Arab history holds many examples of women who enjoyed distinguished social, political, and literary careers. The role of women in public life is lauded by the

Prophet Muhammad and many Muslim authorities. Hence, the correct and genuine understanding of culture and religion should foster an open attitude to women's participation in public life.

The two main areas, however, where women still get noticeably bad representation are justice and *shari'a*. Although women graduating from law colleges constitute one-eighth of the graduates and women graduating from *shari'a* college constitute one-fourth of the graduates, female representation in both the legal and justice systems in Syria is very low indeed. This reflects badly on both the legislation and implementation of laws concerning marriage, child custody, divorce, benefits, etc. It is in these areas that Syrian women still need to introduce radical changes to both the existing laws and the practices which ensue, as well as introducing new laws required by modern society, such as laws concerning nationality and spouse battering.

Although according to the true spirit and the letter of Islam every Muslim woman is entitled to preserve her right to divorce her husband and to have this right registered in her marriage contract, this right is rarely acted upon in all Muslim countries. Apart from books on Islamic *tafsir* (interpretation of the Quran), this right is not mentioned anywhere else. Further, this right is not discussed in the two places where it matters most: schools and courtrooms where marriage contracts are drawn up. If a woman who happened to learn about her right requests that it be mentioned in her marriage contract, there is no guarantee that the husband-to-be will accept such an "improper" condition. It is considered socially unacceptable for women to ask to preserve their right to divorce their husbands. Very few men would want to get married to such a "risky" woman. In some cases, a man has the right to divorce his wife without her attending the court, and compensation which he is supposed to pay her is rarely paid. It is important to note that in most cases it is the man who owns the house, and once divorced the woman must leave. The law completes the chain of injustices by allowing the man to keep his children because the woman has no proper home for them. If she happened to have a home of her own, then she would be allowed to keep the boy till the age of nine and the girl till the age of eleven, provided she does not get remarried.

What is worse is that Syrian women cannot pass their nationality on to their children. Nationality in the Arab world is the divine right of the male population. Hence, a Syrian woman, for example, who marries a Tunisian gives birth to Tunisian children, even if she gives birth to them in Syria. This is creating problems for Arab women in different Arab countries with intra-Arab marriages. Thousands of

Syrian women are married to Egyptians, Kuwaitis, Iraqis, and other Arab nationals, and when they came back to Syria with their children they find that their children cannot hold Syrian nationality. This, of course, deprives them of many rights, including the right to enter government schools. This is true of all Arab women in all countries and it is now the most urgent issue which Arab women have to tackle. In my opinion, there are two issues where modern life requires urgent legislation of new laws giving women the right to divorce and to pass their nationality on to their children. But how can this be achieved so long as women enjoy no real say in decision-making positions, both political and legislative?

Yet, in the last 20 years women in Syria have become MPs, ministers, and ambassadors and have held high executive jobs both at governmental and private offices. And 9 percent of our parliament members are women. We have had one woman minister for the last 14 years and one woman ambassador since 1988, besides a good percentage of women working at senior levels in government and political party offices. There is a Women's Union in Syria which strives to improve women's lot. It works under the instruction of the government, although it has the liberty to pursue its own agenda for the advancement of women's cause. This organization has had its ups and downs, but perhaps its most remarkable achievement is the excellent service it has offered regarding nurseries and kindergartens in order to help working women carry on with their jobs along with having family. It is compulsory in Syria to build nurseries and kindergartens in all working places where more than ten working women are employed. At schools, universities, factories, government offices, and civil servants offices both nurseries and kindergartens are readily available. They are clean, efficient, and they have their own transport to collect babies and children from their homes and return them at the end of the working day. Babies are fed and changed and quite well looked after in these nurseries. The Women's Union also runs courses against illiteracy and courses for teaching housewives skills and crafts. But the problem with this Union is that it does not conceptualize women's problems and does not have a vision for a better future for all women. Moreover, the Union's legislative and political powers are limited: hence its capacity to change laws in favor of women's rights and full equality is also limited.

Part of the reason why so much effort has been invested in childcare is that the family is such an important unit in our society. Working women get three months full-paid maternity leave, one month half pay, and up to a year of unpaid leave. For a year after childbirth they get one hour a day off for nursing and there is no apprehension at employing women who are in the process of forming a family; it is part of the social package. A new presidential decree was issued in 1993 making Mother's Day a public holiday, with a great deal of publicity about the role of mothers (not women) both in the family and in society at large.

The system in Syria has its advantages and disadvantages for women who aspire for equality and emancipation. On the one hand, women are held in high esteem and therefore rape outside the home is very rare: it is fairly safe for women to walk in the streets, although no place can be absolutely safe. It can be said that violence against women in the public sphere is very low. Yet this social system which places women on a pedestal forces women simultaneously to shoulder a double responsibility both at home and in the workplace. Over the last few decades, neither our social system, our legal system, nor our food production system has changed. Women's work outside the home constitutes a second burden that women must accomplish in addition to women's work within the home. Indeed, women who spend eight hours a day working for a living still have to prepare the same meals as their grandmothers who were full-time housewives used to prepare. It is obvious that this social attitude insures the continuity of male domination. This period seems to be the period of the superwoman, who is super-professional, super-wife, and super-mother, and the more efficient she is at performing all these tasks, at once, the more rosy her social reputation and status are bound to be. This high esteem for the role of women in preserving the family as a happy social unit taxes women's choices, their health, and even their life. According to custom, no woman is supposed to put her career or even herself ahead of her family and children. Yet, many a woman is abandoned or divorced after accomplishing her role as mother and the middle-aged husband opts to marry a younger wife. These women in their fifties start to suffer from loneliness and boredom. At that age their children are in most cases out of the home and there is no need for mother to bake cakes or spend hours of her day preparing their favorite *dolma* (stuffed grape leaves). The role which she performed for decades is no longer necessary and she recognizes in herself no other use or function. Again, housewives have no pension and therefore in their old age they are either at the mercy of the husband, or if they lose their husband, they can be thrown into poverty and want. The acceptable social norm is that children should take care of their parents, and it is socially disgraceful for children to abandon their mothers or fathers in their old age. This is about the only security that women who do not work outside the home can rely upon. But there is no assurance that all children will comply with social norms and it is inevitable that some women will fall prey to the vulnerability of their situation.

It would seem that in Syria women are never battered within the home, because pride in one's family usually prevents women from speaking out. Whenever a battered woman's case becomes known, it is treated as a personal rather than a social issue. A battered woman, here, is more reluctant to talk about her problem than women in other parts of the world because her marital life is of central interest to her parents, brothers, and members of her extended family. Based on my personal experience, I would say that battered women can be found in all social classes, although there are no statistics or figures. Battered women are caught in a vicious circle. Often they have no place of their own and no independent income. In a society where marriage, family, and children are held in such high esteem, it is understandable to find women prepared to put up with anything rather than sacrifice their position in the society: a position that depends almost totally on their marital status and marital reputation. Moreover, whenever women decide to bring their problems into the open, society manages to put the blame on them and they find themselves both victimized and accused. Hence, learning from each other's experience, most battered women silently bear their lot without invoking further social resentment against them, and this is the case more often in urban areas than in rural areas.

The village community is a small community in which no secret remains hidden for long. Therefore, battered women in the village are quickly identified and their problem is dealt with as a social problem. Here, family and even neighbors have their say, and the man is usually subjected to social pressure that could be the cause of his loss of respectability and status in the village community if he continues in his anti-social behavior. The woman also receives a lot of social support from other women and from the elderly in the village.

The major ruling party in Syria is the Baath Arab Socialist Party, which leads a coalition of national unity. All parties in the coalition are quite small apart from the Baath Party. The Baath is a secular party that advocates equality among all ethnic groups, religions, and sexes. The constitution of the party dwells at length on the importance of achieving equality between men and women and on the national benefits which would result from such equality. In practice, however, none of the leaders of the Baath party seem to be great supporters of women's rights. Although they are members of a secular party, Baath Party members support traditional morality (Christian or Muslim) when it comes to women's issues. Any demands for establishing more equal laws for women are often met with the argument that we are a religious society and we cannot anger the fundamentalists of both religions. So, as women, we are truly confused as to whether we belong to a secular state or a religious state. According to the laws, women are equal and should enjoy equal pay and job opportunities. But women still suffer from unequal laws regarding marriage and divorce, child custody, and other personal status laws. Furthermore, as long as women are not able to pass their nationality on to their children, they are not considered true citizens of the state.

Notes

1. Halim Barakat, *The Arab World: Society, Culture and State* (Berkeley: University of California Press, 1993), p. 97.
2. Ibid., p. 107.

8

Women and Public Participation in Yemen

Sheila Carapico[*]

Although still old fashioned when compared with their Levantine or North African sisters, constrained by patriarchal social structures, and limited in their earning capacities, Yemeni women play at least a token role in contemporary political and economic life. They may well be the most "liberated," though not the most privileged, women in the Arabian Peninsula.

When looking at the civil rights and public participation of Yemeni women, it is important to note their different roles in the North, in the former Yemen Arab Republic (YAR), and in the South, in the former People's Democratic Republic of Yemen (PDRY).

In North Yemen, the three decades after the 1962 overthrow of the Zaydi Shi'a imam saw an increase in veiling and seclusion, as the emerging bourgeoisie sought to imitate the restrictively prim and proper lifestyles of the "ladies" of the old gentry of *"sayyid"* families. Although relatively liberal social legislation allowed such rights as pregnancy leave, voting, driving, travel, running for office, and property ownership, and several women were prominent television broadcasters, in most Northern cities and districts women covered their faces, left school early, and avoided public places. The prevailing ethic was that only dire economic necessity would drive women into markets, factories, or offices. In the countryside, of course, women's contribution to farming and herding was vital.

* This essay was first published in *Middle East Report,* issue #173, November-December 1991. Reprinted with the permission of MERIP/Middle East Report, 1500 Massachusetts Avenue, N.W., #119, Washington, D.C. 20005.

In South Yemen, by contrast, or at least in the formerly British port city of Aden, home to 40 percent of the PDRY's population and the Arab world's only genuinely Marxist regime, unveiled females represented roughly a third of all students, teachers, medical personnel, civil servants, and factory workers. Women were also a visible minority among lawyers, judges, directors, and administrators. As in the North Yemeni hinterland, however, small town and rural dress and behavior varied considerably by region. In distant Mahara, for instance, bare-faced tribeswomen were far more assertive than the demure housebound ladies of the Hadhrami towns.

Over protestations from the religious right, liberal and progressive women and men in the unified Republic of Yemen have managed to hold on to all the legal rights enjoyed by women under either previous regime. The resistance of many conservative *shari'a* scholars to the notion of female judges was resolved with the appointment of one woman to the newly-created 15-judge Supreme Court. Women have also retained or been appointed to positions, including a deputy minister of information, a dean of education, department heads in education, health, social affairs, and the ministries, and a few parliamentary seats. A recent survey found 2,000 professionally qualified women in education, health, communications, law, business, and other fields.

As to urban fashion, the convenient barometer of social freedom, some compromises are evident. Several thousand Adeni women whose own or whose husband's jobs have relocated them to the cooler, more conservative climate of Sana'a almost invariably don a scarf and cloak before leaving the house, while young Sana'ani women from all classes are increasingly abandoning the "traditional" full veil in favor of this more modern look. Several popular new "coiffure" shops also show that fewer women now cover their heads indoors. Even women who wear veils now consider the bare-faced look as perfectly acceptable Islamic dress. By contrast, the distinctively Saudi-style veil, conspicuously marking women whose families were expelled from the kingdom in November 1990 on account of Yemen's position in the Gulf War, strikes Sana'anis as stuffy and pretentious.

Neither the public position of 2,000 professional women nor urban streetwear affects the lives of ordinary townswomen and their country cousins. Their concerns are more those of their families than of women per se: marriage and childbirth, and, increasingly in this time of economic calamity, the loss of migrants' earnings, growing unemployment, high inflation, overburdened and underfinanced social services, and diminishing returns from traditional agriculture and crafts. Most are married young. While few are so tied into the medical health-care system as to utilize gynecological birth control, improved emergency care and widespread immunization for childhood diseases have boosted fertility while reducing infant mortality. The result is that unified Yemen now boasts one of the world's highest rates of natural population growth. Blocked by lack of education or capital from professional careers, blessed with eight children before her thirtieth birthday, and facing severe strain on the national economy, a typical Yemeni women would readily trade the "status" of the veil for a steady cash income.

PART FOUR

Women and Education

9

Formal Education and Training in Non-Traditional Jobs

Samira Harfoush-Strickland *

When speaking of education, training, and employment opportunities for women in the Arab world, it is not easy to generalize. We are talking about twenty-two countries with an equal number of educational systems. Clearly, these countries have a number of factors in common, such as religion, language, and socio-economic similarities. However, they are still different in many ways; in the way they interpret religion, speak the Arabic language, the way their socio-economic and political structures are set up, and in their level of tolerance for female education and employment.

Formal education for Arab women is less than 200 years old. The first modern school for females opened in Egypt in 1829. Egypt was the first Arab country to pass a compulsory education law in 1932, yet this law was not implemented for girls until after Egypt became independent in 1952. Lebanon was the second country to follow Egypt, opening its first school for girls in 1835, followed by Iraq in 1898. The Arab Gulf countries did not offer formal education for their female population until after the first quarter of the present century: Bahrain was first in 1928, followed by Kuwait (1937), Qatar (1954), the United Arab Emirates (1955), Saudi Arabia (1960), and Oman (1970). Cairo was the first to open a female secondary school

---

* This essay was first presented as a paper at a conference entitled New Faces of Arab Women, sponsored by the Institute for Arab Women's Studies and the Middle East Institute, held in Washington, D.C., March 1992. Reprinted by permission.

in 1925, with 40 female students from the upper class enrolled, and by the late 1930s, women began to be admitted to universities in Egypt, Syria, Lebanon, and Iraq.

Females are heavily concentrated in the arts, the social sciences, and education. The majority specialize in areas that are considered appropriate for women in their societies: education, social sciences, liberal arts, and medicine (especially nursing). Female employment and opportunities to work are limited to those that require high school or university degrees and in areas related to their training, i.e., the professions, such as teaching and nursing.

A multitude of factors affect the educational and technical training opportunities available to Arab women, including: 1. access to education; 2. continued participation; 3. program objectives; and 4. social, cultural, and religious beliefs and traditions. In almost all Arab countries access to education depends heavily on social class and academic achievement; in general only a small percentage of first-year primary students (both males and females) ultimately reach the final year of secondary school.

Most rural and lower-class students, especially females, are eliminated by the rigorous selection in Arab educational systems. As a result, the main beneficiaries of modern education continue to be mostly urban males from diverse socio-economic backgrounds and middle- to upper-class women.

Especially in rural areas, females are often withdrawn at an early age from the education process by their families because the family sees no direct benefit in further education for girls. The sex enrollment imbalance increases progressively as the level of education increases. Arab countries have always given priority to the education and training of males. When resources are scarce, families regard investment in the education and training of their sons as more beneficial than investing in the education and training of their daughters. A son must provide financial support for his own family as well as any family he will eventually raise. By contrast, the daughter's stay with her family is considered to be temporary. As soon as she is married, she will join her husband's family and consequently any investment made in her education is considered a financial loss.

Historically, the honor of an Arab family has been tied to the purity of its women. Even today, it is important for a woman to maintain her virginity until her marriage. Consequently, segregation is perceived as a means of controlling female sexuality. In Arab countries, except for private schools and universities, students are generally segregated by sex at all levels of education. In Saudi Arabia, a more traditional country, segregation of the sexes takes place at all levels of education, including the universities.

A female's access to education and training opportunities depends to a certain degree on how cultural and religious beliefs define her role in society. Traditionally, Arab culture has defined the role of women as that of caretakers of their families. In the system which has evolved in the Arab world since ancient times, men have the responsibility of protecting and providing for women. However, this system is now in a state of transition, since in the modern world few men can continue to provide for all the women in their family. More and more women will need to join the workforce. The traditional view of men's and women's roles is reinforced by the way men and women are portrayed in the textbooks. As in most other cultures, women are rarely portrayed as electricians, mechanics, or industrial machine operators, but are always depicted as loving, sacrificing wives and daughters, or perhaps as teachers and nurses. Men are portrayed as manual laborers, technicians, doctors, and engineers. It is only natural, therefore, for schools to emphasize home economics for girls and industrial arts for boys. In sum, careers that are suggested for females in school are an extension of their traditional domestic roles.

Another deterrent to the education of women is the early marriage age for females generally in rural areas. Early marriage prevents women from having the opportunity to continue their schooling. Most technical, non-traditional training requires a minimum of nine years of schooling, but females are usually withdrawn from the school system between the seventh and the ninth grades.

While the overall educational status of Arab women improved substantially between 1965 and 1990, there are a few factors that still have a negative impact on women's education. These factors are: 1. illiteracy (parents' generation); 2. low enrollment; 3. educational wastage (dropout, withdrawal); and 4. sex disparities or the gender gap.

Available research on female education in the Arab world reveals a number of factors that hinder the entry of females into primary education. These factors are: 1. unavailability of schools for females only; 2. lack of female teachers, particularly in rural areas;[1] 3. low social status of teachers;[2] 4. parental ignorance about the benefits of completing education;[3] 5. early marriage age for females; 6. domestic responsibilities for brothers and sisters; 7. lack of transportation to and from schools;[4] 8. limited job opportunities after graduation; 9. lack of school facilities; 10. the widespread belief that an educated female is less likely to get married; 11. lack of water and electricity in rural areas causing females to have to fetch water and wood for family consumption.

By the year 2000, the population of the Arab world is estimated to reach 234 to 280 million. About 130 million students will need education, 50 percent of whom are females, who will require 7 to 8 million teachers. If ten percent of college age students attend higher educational institutions there will be a need for 540 universities instead of today's 85. If spending on education continues to decrease (as it has across the Arab world since 1970, from 5 percent of GDP to 4.7 percent), a greater portion of the society will not be educated and the major segment of the population that will suffer the consequences is most likely to be female.

Notes

1. All-female schools prefer to have all-female staff, since this encourages the parents to enrol their daughters.
2. While this applies to both sexes, yet women tend to shy away from jobs with low social status, finding refuge in marriage.
3. Some parents view the education of daughters as unimportant since daughters may end up by getting married and becoming housewives.
4. In some rural areas, children of primary school age must walk a considerable distance back and forth from school. While parents allow boys to walk this distance, it is not considered safe for girls

10

Women and the Nursing Profession in Saudi Arabia

Nagat el-Sanabary
*

Research on women's work in Islamic countries suggests that acceptance of women's participation in an occupation rests upon identifying it as appropriate for Muslim women.[1] This is generally true and helps explain the acceptability of teaching at all levels, and the generally high levels of women's participation in the medical profession in most Muslim countries. But how can we explain the low participation rate of women in a "culturally appropriate" female occupation such as nursing? In this paper I argue that deeming an occupation culturally appropriate is not enough to harness popular support and guarantee women's participation it. Other factors, such as prestige, class association, general reputation, and the potential moral and social risks of women's occupation involvement are implicated. By focusing on nursing, this study explains the dynamics of women's educational and occupational choices, and identifies the opportunities and challenges facing the development and utilization of health "woman-power" in Islamic countries.

In most Western nations, nursing is a female occupation, while the prestigious medical profession is predominantly male. The situation differs in Islamic countries, where women's participation is low in nursing and high in medicine. The disparity is paradoxical considering that these countries consider both nursing and medicine culturally appropriate female professions. Nonetheless, medicine is the

* This essay is a shorter version of the paper entitled "The Education and Contribution of Women Health Care Professionals in Saudi Arabia," published in *Social Science and Medicine*, vol. 37, no. 11 (1993), pp. 1331-1343. Reprinted with the permission of Elsevier Science Ltd., Pergamon Imprint, Oxford, England.

most acceptable and prestigious profession for Muslim women, whereas nursing remains a low-status occupation shunned by both women and men. Consequently, despite the need for female doctors and nurses, popular demand is high for medicine but low for nursing. This discrepancy has created a major problem for traditional gender-segregated Saudi Arabia for over 30 years. Ironically, the same factors that promoted women's participation in nursing also mitigate against it. Popular attitudes toward nursing keep women from getting the training they need, or utilizing their skills after graduation. This problem has obstructed Saudi Arabia's efforts to solve its nursing shortage by recruiting women for this "culturally appropriate" occupation.

This problem is not unique to Saudi Arabia but is found, at different levels of intensity, in all Arab countries, especially the rich.[2] In a 1973 article, Khoury noted that nursing was not fully appreciated as a career for young Kuwaiti women, a situation which led them to seek prestige in other professions.[3] Similarly, in 1980, Meleis and Hassan argued that a crisis confronted the nursing profession in the Persian Gulf countries, threatening "not only the quality of nursing care available to the people who live in the area, but the very future of nursing itself."[4] Kronfol and Affara also maintain that, in Bahrain and the Gulf in general, "the shortage of nurses constitutes the primary limiting factor to the effective provisions of health care."[5]

BACKGROUND

Popular Western literature about Saudi women focuses primarily on their veiling, gender segregation, and limited options. It fails to recognize that these women are caught in the grip of vast social changes, that they face difficult choices, and have indeed made major progress in various spheres of life over a relatively short time. Scholarly research has documented the changes. Altorki revealed the major progress in the lives and opportunities of elite urban Saudi women as well as women in small towns, and Parssinen, Gerner, el-Sanabary and Ramazani described major changes in the educational, personal, and occupational situations of Saudi women over the past three decades, although they also noted certain persistent problems and constraints.[6] Sudden oil wealth provided great opportunities for development, but traditional cultural and religious attitudes, as well as the country's educational and employment policies, have been a major constraining factor. The changes that have swept over the country affected people unevenly, having a greater impact on economic than social infrastructures. These uneven changes are evident in the evolving situation of Saudi women, and their generally low labor force participation.

Three development areas underscore Saudi Arabia's need for female health-care professionals in the midst of rapid socio-economic change: (1) the vast expansion of female education and the desire to provide culturally female-appropriate occupations; (2) the astronomical expansion of health-care facilities and the government's commitment to train needed health workers; and (3) the country's heavy reliance on expatriate health personnel and the desire to replace them with Saudis.

Saudi Arabia, formerly a poor nomadic tribal country, was catapulted into the twentieth century by the oil wealth of recent decades, which made it a middle-income country. Its new-found wealth dramatically changed all spheres of society, especially the educational and health sectors. Beginning in the early 1960s, the government embarked upon a massive development program facilitated by systematic planning and financed by oil revenues. Despite the unprecedented changes, the Saudi government has maintained a determination to modernize without deviating from traditional social and religious values, especially those pertaining to women. Accordingly, the genders are separated in education and employment, and veiling in public is mandatory. Major educational and economic changes have occurred within this traditional framework, the most dramatic of which has been the vast expansion of female education, and the increase in women's employment, especially in teaching, and, to a lesser extent, in social work, nursing, medicine, and a few other occupations.

DEVELOPMENT AND EXPANSION OF FEMALE EDUCATION AND THE NEED TO PROVIDE FEMALE-APPROPRIATE OCCUPATIONS

Prior to 1960, Saudi Arabia had no public schools for girls, and no women were employed outside the home. During that year, the government opened its first primary schools for girls, under the auspices of a separate agency, the General Presidency for Girls' Education (GPGE), thereby marking the beginning of a new era for Saudi women. Prior to that date, a number of private schools were open in the main Saudi cities: Jeddah, Riyadh, and Makah. Gradually, a separate full-fledged system of girls' education emerged that now provides free schooling from the primary to the doctoral level. In 1988, more than one million (1,129,500) girls and young women were enrolled in

Saudi schools and colleges: 770,370 in primary education, 308,700 in intermediate and secondary education, and 50,430 in higher education. Females made up 45 percent of the enrollment at the primary levels, and 39 percent at the college and university levels.[7]

The increase in female education has led to a gradual and steady rise in women's participation in occupations designated suitable for Muslim women. According to Saudi government policy issued in 1970, the two main objectives of girls' education were: to prepare them for their roles as mothers, and "to perform those jobs which suit their nature like teaching, nursing, and medicine."[8] These occupations are an extension of women's domestic roles, and utilize the stereotypical women's qualities of caring, nurturing, and service to others. They are also deemed culturally and religiously appropriate because they help maintain gender-segregation through women's work with other women in segregated work environments. This condition applies easily to education but not to the health sector. Therefore, teaching and school administration are the most widely held occupations by Saudi women, particularly at the primary and secondary levels. In 1986, 44,653 Saudi women were employed as schoolteachers and administrators by the GPGE, having replaced Egyptian and other Arab women. Another 1,273 were working in the universities. According to the Civil Service Bureau, over 88 percent of Saudi working women, in the non-agricultural sector, were employed by the GPGE and the universities (85.9 percent and 2.4 percent respectively) as compared to only 7.4 percent employed by the Ministry of Health (MOH).

VAST EXPANSION OF MEDICAL FACILITIES

Since the 1950s, the goal of official government policy has been to provide health-care for all citizens free or at nominal cost. Oil wealth has prompted astronomical growth in health-care facilities and personnel. Since 1980, the MOH has emphasized preventive health measures: a massive vaccination program, environmental health and hygiene, health education, early screening, primary care, and maternity and child-care.[9] The number of public and private hospitals, dispensaries, and primary care centers has skyrocketed. By the 1980s, Saudi Arabia had established some of the most advanced and best equipped hospitals in the Middle East.

To staff its expanding health facilities, the Saudi government recruited vast numbers of foreign health-care providers. Between 1970 and 1980, the number of doctors increased 4.5 times, and the number of nurses tripled. The country needed to expand its own supply of Saudi health professionals. The Third Development Plan (1980-85), emphasized health staffing. It stressed the necessity "to increase the public awareness of the need for and utilization of health training programs, especially nursing education for girls."[10] In the meantime, the MOH forged ahead with the expansion of facilities and personnel. During the Fourth Development Plan (1986-1990), it expected to add 45,500 new positions in the health sector. The ratio of physicians and other health-care providers to the population increased dramatically. For instance, the number of physicians per 10,000 inhabitants rose from 3.8 in 1975 to 6.7 in 1980. The target during the Fifth Development Plan (1990-95) is one physician per 500 inhabitants and one nurse and health technician per 225 inhabitants. Achieving this ambitious objective required the training of 4,200 physicians, 565 specialist physicians, 5,880 nurses, and 7,560 health technicians.[11] The numbers are almost overwhelming and only a small fraction can be trained by Saudi medical and nursing colleges, especially the latter because of the factors outlined later in this paper.

CONSTRAINTS ON WOMEN'S PARTICIPATION IN NURSING

As noted above, Saudi officials, writers, and religious leaders sanction nursing as a suitable occupation for Muslim women. So what are the constraints on Saudi women's participation in nursing education and practice? They are numerous and complex.

The first pertains to women's work generally. In Saudi Arabia and elsewhere, gender-role expectations and female socialization are a major obstacle to women's entry into the workforce. The prevailing view is that a woman's place is in the home and that outside employment is justified only when necessary. The pressure to get married, and to stay at home and care for their families, compels many young women to either forgo employment completely or to choose an occupation such as teaching, which is easy to integrate with family responsibilities. Very few are willing to venture into a demanding education and career, unless it has the prestige that justifies the sacrifice, such as medicine. Saudi society has not fully accepted the idea of women's work outside the home, despite the thousands of employed Saudi women, most of whom are in the education sector. The ongoing debate about women's role in the family and society and the potential threats to family from women's employment has not abated. Several conservative Saudi and other Muslim writers continue to write extensively on women's work and its potential effects on society. Full-sized books as well as pamphlets have been written debating the issue of women's roles in society. The following titles are revealing: *Remain in Your Place and Be Graceful, Women's Work in the Balance, The March of Saudi Women: To Where?* Such books speak at length about women's primary role in the family, oppose women's work, and warn of the anticipated breakdown of the Saudi family as a result of women's employment. They cite perceived ills of Western societies: "moral deterioration," the "collapse of family values," and "the loss of children," blaming them all on women's work outside the home. They contrast this situation with "ideal Islamic society and values," extol the virtues of motherhood, and exaggerate the danger of women's work. They do, however, sanction teaching, medicine, nursing, and social work as culturally and religiously appropriate feminine occupations. Their writings convey a conflicting message to Saudi women, by telling them in one and the same breath that it is their duty to serve their country in appropriate occupations, and that their place is in the home. Only teaching gets the full endorsement of those writers because of its congruency with women's traditional roles and its fully segregated work environment. The following are just a few samples of their writings.

Suhaila Zein el-Abedeen, an influential conservative Saudi woman journalist, opposes women's employment outside teaching. She argues, however, that nursing education should be made compulsory at all stages of female education, starting with intermediate schools, to insure that women have the nursing knowledge they need to perform their duties as mothers in peace time, and to shoulder their responsibilities toward their country in war times.[12] Another Saudi writer, a Western-educated physician, Mohammed Ali el-Bar, a staunch opponent of women's work, concurs. He points out that the role of women in nursing the wounded and sick, and serving the fighters by providing them with food and water, is an important role in the battlefields, a role played by the mothers of the Muslims and pioneering women in the early Islamic period. He mentions Rufaida, a Muslim women who nursed the wounded in the battle of al-Ahzab, and other women who practiced medicine in various periods of Islamic history.[13] Yet he stresses that these duties are only required in times of emergencies, and he exhorts contemporary Saudi women to stay at home because of alleged dangers of women's work and the "unavoidable" moral corruption that results from the intermingling of the genders.

Ahmad Mohammed Jamal, another staunch opponent of women's work, has written extensively about the pernicious effects of women's work, especially where women and men work together. He recognizes women's right to work as "a teacher, physician, nurse, or midwife in female environments only where there is no intermingling of genders, and no fear of the corrupting influence of such intermingling."[14] Jamal argues that Saudi women, by virtue of their Arab-Islamic society, do not need to compete with men for jobs except those that are fit for them, such as needlework, sewing, and teaching girls. He adds that some Saudi women actually perform the kinds of occupations that suit women's abilities and domain. They are the teachers, school administrators, and physicians who educate and treat other women.[15] He also cites the example of courageous Muslim women nurses during the early Islamic period. But he affirms that he mentions them only to demonstrate their courage, and not to encourage contemporary Saudi women to follow their example in the battlefields since "military warfare has advanced and no longer needs women to satisfy the thirst of the warriors, or care for the wounded or the sick."[16]

These writers also oppose support systems that enable married women to work and care for their families. Child-care is a concern, especially for women who cannot afford live-in nannies or who have no extended family members to care for their children. But these writers reject child-care centers for their alleged harmful effects on children. Their writings reflect the attitudes of a broad segment of traditional Saudi society, not the younger generations of educated men and women, who have read and traveled widely and recognize the need for Saudi women to assume new roles and contribute to national development.

In addition to the general resistance to women's employment among the traditional strata of Saudi society, several other reasons specific to nursing discourage women's entry into the profession. The first is a negative image and a deep-seated prejudice against nursing. This is not peculiar to Saudi Arabia but is found in other countries as well. The image of the nurse as a doctor's helpmate is a worldwide stereotype that has persisted for decades. In most Arab and Islamic countries, a stereotype of the nurse as a subservient uneducated female hospital worker discourages many Arab women from entering nursing. A World Health Organization (WHO) report indicates that "the public image of the nurse appears to be particularly negative in countries where strong cultural traditions severely restrict the participation of women in paid occupations outside the home. As a result, nursing functions in these countries are performed by women of lowest social class — a situation reminiscent of the earliest days of nursing" in the West.[17] Therefore, few young women study nursing by choice but only as a last resort when their grades do not qualify them for more prestigious fields of study.[18]

A Saudi woman professor, Samira Islam, a former dean of the colleges of medicine and medical sciences at King Abdelaziz University and a consultant to the World Health Organization, spoke about the negative image of nursing in Saudi Arabia. Citing evidence from her professional experience, she reported that the general public and members of the health team, especially physicians, lack an understanding of the nature of the nursing profession. Negative perceptions often pop up in professional discussions, she said, and medical educators consider nursing students less intelligent and less capable. In her view, physicians have a "superiority complex" and consider anyone else in the medical team inferior to them. They view the physicians as the boss and the rest as "apprentices or laborers." She stated, "People like to look up, they like power and prestige." She noted that even women physicians who spent their freshman year in the same class with nursing students still look down on nurses and consider them inferior. She added, "The problem is not just with the girls who like power, fame, and glory by having a medical degree or being a physician, but also with the medical team ... We try to convince the physicians that the nurses and other paramedical personnel are colleagues, not servants."[19]

Work conditions are another problem that hamper women's participation in nursing but less so in medicine. First, is the difficulty to integrate nursing with women's family responsibilities because hospital work involves long hours and night shifts. This is especially a burden in view of women's restricted mobility and lack of autonomy. Saudi women's inability to drive makes it very difficult for them to commute to their jobs. Furthermore, parental opposition to women's living away from home prevents them from accepting positions in the villages that need their services the most. The second is a more formidable obstacle: the intermingling of the genders in hospitals. Women nurses must interact with Saudi male physicians and patients, as well as with non-Saudi physicians and other health-care providers. It is generally believed that such intermingling in the workplace, which is unavoidable in hospitals although prohibited by Saudi law, promotes immorality. Thus, contrary to Western literature that associates nursing with such characteristics as virtue and purity, the taint of immorality associated with nursing in Saudi Arabia and some other Arab countries is the most damaging to the profession and the peace of mind of the women who want to pursue it. The concern over a woman's reputation and honor limits women's access to and persistence in nursing. My interviews with Saudi nursing students, as well as those who have transferred from the nursing colleges, confirmed that most parents oppose their daughters' desire to become nurses. Likewise, some men interviewed for Saudi newspapers have stated their objection to their sisters', daughters', or wives' entry into nursing due to the moral "hazards" involved. Sadly, some practicing Saudi nurses refer to harassment, or "annoyances," on the job, which impel some nurses to quit. Those who persist often risk their reputation and pay a high personal price: possibly forfeiting marriage altogether. One of the earliest graduates of the health institutes stated that should she marry and have a daughter she would never allow her to become a nurse so as to spare her what she herself has endured.

Ironically, while sharing the same working conditions, medicine has not been stigmatized like nursing, but enjoys high prestige and status, which makes it the most favored and prestigious educational and occupational option for Saudi and Muslim women in general. In contrast to nursing, the demand for medical education is so high that every year, more than four times as many women apply for admission to medical school as those accepted. The opposing images of the two professions prompt women to gravitate toward medicine and shy away from nursing. In Saudi Arabia, as in the other Gulf states, the association of nursing with menial work, requiring no intelligence or education, relegates it to those occupations below the dignity of most Saudis, male and female, that are better left to foreigners. The low educational association relates to the history of nursing education in Saudi Arabia, where it evolved as a vocational education program. As such, it suffers from the general stigma of being the catch-basin for the lower classes and those who cannot make it academically.[20]

Class is a related problem. As with women in most Third World countries, women's socio-economic background has a major influence on their educational and career choices. The wealthy and more advantaged groups are more likely to enter prestigious occupations and professions than the socially and economically disadvantaged who are less likely to pursue higher education. In wealthy Saudi Arabia, despite democratization efforts and free education, the majority of the females who graduate from high schools and enter colleges come from middle- and upper-class backgrounds. As with other Islamic countries, women of the social elite choose the prestigious field of medicine. For these women, education is a status symbol. Very few, if any, are willing to risk their social prestige by entering low-class associated nursing.

SAUDI WOMEN NURSES AND HEALTH DEVELOPMENT

These attitudes have discouraged many Saudi women from entering nursing, thus helping exacerbate the existing nursing shortage. Those who have entered the profession remain underdogs: their status is low, and their power limited. They are maligned by the stereotypes and negative propaganda. Consequently, the nursing profession in Saudi Arabia is still predominantly female and foreign. The latest available figures indicate that the proportion of female Saudi to non-Saudi nurses was only 6.5 percent (1,388 Saudis and 21,269 non-Saudis); comparative figures for males were 1,431 Saudis and 4,178 non-Saudis, at a ratio of 34 percent.

Despite the problem and dilemmas, Saudi women who have entered nursing, although small in numbers, have contributed to health development in their country as individuals and professionals. The greatest contribution is credited to the first Saudi nurse-midwife, Saudi Arabia's Florence Nightingale, Lutfiyyah al-Khateeb, who received a nursing diploma from Cairo, Egypt, in 1941. Upon her return to Saudi Arabia, she dedicated her life to uplifting the educational and health conditions of Saudi women. She lobbied for female education, nursing, and medicine, and was instrumental in establishing the health institutes, and became the first director of the one in Jeddah. Her efforts on behalf of Saudi women — which are recorded in her memoirs, and acknowledged by those who know her — are a testimony to the commitment, resilience, and courage of women in the face of seemingly insurmountable obstacles. By championing the cause of female education and health, she laid the foundation of Saudi women's empowerment. As a pioneer and social reformer, she was the driving force behind the founding of government education for girls and health-care facilities for women and children. Single-handedly, she taught women about care during pregnancy and delivery, proper child-care, nutrition, sanitation, and the risks of childbirth. Under the motto "Prevention is better than the cure," she called for massive immunization against contagious diseases such as diphtheria, whooping cough, tuberculosis, polio, typhoid, cholera, tetanus, typhus, and the plague, and for improved sanitation practices. She called upon every citizen to urge pregnant women to make full use of primary health-care centers and hospitals for prenatal care and safe deliveries. Her campaign for the establishment of a specialized maternity and obstetrics hospital succeeded in persuading the government to convert a newly established eye clinic into a maternity hospital staffed by Arab physicians. She won the support of the Saudi leadership and the common people for her ideas, mission, and common sense views on education, nutrition, sanitation, and clothing. Her success was largely due to her work within the framework of the prevailing traditional cultural and religious values.

Saudi Arabia has come a long way since the pioneering work of Lutfiyyah al-Khateeb. The country has changed and women have assumed new roles. Either by necessity or choice, hundreds of Saudi women have disregarded the prevailing stereotypes and restrictions by taking advantage of the available opportunities to train for and practice nursing. In 1989, according to government statistics, 1,388 female Saudi nurses were working in hospitals, dispensaries, and primary health centers run by the Saudi Ministry of Health.[21] Many others are employed in the military hospitals run by the Ministry of Defense; in clinics for female students and staff operated by the General Presidency of Girls' Education; and in numerous private hospitals and clinics in the main Saudi cities. Whether they choose nursing because it is their only option, to take advantage of the stipend, to obtain a needed job, or to alleviate human suffering, these women are providing essential health services and contributing to the welfare of their families, communities, and wider society. One hopes that they will ultimately succeed in changing the public's attitudes toward women and their role in society, and help pave the way for other women making educational and career choices.

Currently, the number of these women is too small to make a dent in the existing nursing shortages. This situation limits their role in alleviating the numerous health problems that still affect the country and require the attention of Saudi nurses and other health-care providers. These health problems underscore the need for health-care and education of women, the primary health-care providers, and an urgent need for Saudi female health professionals and health educators.

These health problems cannot be effectively solved by foreigners, but need Saudi health-care providers, especially women, cognizant of local conditions, and sensitive to Saudi women's needs and concerns. Continued dependence on foreign health-care providers interferes with the proper delivery of health-care to the Saudis, especially women, because of the communication problems resulting from differences in language and culture between the health-care providers and patients. The same problem exists in other Gulf states. In Kuwait, for instance, Meleis noted that "visiting health-care professionals who are there only for a limited period, no sooner having adjusted to their clients and the clients to them, find that it is time for them to leave. Therefore, health-care clients have to continuously adjust to new workers ignorant of the culture and system."[22] Hence, the goal of Saudization, or achievement of some balance between the numbers of Saudi and foreign health-care providers, is not just a matter of national pride, but of practical necessity also.

Notes

1. N.H. Youssef, *Women and Work in Developing Societies* (Berkeley: University of California Press, 1974).

2. M. Jansen, "Nursing in the Arab East," *ARAMCO Magazine* April-May 1974, pp. 14-23.

3. J.F. Khoury, "Nursing in Kuwait," *Institute of Nursing Review* (1973), p. 14.

4. A.I. Meleis and H.H. Soad, "Oil Rich, Nurse Poor: The Nursing Crisis in the Persian Gulf," *Outlook* 28 (April 1980), p. 238.

5. N.M. Kronfol, "Nursing Education in the Arabian Gulf: The Bahrain Model," *International Journal of Nursing Studies* 18 (1982), p. 89.

6. S. Altorki, *Women in Saudi Arabia: Ideology and Behavior Among the Elite* (New York: Columbia University Press, 1986); S. Altorki and D.P. Cole, *Arabian Oasis City: The Transformation of Unayzah* (Austin, TX: University of Texas Press, 1989); C. Parssinen, "The Changing Role of Women," in *King Faisal and the Modernization of Saudi Arabia*, ed. A. Beling (London: Croom Helm, 1980); D.J. Gerner, "Roles in Transition: The Evolving Position of Women in Arab-Islamic Countries," in *Muslim Women*, ed. F. Hussain (New York: St. Martin's Press, 1984); N. el-Sanabary, "Educating the Second Sex: Saudi Arabia's Educational Policy for Women and Its Implications," Western Regional Conference of the Comparative and International Education Society, Sacramento, California, 1988; N. el-Sanabary, "Higher Education for Women in Saudi Arabia: The Paradox of Educational Reform," Annual Conference of the Comparative and International Education Society, Pittsburg, PA, 1991; N. Ramazani, "Arab Women in the Gulf," *Middle East Journal* 39 (1985), pp. 258-76.

7. *UNESCO Statistical Yearbook* (Paris: UNESCO, 1991).

8. Kingdom of Saudi Arabia, Ministry of Education, *Educational Policy of the Kingdom of Saudi Arabia* (Riyadh: Ministry of Education, 1970).

9. R. el-Mallakh, *Saudi Arabia: Rush to Development* (Baltimore: The Johns Hopkins University Press, 1982), p. 243.

10. Kingdom of Saudi Arabia, *The Third National Development Plan: 1980-1985* (Riyadh: Ministry of National Planning, 1980), p. 83.

11. Kingdom of Saudi Arabia, *The Fifth National Development Plan: 1990-1995* (Riyadh: Ministry of National Planning, 1990), p. 313.

12. S. Zein el-Abedeen, *Maseerat al-Mar'ah al Saudiyyah ela Ayn? (The March of Saudi Women: To Where?)* (Jeddah: The Saudi House of Publishing and Distribution, n.d.), p. 99.

13. M.A. el-Bar, *Amal el-Mar'ah fil Meezan (Women's Work in the Balance)* (Jeddah: The Saudi House for Publishing and Distribution, 1987), pp. 219-20.

14. M.A. Jamal, *Makanek Tuhmadi (Keep to Your Place, Thank You)* (Beirut: Dar Ihyaa al-Uloum, 1986), pp. 131-32. The book was first published in 1964.

15. Ibid., p. 199.

16. Ibid., p. 247.

17. World Health Organization, *Women As Providers of Health Care* (Geneva: World Health Organization, 1987), p. 66.

18. Ibid.

19. Personal interview, July 1987.

20. N. el-Sanabary, "Vocational and Technical Education for Women in the Arab Countries," in *Women and Work in the Third World: Impact of Industrialization and Global Economic Interdependence*, ed. el-Sanabary (Center for the Study, Education and Advancement of Women, University of California, Berkeley, 1983), pp. 253-64.

21. Kingdom of Saudi Arabia, *Annual Health Report* (Riyadh: Ministry of Health, 1989).

22. A.I. Meleis, "A Model for Establishment of Educational Programmes in Developing Countries: The Nurse Paradoxes in Kuwait," *Journal of Advanced Nursing* 5 (1980), p. 290.

11

Women's Education in Jordan

Abla Amawi

As in any other country, the status of women in Jordanian society is different from that of men, and this difference places women in a disadvantageous socio-economic and political position. Yet Jordanian women are not merely helpless bystanders in their society. On the contrary, they have recorded significant gains in comparison to the position of their mothers and grandmothers a mere one or two generations ago, and their priorities in the development process are given official sanction.

In the field of education, Jordanian women have realized important advances during the past thirty years. However, this progress is only slowly erasing the effects of decades of neglect. As recently as two generations ago, few children attended school in Jordan's overwhelmingly rural society, and fewer girls than boys attended and completed primary school. However, more girls are now attending school than ever before. Whereas 59 percent of girls were enrolled in primary education in 1960, a full 92.5 percent were enrolled in 1990.[1] This is 2.1 percent higher than the primary enrollment rate for boys. Some 58 percent of all Jordanian women have now completed elementary education, and 78 percent of Jordanian girls now attend secondary school compared with 80 percent of boys. More women are now attending community colleges and universities as well: by 1988, 40 percent of all university students were females.[2] As a result of the emphasis placed upon female education, female literacy rates have risen faster than the literacy rate for males: from 29 percent in 1970, to 59 percent in 1985, and to 73 percent in 1990. By comparison, male literacy rates rose from 64 percent in 1970 to 89 percent in 1990.[3] Overall adult literacy rates in Jordan are higher than the average rates for the Arab world and for developing countries as a whole.[4]

This overall increase in the percentage of educated Jordanian women has increased their participation in the labor force. The historically agricultural and pastoral nature of Jordanian society dictated that most women work in the home and village economy; only recently have women begun entering a wider workforce. Yet, despite speedy advancements made on other levels, women remain underrepresented in the general Jordanian workforce and are largely concentrated in certain professions or within the state sector. Government statistics reveal that only 10.6 percent of the workforce is female, and of these, only 27 percent are married.[5] This is roughly in keeping with other Arab countries, where women comprise 13 percent of the overall workforce.[6]

The female Jordanian workforce is comparatively skilled and well-educated, and the majority of Jordanian women who work outside the home (46.4 percent) are in professional or technical jobs, including teaching. By contrast, the majority of male workers (41.3 percent) work as laborers.[7] These figures are consistent with other data which suggests that the smaller female workforce is much better educated and skilled than its male counterpart. For instance, while over 75 percent of working women have graduated from secondary school, only 28 percent of male workers have done so.[8] In the legal context, women enjoy equal protection with men under Jordanian labor law and civil service regulations.[9]

Notes

1. The following statistics are taken from UNICEF, *Situation Analysis of Jordanian Children and Women* (Internal Draft Report, 1992), p. 64.

2. Nadia Kamal and Mary Kawar, "The Status and Role of Women in Development in Jordan," paper delivered at Women in the Jordanian Labor Force Conference, Amman, Jordan, Dec. 1990, p. 4.

3. *Situation Analysis*, p. 64.

4. "Human Development in the Arab Region: A Background Paper," unpublished manuscript, United Nations Development Program, Human Development Report Office, 1993, pp. 15-16.

5. Kamal and Kawar, p. 3, and *Situation Analysis*, p. 66.

6. "Human Development in the Arab Region," p. 7.

7. *Situation Analysis*, p. 65.

8. Ibid., p. 65.

9. Ibid., p. 70.

PART FIVE

Women and the Civil War in Lebanon

12

The Case of Lebanon

Hala Maksoud[*]

From its inception, the Arab women's movement has been inextricably linked to the modernizing and nationalist movements; in other words, most Arab women gained feminist consciousness as a result of political involvement. From the early twentieth century, Arab women were visible in the struggle against colonial powers, first against the Ottoman Turks and then against the French. The first record of Lebanese women's political activism is the letter sent by the Organization of Arab Women in Beirut to the Arab Congress held in Paris in 1913. In the early 1920s, women added voting rights demands to their anti-colonial agenda. Following in the footsteps of the Egyptian Huda Sha'rawi, Lebanese women removed their veils in 1923. In Egypt, Lebanon, Palestine, and many other Arab countries, women-led demonstrations were commonplace from the early 1920s on.

When Lebanon gained its independence in 1943, the women's movement focused on gaining full political rights. They agitated for universal suffrage, and intensified the pressure on the Lebanese government until women achieved the right to vote in 1951.

In fact, it can be argued that the problematic in the latter development of the Arab women's movement was inherent in its genesis. The fact that modernizing nationalist men were the leaders in prodding women to participate led to some confusion and to the blurring of many issues. Women were shocked when they discovered the level of resistance men showed when they entered the struggle, because the women's movement was part and parcel of the modernizing movement. The failure of developmental policies and the discrediting of

* This paper was first presented at a conference entitled New Faces of Arab Women, held in Washington, D.C. in March 1992. The conference was sponsored by the Institute for Arab Women's Studies and the Middle East Institute.

the modernizing elites in many Arab countries was bound to reflect on the movement, and to lead to a backlash, with some sectors reacting obsessively to modernization in the name of a return to authenticity.

Notwithstanding this reaction, the Arab women's movement has been, to a large extent, a linear movement, achieving incremental gains over the years. As countries in the region were achieving their independence, women were gaining their political rights and were increasingly visible in most domains.

However, the Arab women's movement has been in general overly preoccupied with political issues, often neglecting social and other matters. This has been one of the main criticisms leveled at it by Western feminists. In light of the fact that most Arab countries live in a period of social transformation, with many experiencing wars and struggles for liberation, it is only natural that although realizing the necessity for social change and the importance of women's issues, the political sphere overrides their concerns, and its immediacy often deflects from other pursuits. In such situations, women's priorities cannot be the same as those of women living in peaceful, post-industrial societies. Thus, although one can assert that the Arab women's movement is an integral part of the global movement toward the enfranchisement of women, and that through the diversity of development with which they are experimenting they are actually contributing to the wealth of the movement as a whole, who can expect the Lebanese woman who has experienced 16 years of war and the devastation of her country to have the same priorities as other women who live in more stable societies?

When it comes to war, Arab women have seen it all. It might sound melodramatic, but in the last century the lives of the Arabs have been punctuated by wars. They have lived through different forms of wars and have experienced their traumatic aftermath, the dislocations, the pain, the killings, and the losses. They have learned to distinguish between various forms of war and their effects on society: wars of liberation, as in Algeria and Palestine; civil wars, as in Lebanon, the Sudan, Somalia, Yemen, and elsewhere; high technology wars, such as the Gulf War; guerrilla wars; protracted wars; and others. All this constitutes a very rich experience, which should enable us to readdress the prevalent scholarship on the subject of women and war, and this is what I shall attempt to do, using Lebanon as a model.

The Lebanese experience of the 16 years of civil war was traumatic to many women. The war has now ended, but its effects in terms of devastation and misery are still vividly present, preventing one from exercising the needed detachment for an objective study. The accumulated experience of the 16 years in Lebanon challenges prevalent scholarship on the subject of women and war. For a long time, theories were accepted which emphatically maintained that all wars have hastened the emancipation of women, either because of women's active participation in combat or because women were propelled into the workforce to replace men. These studies drew on the experience of British women who, after their involvement in the First World War, were granted their political rights. It was argued that through their participation in that war, women changed the attitudes of men who had ridiculed the suffragette movement in the past; they had gained men's respect and imposed themselves in the public domain. The same phenomenon also happened in the United States as a result of women's participation in the Second World War.

Feminist literature on the subject adopted this paradigm and drew on later experiences of women's involvement, particularly in the Algerian Revolution, as well as on revolutionary theory, especially as developed by Frantz Fanon and Simone de Beauvoir, to argue that women, through their struggle in wars of liberation, liberate not only themselves but also their male oppressors from their chauvinism, as well as the occupier from his dehumanizing occupation. Although that literature was developed with particular reference to wars of liberation, it was later applied to all wars, on the assumption that war opens up opportunities for women, which, if properly used, are bound to lead to their empowerment.

I would like to submit that this has not been our experience in Lebanon. I am becoming wary of the insistence on pinpointing the gains made by women through their participation in war, while totally neglecting the negative aspects of that same participatory act. Historically, wars of conquest and civil wars have always been the quintessential domain of men. In war, aggressiveness, violence, and ruthlessness, all typically male attributes, dominate over the feminine attributes of nurturing and caring. Women who participate in wars show that they can be as aggressive as men — perhaps securing male respect but also raising the question whether it ought to be the concern of women to become "like men."

Like their other Arab sisters, women in Lebanon have been involved in the political, social, and literary field since the beginning of this century. The First World War caused dislocation and famine, leading women in Beirut to organize shelters, schools for needy children, clinics for first aid, and to open factories which employed over a thousand women. In 1928, more than one hundred welfare and educational women's organizations were established to serve the community in cities and villages across Lebanon. The Council of Lebanese Women was formed to coordinate their activities and to serve as a platform for the exchange of ideas and experiences. Since that time, the Council has held a yearly conference attended by Lebanese women, many of whom are representatives of organizations. Furthermore, many Lebanese women have participated in pan-Arab and international women's conferences.

Following in the footsteps of Huda Sha'rawi, Lebanese women removed their veils and achieved universal suffrage in 1951. Extremely active in the literary and artistic fields, they had early on insisted on being treated with the respect they deserved from their male counterparts. In 1928, a delegation of women went to the House of the Lebanese Book to place a picture of Warda al-Yazigi, a woman novelist, next to the pictures of the famous male writers. Since then, numerous women writers' pictures have been included in this "hall of fame."

Prior to the civil war, Beirut was the intellectual center and a beacon of enlightenment in the Arab world. In the 1960s and 1970s no writer was considered credible if that writer was not published in Beirut, which had become the intellectual melting pot of the Arab world.

Looking back at the period prior to the outbreak of the civil war, all Lebanese reminisce about those days of ferment and creativity when they believed that everything was within their reach. It is extremely difficult to convey the atmosphere of those days and how seriously the Lebanese were involved in all issues that affected them, the Arabs, and the world in general. Lebanese women were in the forefront of the Arab women's movement; they had achieved great gains and were becoming visible in all social, economic, and political fields. Many seminars, lectures, and conferences were taking place to discuss feminist issues, how to secure a feminist agenda, and Arab women's relations with Third World and Western feminists.

Those were days rich in experience and only students of the subject who are unaware of this rich background can assert, as Miriam Cooke has done in *War's Other Voices*, that the civil war "has brought about an unprecedented feminist consciousness which should be registered before it disappears unnoticed."[1] I would argue that this consciousness originated in the period before the war, when women had time to think about and to analyze their condition. Nearly all of the feminist writers mentioned by Cooke had been published prior to the war and the feminist content of their work has not changed since. During the war, men and women were living with insecurity and anxiety about their personal survival. When abstract concerns such as feminism persist in the consciousness of a society at war, the level of purpose in the debate has diminished, because to have a purpose beyond survival becomes in the minds of people a factor interrupting their quest for self-preservation. In such an atmosphere, there invariably develops a diminishing of political and social consciousness, which is what happened in Lebanon.

Miriam Cooke argues that before the war there were two kinds of writers, those concerned with women's issues, like Leila Baalbaki and Ghada Samman, and those who were mainly concerned with political issues and commitment. This assessment is inaccurate, since Leila Baalbaki was very much in the consciousness of the politicized women of Lebanon, who had championed her cause when she published her book *Ana Ahya* (I Live), the first feminist book in the Arab world to advocate explicitly that women should take possession of their own bodies. When this book was banned by the Lebanese authorities, Baalbaki became a *cause celèbre* for the politicized women of Lebanon. Nor can one argue, as has Cooke, that Leila Usairan had not developed her feminist consciousness prior to the war, since Usairan was holding feminist study groups in the late 1960s and early 1970s, long before the outbreak of the war.

I do not want to spend a great deal of time on Miriam Cooke's book. I mention it as an example of feminist theory applied as a rigid framework rather than an analytical tool. With regard to Lebanon, the most important observation which can be made is that, as a result of the breakdown of the social order, people clung to family and tradition, and extended family ties became stronger than ever. One positive outcome of this is found in the psychiatric studies of the effects of the war on Lebanese children, which found that the children were not as affected by the traumatic experience as expected because the extended family and close social relations provided a strong protective support system which gave them, despite the trauma, a great deal of security.

Another result of the breakdown of the state machinery was the total disruption of services usually provided by the state. Water, electricity, sewage, garbage collection, and other services usually taken for granted by city-dwellers were totally disrupted. This led to an increase in women's chores in the home and to a renewed emphasis on traditional women's roles, which adversely affected women. This was compounded by the rise of the fundamentalist movement in Lebanon which put the feminist movement on the defensive.

Employment figures show that following the war the number of women in the workforce has decreased, and in education, where men and women had almost achieved parity, figures now show a greater

disparity. It has often been asserted that because of the deconstruc-
tion of society as a result of war women can construct new roles. What
happened in Lebanon, however, was exactly the opposite. The decon-
struction of society led to the arrest of progress, the stifling of creativity, and to the reduction of concern for basic needs. Women, instead
of being free to construct new roles, were in fact consumed with old
traditional roles and domestic duties. Women's understanding of the
need for change and their accumulated experience during the pre-war
period, which had changed their perceptions of themselves and men's
perception of them as well, were lost in the daily battle for survival.

One thing we all learned from the Algerian experience is that, without
its articulation, experience has no meaning. From that perspective, even
if some Lebanese women felt empowered as a result of their personal
participation in the war, this has not translated into gains for women,
because they were not organized as women around an agenda. In
fact, the only organized women's activities during the war were demonstrations and sit-ins against the war. The war marginalized women;
they found themselves organizing, together with other marginalized
sectors of society, non-violent protests against the war and trying to
reconstruct out of the debris some modicum of normality.

We come back to the question, what was the impact of the war on
Lebanese women? I would say that it sidetracked women from concentrating on developing their communities, which is a precondition
for improving the status of women. Most Lebanese women who suffered through this war were despondent bystanders witness to the destruction of their country and their earlier achievements, who
yearned for peace in order to devote their energies toward the reconstruction of their society so that men and women might together pursue their right to authentic freedom and liberation.

Notes

1. Miriam Cooke, *War's Other Voices* (New York: Cambridge University Press, 1987).

13

The Effects of War on Women in Lebanon

Julinda Abu Nassr

Lebanese women radiated with life and beauty before the war. During the war, they struggled to remain afloat, living under harsh circumstances and in the most destructive and discouraging circumstances, without much notice taken of their opinions about the political, military, or economic conditions of what had become a war-society. But Lebanese women saved the most precious things in life: the family and their integrity, and consequently their country.

When we speak of war and society, and when we decide to concentrate on women as half of the population and an integral segment of society, we are encumbered with conceptual and practical variables. The situation is complex, and therefore we must divide our issue into parts, and the parts into chapters. The first part can comprise the effects of the war on women, with chapters analyzing psychological effects, stress syndromes, as well as economic, health, infrastructure, environment, child-care, social costumes, humanitarian activities, legal and human rights, not to mention gender relations. The second part involves the coping strategies of women, both conscious and unconscious. The chapters of this part would represent the actual developments and unfolding of part one.

Hence the situation is paradoxical, because, along with the laws of destruction, new life-affirming laws of survival emerge, asserting the never-ending human ability to start from scratch time after time. The involvement of the women of Lebanon in the destruction was practically non-existent. They did not initiate the war, nor did they encourage it. In fact, it disregarded their existence altogether. Women had no say over when the war started, neither in the decision-making processes, nor in the efforts to achieve reconciliation. Their roles were those of the recipients of the consequences and the outcomes of the war on the one hand, and the makers and manufacturers of the laws of survival on the other hand.

EFFECTS OF THE WAR ON WOMEN

In very simple terms, the war made life extremely difficult, not to mention dangerous. It caused at least partial destruction of the country's infrastructure. In addition to the loss of safety and security, basic domestic facilities were hardest hit. Hence, food supplies had to be secured in very hazardous conditions, water, electricity, and other basic necessities were barely available. Sending the children to school became a daily ordeal for the parents as well as the children. And the list goes on. Women, being the basic managers of domestic and family affairs, were under tremendous pressure and had to rely on primitive and other resourceful means to secure their needs. "It was difficult to satisfy even life's elementary needs, but the extremity of the situation channeled women's inventiveness and initiative. They adapted traditional methods meant for a different era and environment, the war-torn environment."[1]

Another major effect on the women was the absence of men and husbands. A majority of the men went off to battle, and many died, leaving widows with families to sustain. Others migrated to work overseas in the Gulf, Africa, Europe, and the Americas in order to sustain their families financially. Women were suddenly heads of families, with little if any previous experience or preparation. With inflation rising to 300 percent in the mid-80s in the middle of the war (and reaching 1,000 percent in 1992), financial resources became scarce. Many women had to leave their homes and secure jobs. Consequently, Lebanese urban centers witnessed an increase in female labor force participation. In a sample survey conducted in 1990 in Beirut that included women from various locations and religious groups of the city, the main reason cited for working was financial or economic need. Eventually, women began to establish private business enterprises and climb up the ladder of the corporate hierarchy.

In the traditional rural villages, young girls of marriageable age according to social customs also suffered from the absence of appropriate male suitors. The consequence proved to be a positive development for them, for they resorted to seeking higher education. Consequently, student gender ratios approached male/female parity in the universities, and increased even further for females in secondary schools, which had previously been characterized by a significant drop-out rate among female students approaching the traditional age of marriage.[2]

COPING STRATEGIES

The most tragic effect of the war on rural Lebanese women was displacement. Over 700,000 Lebanese were forced to move away from their towns and villages of origin and settle haphazardly in the capital, its suburbs, and Mount Lebanon.[3] Fortunately, these women were approached by grassroots organizations and NGOs like the Institute for Women's Studies in the Arab World to help them sustain their families and integrate them in the labor force. Based on intensive market research to insure the relevance and need for these skills, displaced semi-literate women were offered training workshops. They were taught embroidery, knitting, operating factory machines, and other similar skills. The workshops were complemented by instruction in basic living skills in home management, child-care, family planning, health, nutrition, environment, law and legal rights from a kit produced by the Institute. Finally, the Institute helped them secure jobs and market their products. At least 500 to 1,000 women benefited from this project in its first three years.

As far as military conflicts were concerned, Lebanese women proved to be an impressive source of humanitarian and medical first aid assistance. Women's major achievement was to hold together the collapsing structures of Lebanese society. They patched up the lack of adequate social and medical services by volunteering to work in social welfare organizations, both national and international, such as the Red Cross, the YWCA, the Child Welfare Association, the Child Care Association, Family Planning Association, Catholic Relief Services, Near East School of Theology, Terre des Hommes, the United Nations Development Program, and various local women's groups.[4]

They coordinated relief actions for refugees and displaced families by providing food rations, blankets, clothes, medical treatment, and shelter. Some women even traveled overseas to collect help and funding, and to stay up-to-date with educational developments and other sustainable development programs.

Lebanese women also protested war activities by sending communiqués — which were all left unanswered. Peace marches organized by individuals and women's groups were shrewdly dismantled by angry war-profiteering politicians.

Women reopened schools and resumed education at the beginning of the war in 1975, after a long period of closure. Hence, in November 1975, one school opened after a few women teachers decided to take up their duties and perform as well as could be expected. The school soon swarmed with children and other schools followed suit.

Women also formed the majority of schoolteachers. As a professor in a university, a trainer of preschool teachers, and a consultant for schools in the country and across the region, I am proud to confirm the gigantic, superhuman role performed by women in an effort to keep schools and classes going against all security odds, to maintain a respectable and advanced level of education and to deal with all traumatic situations and reactions of children and students caused by war conditions.

However, probably the greatest achievement of Lebanese women during the war was the role they performed inside their homes. In their determination to provide all the necessary domestic needs they insured that children had a home to return to. Many women would tell tales of how they saved their husbands, children, and relatives from the violent circumstances around them. Despite the absence of law and order, civil codes of behavior were maintained to the best possible level. It is true that chaos did produce some anomie or alienation from accepted norms and values by releasing latent aggression in adults as well as children, but generally speaking, the situation could have been much worse.

Women's sacrifices and strict attention to family needs saved the family structure in Lebanon. The family is the most powerful and important social unit in Middle Eastern society. Therefore, by saving it the Lebanese women saved the country and its future.

CONCLUSION

My mind becomes crowded with all the relevant details, actions, achievements, and resourcefulness of Lebanese women and the ways they survived the war. The list of women's achievements is long. They sustained an entire country on the constant brink of collapse in a never-ending and ever-increasing state of chaos and anarchy. And in the process they lost loved ones, homes, and personal opportunities. They did all of this in a predominantly patriarchal society that values men more than women. Yet women of Lebanon proved themselves in their country and in the international community.

In post-war Lebanon, women are reaching political posts, and recently three women became members of the new parliament. They are raising their voices to have the Lebanese government ratify the Convention for the Elimination of All Forms of Discrimination Against Women; they are getting directly involved in the worldwide and national campaign for a cleaner and safer environment; and they promise to overturn discriminatory legislation curtailing women's civil rights, notably to conduct business transactions without the required endorsement of a man. In an interview conducted with the female deputies, they were determined to become involved in decisions concerning national and international affairs, such as the return of the displaced to their homes, the retreat of foreign forces from Lebanon, the preservation and improvement of the educational system, the battle against soaring inflation and an acute economic crisis, and other national issues.

Some writers have attributed the involvement of Lebanese women in the government, the labor force, the economy, education, and health-care to the war; specifically, to the fact that women were filling the gap created because many men were either killed or had gone into exile. I believe that Lebanese women have historically been demanding a greater share in the country's development and that they were preparing themselves for this role all along by achieving higher education in all fields and by struggling to achieve a high profile in society by all means at their disposal, and that the war has not deterred them.

Notes

1. See Jullette Haddad, *Al-Raida* (Beirut), November 1, 1984, no. 34.
2. Hannania, *Women and Education in Lebanon*, monograph by the Institute for Women's Studies in the Arab World, 1980.
3. Iskandar and Baroudi, 1984.
4. "Women as Peace Makers," *Al-Raida*, August 1980.

14

Lebanon's Civil War Through Different Eyes: An Interview with Jean Said Makdesi

Suha Sabbagh

You have written an autobiogaphical work about your experience in Lebanon during the last few years.¹ What was the driving force behind your motivation to write?

I was motivated primarily by the desire to communicate my experience to others. I wanted to record what was happening, perhaps because it was so difficult for me to accept rationally the real situation. By recording it I would then become a witness to what was happening and, in this respect, I would confirm to myself and to posterity that these things actually happened and hopefully that they will not be allowed to happen again.

In a sense, writing is a form of experiencing these events on two levels: the first is the lived experience and the second is its recreation in language. The relation between the two is not very clear to me at this point, since I am too close to the actual event, but I believe that writing confirms — it is an act of witness — that terribly ruthless acts were indeed committed. I believe that the number of autobiographical works written by women writers in Lebanon may well be motivated by the desire to present to the world a human record of the war.

There were some women, of course, who wrote from a specific political angle. I chose to write on behalf of the victims of the war, since their voices are rarely heard. By victims, I mean the non-combatant population. Political parties have enough spokesmen. The unarmed men and women have been left to fend for themselves; it is their predicament that I seek to record.

I also wrote to record the daily realities of life in situations that few people outside of Lebanon can fathom. I did not seek to conduct a political analysis, since there has been enough said on the subject. There is an element of social history in the work, since it is a record of how people reacted to major historical events. My book reads, I hope, like a map, and shows the resilience of the human spirit in times of adversity.

Since the intifada on the West Bank and Gaza, we have been exposed to images of violence and bloodshed every night on the evening news. How does this street fighting compare with the experience of Lebanon?

The intifada is much easier to understand and analyze. There are occupiers and occupied; the lines are clear and tightly drawn. The individual has a single identity, and belongs to one camp or the other. In Lebanon the situation is far more complex, since in the years of conflict individuals have recognized in themselves more than one identity. This can be emotionally devastating, especially when a militia is in charge and can pass life or death sentences based on what it perceives to be one's single identity. Responses to situations are not as clear either, and life in general becomes far more emotionally demanding. Over the years, alliances have shifted between the parties to the conflict, and hence also the identity of individuals vis-à-vis the war. The impact of this is draining.

There is also the cultural dimension to the conflict in Lebanon. The situation is far more complex than on the West Bank and in Gaza, in that all parties to the conflict are of similar cultural background but perceive themselves differently. If there is any clear-cut definition it is between the armed and the unarmed, the militia and the civilians. In this dichotomy it seems to me one side is victimized no matter which party it belongs to and I have chosen to speak for these victims.

Where do women fit into the quagmire that is Lebanon? How has the war changed their role and their perception of self? Are there any feminist issues being raised at the present time?

When the most important issue is daily survival it is very difficult to think of bringing up feminist issues. But the war has changed the role of women and made them far more independent. Women are left to handle the crises created by the political situation. They are the ones who have to find food to place on the table. They are responsible for the safety of their children in extremely dangerous situations.

Women will no doubt emerge a lot stronger from this experience which was a test of their strength. While this is not the time to discuss the issue of equality, women have gained greater autonomy by default and they will, no doubt, have trouble relinquishing this new-found power.

The traditional role of women provided a form of security and a source of control. I have known many women who used the traditional respect accorded to them in our culture to resist the militia and, in some cases, to save the lives of members of their families. In these cases, women simply used the system of traditional values in the current political context and it worked in instances when otherwise only superior physical power could have worked. While the militia had no fear of the unarmed population, traditional respect for women inculcated by their upbringing was hard to overcome. I am not saying that in all situations this respect works, only that women have often used it to protect themselves.

What, in your opinion, will be the impact of this change on the role of women in the future?

I believe that we shall see a situation that is similar to that following other wars. After war, women who have had to handle all family responsibilities in the absence of their husbands have often found it hard to relinquish the powerful role they had been forced to assume. Here in Lebanon, many men, heads of large families, have had to leave the country for economic reasons, seeking work where they could find it abroad. Their women, who learned to fend for themselves during the times of danger, will find it very difficult to yield the autonomy thus thrust upon them when the situation normalizes and the family is reunited. This is only one of many examples of what I am talking about. Another is the strain imposed by months at a time of enormous stress on people living at very close quarters, such as a shelter or at home, without work or entertainment to lighten the burden. The results of the strain that the current situation has placed on marriages in Lebanon have yet to be seen.

As for the woman's movement, it seems clear to me that most social demands were suspended during the war. The demands of women for greater equality under the law, for better social status in general, were naturally suspended as well. This is especially true since women had absolutely no place or representation in the military power establishments which governed during the war. I believe that now the war has come to an end, the demands of women will once again be voiced, but this time by women made stronger by their terrible experiences. There will also, I feel sure, be a great public debate on the point, as the perception of the required status of women is at the core of many difficult cultural and political questions which still need to be settled.

Notes

1. Jean Said Makdesi, *Beirut Fragments: A War Memoir* (New York: Persea Books, 1990).

PART SIX

Palestinian Feminism
and Nationalism

15

Palestinian Women and Institution Building

Suha Sabbagh

Raymonda Tawil, a Palestinian activist who was living on the West Bank during the Israeli occupation in 1967, correspondent to various foreign journals and editor of the Palestinian journal *Al-Awda,* became fairly well-known in the United States and Europe through her contact with Western reporters and foreign diplomats visiting the West Bank. Her autobiography, *My Home, My Prison,* was one of the earliest sources to offer information on the way that Palestinian women organized in reaction to the punitive measures imposed by the occupying military government. In her book, Tawil offers important details about specific events which led to women's active involvement in resisting changes imposed by the Israeli military government such as changes in the school curriculum, and women's participation in demonstrations carried out against the demolition of homes.

Tawil describes the condition of the refugees evicted from their homes and settled temporarily around her house during the first few days of the 1967 invasion. Her first efforts were to provide food, shelter, and medical care. Together with Sahar Khalifeh, who has since become a well-known author whose novels have been translated into nine languages, she set off to get the Israeli authorities to open up the UNRWA warehouse (United Nations Relief and Works Agency) to provide food for the refugees. Tawil, who grew up in the coastal city of Acre after 1948, was able to communicate with the soldiers in Hebrew. The two women's move was bold since at that point no one knew what to expect from the occupying power. Their action was pragmatic and devoid of any ideological posturing. When some local men objected to their behavior, both because as women they were not supposed to ride in a jeep with the soldiers, and on nationalistic grounds, the two women responded by saying, "We now have a lot of mouths to feed and a lot of displaced people to care for and this will determine our agenda." This early reaction in many ways set the tone of the agenda of the women's organizations in later years. Palestinian women on the West Bank and in Gaza have maintained the same directness in their approach to solving the problems faced by the community.

By and large, in the early days of the occupation, women organized as an extension of their nurturing role. Any problem touching on the life of the family, education, food for needy families, medical care, etc. became the domain of the Arab Women's Union, whose activities are recounted in Tawil's autobiography. In this early phase, women's position shifts from being the guarantor of life in the maternal context to becoming protector of life and family concerns in the political context. However, it is incorrect to assume that women have no ideological views. Although their approach is basic and is concerned with survival, women's organizations also belong to different ideological factions within the Palestine Liberation Organization (PLO), and the nature of their involvement is influenced by their views. The Arab Women's Union, whose membership consists of middle-class women, is mainly a charitable organization, while other organizations are more involved with vocational training and self-help.

WELFARE ORGANIZATIONS MARK THE FIRST PHASE

The Society for the Resuscitation of the Family, In'ash el-Usra, headed by a dynamic and self-motivated woman, Samiha Khalil, was founded in 1965, two years before the Israeli occupation of the West Bank and Gaza. The objective of this organization was to help women, especially single heads of households, to increase their income. In 1965 the budget of this small organization was $500. By the time Israel forced the organization to shut down in 1988, on the grounds that "it was teaching the slogans of the intifada," it was the largest organization of its kind in the West Bank, with an annual budget of $420,000. This organization was helping 15,000 women which included 4,800 women employed in traditional Palestinian embroidery projects in their homes, 152 full-time employees of the society, and 200 young women registered each year in vocational programs. Through this organization, 1,500 families were receiving sponsorship aid of $500 a year, including military prisoners and their families.[1] In'ash el-Usra is not the only organization of its kind. Palestinian society has a high rate of women who are single heads of house-holds, either because their husbands are in jail or because they are employed in Gulf countries. Samiha Khalil realized that women have to rely on each other through a networking system to increase their income, and this welfare organization performed a very important role by providing financial, medical, and scholarship aid programs.[2]

WOMEN'S WORK COMMITTEES

A new form of women's organization began to emerge in the late 1970s, the four women's committees which were also affiliated with the four main factions of the PLO.[3] While the welfare organizations were run from the top down, generally by urban middle-class women who wanted to help women with less income, the new organizations were more democratic and stressed self-help over welfare programs. The younger generation of women felt that welfare organizations did not stress independence and women's issues, focusing instead on as-sistance programs. The women's work committees stressed forming cooperatives for food processing and for agricultural products. They offered literacy classes, health education, office skills training, and food processing. They also provided women with day-care centers so women could feel secure that their children were safe while they were improving their survival skills. Most importantly, they engaged women in political discussions which soon turned into discussions about women's issues and women's rights.[4]

At the start of the intifada, when directives were issued by the United National Leadership of the Uprising (UNLU) calling for strikes or marches to take place, the women's committees would translate them into a call for action by women and pass them on through their networks. They organized marches in which women called for the liberation of the land and for equality for women in a new Palestinian state headed by the PLO. At the beginning of the in-tifada, Israeli soldiers hesitated to use force against women and women turned this constraint to their favor. In more conservative vil-lages, women's participation was smaller, yet signified a shift in what constituted women's territorial domain. The women's committees also benefited from the increased political awareness of women by drawing many new members to join the ranks of these institutions. They attracted women by offering classes in first aid and health edu-cation to compensate for poor access to medical centers in times of curfew. They also increased their day-care hours to make it possible for women to participate in the intifada.

POPULAR COMMITTEES

The intifada saw the emergence of a mass base, an informal system of organizations called the Popular Committees designed to insure the needs of the community and enable them to resist, which consisted of men and women working side by side. Members of the women's committees also joined the Popular Committees and transferred to them their institutional know-how. The two forms of committees were able to supplement each other's programs. The Popular Committees were based on the principle of extending the care and support once reserved to members of one's extended family to all members of one's community. Under curfew and under restricted forms of mobility, one's neighbor is more important than a cousin who lives in the next village. Each neighborhood has a committee to deal with emergencies and ongoing services and supplies: to provide food and baby milk, guard the neighborhood, maintain the clandestine education system, visit prisoners, and to develop and staff the so-called "defense system." This last committee, the most visible one, consists of the *shabab* (youths) who engage the army by throwing stones.

With the exception of the defense committees, all other committees had more than 50 percent female members. It is not difficult to see that women were more efficient in assessing the food and baby food requirements of households, the first aid needs, and the urgent medical care needed, especially in cases of childbirth. The committees sought to meet these needs as best they could because schools were closed. Women developed a clandestine education system in their basements and in community buildings which was illegal; if discovered, the teachers risked a prison sentence and a heavy fine. Pupils who attended had to hide their destination and their books from soldiers, and because of the surrounding anxiety and tension, many were not able to show the same concentration as they might have in a regular school.

Women's committees matured in the process of lending their skills to the intifada. Before the uprising, competition was the norm between committees affiliated with the different political factions, which sometimes led to the duplication of the services offered in certain villages. During the intifada, all committees learned to work together and to coordinate their activities, a step which brought together activists from the various factions. Some analysts have argued that the agenda of the Popular Committees constituted a regression in women's rights because it was an extension of women's traditional role of caring for the sick and the needy, which was vital to the resistance but did not

necessarily benefit women.[5] Others argue that while women's position was not significantly altered, their participation has earned them
a stronger role in family decisions, including greater control over finances, their own mobility, and the education of their children.

During the intifada, women were engulfed in the resistance movement, pushing their own issues aside. However, the Algerian example
was very much on their mind. Later, years into the intifada, women
were ready to go back to their hard-won agenda. Issues under discussion in the Higher Women's Council include the draft legislation on
women's issues to be passed by the interim Palestinian Authority and
a new Palestinian state.[6] There seems to be a consensus that women's
struggle for equal rights has only just begun.

WOMEN'S FOOD COOPERATIVES

In an attempt to meet the directives of the United National Leadership of the Uprising (UNLU) to boycott Israeli goods, the women's
committees established food cooperatives to produce jams, fruit
juices, canned fruits, pickled vegetables, biscuits, and breads. Women
did not have to learn new skills, since canning is practiced in most
Palestinian households. Methods of food preservation had to be improved and products were sold through shops or directly to custom-
ers. The effectiveness of the cooperatives in providing an alternative to
goods imported from Israel was limited; however, the experience afforded women a taste of economic independence and set an example
of how women can contribute to the market while simultaneously
creating jobs.

Um Khalid, a 48-year-old worker in an agricultural cooperative in
her village near the city of Ramallah where she works with twelve village women, had the following to say about her work and her new
sense of self: "Now I feel that I'm able to fight for my full rights as a
woman and as a human being. I am no longer just a housewife. No,
I'm part of the workforce which is creating the direct change in my
society .... By being productive, I can also be a full partner in establishing the structure of our society."[7]

Another successful cooperative, called Our Production Is Our
Pride Cooperative, has two branches in the West Bank and was
formed shortly before the intifada. Its 22 women workers attended a
course in marketing, production methods, and bookkeeping. Decision-making is shared and so are the profits. Their jars of pickled cu-
cumbers, olives, and stuffed eggplants are popular products in shops
around the Jerusalem area. Many cooperatives give women work to

perform at home, in between household chores such as embroidering traditional dresses and other items.

Assessment of the impact of cooperatives and other forms of home economics on women's lives indicates that increased income does not automatically alter the gender gap. Women still do their household chores in addition to their work outside the home. Yet, participation in the cooperative decision-making process seems to have altered their perceptions of themselves. As one female worker put it: "As rural women, we have been working on the land all our lives, but we did not take a role in the decision-making and we never dared to ask to be paid by our husbands or fathers. Now we can work as we did, but with more organization and taking part in the decision-making."[8]

WOMEN'S RESEARCH CENTERS

If documentation of women's participation can safeguard against the obliteration of women's rights after independence has been won, then Palestinian women's rights are well insured. Several research centers belonging to different political factions publish regularly on women's issues. The Women's Affairs Center located in Nablus, headed by Sahar Khalifeh, publishes a quarterly journal in Arabic. The center trains researchers who have published studies on women in agricultural cooperatives; on the exploitation of nurses by local hospitals; the choice of a career in journalism by women; and assessment of the women's movement in the occupied territories. In addition to interviews with local activists, the journal has also published translations of articles by Robin Morgan and other Western feminists. Among its many activities, the Center sponsors lectures and house meetings to raise women's consciousness on women's issues. Other research centers are doing similar work.

The Women's Resource and Research Center in Jerusalem publishes a monthly popular women's magazine, *Al-Mara'a*, which deals with the social issues facing women. It has published an economic study entitled "The Socio-Economic Conditions of Female Wage Labor in the West Bank," which addresses such issues as vacations and health insurance available to women, training available for women, and an assessment of women's awareness of their labor conditions; and another paper entitled, "Women Street Vendors," which assessed women's income and status in society. The Center holds conferences and lectures in association with women's committees to inform women about their rights. The committees have carried out a campaign and published information pamphlets on violence against women in the home, and they hold consciousness-raising sessions in which women discuss their rights and their role in society.

The Palestinian Research and Development Group, known as Bisan, located in the Ramallah area, published the proceedings of a women's conference entitled "Together Toward Enlightenment and Equality,"[9] held on December 14, 1990 and attended by nearly 500 people. Its five academic papers and four workshops were highly critical of the gains made by women. A participant summed up the mood of the day when she said, "This is the first time we say out loud that there isn't a fundamental change in the role of women in Palestinian society." One of the papers dealt with the "Intifada and Social Issues,"[10] in which the author addresses the reasons behind the retreat from female participation during the second phase of the intifada. Another panelist argued that women's status has not been altered in proportion to their contributions to the national struggle. Women continue to be perceived exclusively as protectors of the home and have not been fully represented at the political level, which can be seen in their representation in the Palestine National Council, which does not exceed ten percent. A third paper, "Intifada and Social Norms" states that the austere culture which developed during the intifada did not benefit women. Other centers published studies on the role of women, children, and the family. Should Palestinians have their own state, these studies may provide an analysis of social and development policy on which a new government might base its policies. It is to be hoped that through the documentation of their significant role, women will be able to achieve equal rights within the framework of a democratic Palestinian state.

CONCLUDING REMARKS

The emergence of women into the forefront of the intifada is a reflection of the interdependence of the national and the gender-based struggles. As two women authors from the occupied territories put it: "Just as the intifada in its initial stage offered remarkable opportunities for the development of the women's movement, the obverse is also true; the women's movement in the occupied territories, inextricably tied to the national movement, reflects each twist and turn of the national fortune. The shape that the fledgling women's movement will take in the future depends on the political future of the territories occupied by Israel."[11]

Women on the West Bank see their future as tied to the fate of the national liberation struggle. And, one might add, on the future of the

U.S-sponsored peace negotiations and its resulting "Palestinian Authority."

Notes

1. For information on In'ash el-Usra, see Orayb Najjar, "Palestinian Self-Reliance on Trial," *The Christian Century*, November 23, 1988, pp. 1070-1072.

2. Even when the society faced a severe financial crisis in 1984, Khalil refused offers of aid from organizations that did not support the principle of self-determination for Palestinians. She refused funds from American organizations whose money comes from the U.S. Congress, on the grounds that the same Congress finances Israel, which in turn transgresses against Palestinian rights.

3. The four women's committees are affiliated with the following political groups — Federation of Palestinian Women's Action Committees (FPWAC): the Democratic Front for the Liberation of Palestine; Union of Palestinian Working Women's Committees (UPWWC): the Communist Party; Union of Palestinian Women's Committees (UPWC): the Popular Front for the Liberation of Palestine; and Women's Committee for Social Work (WCSW) supports Fatah.

4. Joost Hilterman, "The Women's Movement During the Uprising," *Journal of Palestine Studies* 20;3 (Spring 1991), pp. 48-57.

5. See Islah Jad, "Impact of the Intifada on the Palestinian Family," in Suha Sabbagh (ed.), *Gender in the Intifada* (Washington, D.C.: Institute for Arab Women's Studies, forthcoming).

6. See the draft document reprinted below, pp. 258-61; and Phillipa Strum, *The Women Are Marching: The Second Sex and the Palestinian Revolution* (New York: Lawrence Hill Books, 1992), p. 161.

7. Saida Hamad, "Intifada Transforms Palestinian Society Especially the Role of Women," *Al-Fajr*, March 13, 1989.

8. Ibid.

9. The Bisan Center for Research and Development is headed by Izzat Abdel-Hadi. Eileen Kuttab is director of the Women's Research Committee.

10. Eileen Kuttab argues that the intifada consists of two phases. In the first phase, women performed a much more important role. The second period was characterized by a relative decline in the intensity of struggle and a retreat in women's rights. She cites the following reasons for the decline in women's participation in the struggle: 1. The lack of a policy on the part of the national forces to liberate women from the constraints of traditional norms; 2. Both the women's movement and the national forces lacked a clear and pragmatic agenda for dealing with women's issues and a clear women's program; 3. Women formed an important part of the popular committees and local committees: when these committees began to decline, so did women's participation; 4. The rise of fundamentalism brought about the segregation of the sexes.

11. See Rita Giacaman and Penny Johnson, "Intifada Year Four: Notes on the Women's Movement" in Sabbagh, *Gender in the Intifada*.

16

The Declaration of Principles on Palestinian Women's Rights: An Analysis

Suha Sabbagh

On September 13, 1993, Yasir Arafat, chairman of the Palestine Liberation Organization, and Yitzhak Rabin, prime minister of Israel (assassinated on October 4, 1995), shook hands on the South Lawn of the White House while President Clinton looked on approvingly. What will this handshake, touted as the most important and most televised handshake of the century, mean for Palestinian women on the ground? Will this handshake lead to change in the direction of bringing about equal rights? Or will it simply lead to a perpetuation of the status quo in gender relations once a new Palestinian government is established. In Arab culture and traditions Arab men are considered as the guardians and protectors of women, justified in the name of the words of the *shari'a: "Al-rijal quayyamun a la al nissa"* (men are the protectors and providers for women). In the present context, this statement could become a tool to distance Palestinian women, who for many years aided in maintaining the fiber of society under occupation, from competing for coming job opportunities or seeking higher offices.

To insure that their rights will be guarded during the upcoming period of political transition, women on the West Bank have been actively involved in drafting their Declaration of Principles on Women's Rights (see Appendix A). If they succeed in incorporating this document into the constitution of a new Palestinian state, this will mark the first time in the history of the West Bank that women will have buttressed their struggle for equal rights with a document that constitutes the cornerstone of Palestinian national rights.

It is interesting to trace the path which transformed this document from a draft proposed by the General Union of Palestinian Women, residing in Tunis and somewhat cut off from women's groups in the occupied territories, to the semi-final third draft supported and signed by most of the women's organizations, including some who oppose the Oslo agreement but who see this draft as empowering to women. As might be expected, the final document displays symptoms of being a "tired text," or a text that has been worked over to the point of losing its directness in projecting women's demands. This symptom is an indication of the amount of time spent in discussion, compromising, and outright haggling between the various women's groups which prepared the final document. The two previous drafts were written by groups that shared a greater degree of consensus, while the third draft which became the final draft was endorsed by most of the women's organizations, ranging from the conservative In'ash el-Usra, headed by Samiha Khalil, to the more progressive groups, such as the Bisan Center in Ramallah, headed by Eileen Kuttab (see interview, pp. 121-26). Each organization in this vast spectrum has its own agenda and political affiliation and this is reflected in the demands made in this document.

The women who attended the meetings to ratify this document are impressed with the fact that it reached this semi-final stage and that such a large number of the women's organizations have signed on to it. After the dust has settled, it will perhaps be advisable to rewrite this third draft in a way that will reintroduce the directness of women's demands exhibited in the second Tunis draft without altering the delicate balance achieved by all groups and without disturbing the more democratic nature of the last draft.

COMMENTS ON THE SECOND AND THIRD, SEMI-FINAL DRAFTS

Both draft documents were signed in the name of the General Union of Palestinian Women, an umbrella organization which is part of the PLO, formed in 1965, which includes women from all four main Palestinian political factions. In the past, women's groups in the occupied territories had little contact with the leadership structure of the General Union of Palestinian Women. Headquartered in Tunis, the latter group was coopted by the leadership, where female participation in the PLO structure verged on little more than tokenism. Cut off from the leadership structure, the women's movement in the occupied territories developed a more serious agenda, focusing on issues of equality and exceeding the "feminine" activities of women's groups outside the West Bank. Because their demands were based on women's essential role in preserving the very fiber of society during the intifada and prior to that, women on the West Bank felt more secure in making these demands. The final document was written on the West Bank, on national soil, where women's contributions are well recognized; consequently this draft reflects a more self-assured posture. Women do not feel the need to reiterate first the means by which they contributed to the national struggle since these are well recognized facts.

When one analyzes the "we" of the second and third drafts, it becomes evident that the final or third draft projects a less hierarchical and more democratic tone generally absent from the second draft. In the second Tunis draft, the "we" of the speaker is univocal: it stands for the General Union of Palestinian Women who speak for all Palestinian women. Not all women belong to this organization; yet the text states, "We, in the General Union of Palestinian Women (GUPW), declare in the name of all Palestinian women that we look forward to assuming — on equal footing — the responsibility in the independent stage ... ," etc. Implied here is a certain hierarchy whereby the GUPW places itself in the position of speaking for all women, yet the categories of women are not even mentioned.

Who is the "we" of the speaker in the third draft? Although the document is also written in the name of the GUPW, in the section entitled "General Provisions," "we" is defined as "the women of Palestine, from all social categories and the various faiths, including workers, farmers, housewives, students, professionals, and politicians [who] promulgate our determination to proceed without struggle to abolish all forms of discrimination and inequality against women." Of course, the women who wrote the draft are not all the ones listed above, yet there is a more democratic spirit in that the different categories of women are at least listed as the ones who stand behind this statement.

It is equally interesting to compare the areas in which each group of women buttresses women's demands. In the first paragraph of the second draft, the writers feel compelled to bring up first and foremost the issues that still concern the whole Palestinian society, such as "Zionist settlements are set up on large parts of it [Palestine]." This is a reflection of the fact that the women's agenda in Tunis has always prioritized the national issue over equal rights for women. The writers also state their concern first for the national agenda: "The people, and its political leadership, has yet to achieve a number of its national

goals, such as the right to return, self-determination, and the establishment of the independent state." Later on, the writers buttress
their demands for equal rights in "the Palestinian Declaration of Independence," followed by "the Universal Declaration of Human
Rights," on which the former is based, and on "international charters
pertinent to political, legal, civil, and religious rights, as well as with
the various conventions that aim at the elimination of all forms of discrimination."

In the third and final document, the authors do not feel compelled
to state first their concern for the national issues and agenda. This is
a reflection of the fact that the women's groups on the West Bank
have had a separate women's agenda; it is also a reflection of the fact
that the third draft was written at a later period. Since the signing of
the peace agreement, women on the West Bank have felt the urgency
of pushing for a women's agenda because the failure to do so at this
moment could mean that Palestinian women will not reap the benefits of their long and hard struggle for both national and equal rights.

What is curious about the opening paragraph of the third and final
document is the emphasis placed right at the outset on the need for
the government to respect the rights of minorities: "The rights of minorities will duly be respected by the majority, as minorities abide by
decisions of the majority." This right is stated even before the "public
rights of men and women." One must assume that religious and political minorities present at this meeting somewhat felt the need to insure their rights as such before insuring their rights as women, by
including this section from the Palestinian Declaration of Independence.

Another interesting feature of the third and final document is that
on more than one occasion the document seeks to insure the rights of
"women and men." I suppose that this is a tactic to avoid confrontation with men and also within the women's movement with more
conservative groups. Although the stated objective of the document is
to "enhance the principle of equality between women and men in all
spheres of life," the binary opposition which governs this text is not
always the relation of men and women; rather it is the relation of men
and women to society.

The body of the text stresses three main areas in which women
seek equal rights: political rights, civil rights, and economic, social,
and cultural rights (these last three are lumped together). Their order
in the text clearly reflects the concerns of the authors. First and foremost, under political rights, is the right to vote and run for office. At
this historical juncture women fear becoming disenfranchised from

the political arena now that their participation in the process of liberation is no longer necessary. Women seek guarantees to represent the
state in "international and regional organizations as well as in diplomatic corps."

Based on the interpretation of the *shari'a*, in some Islamic countries women are not considered fit for certain judicial positions, specifically that of judge, because allegedly their emotional fluctuation
can cloud their judgment. While this statement does not address this
issue directly, yet implied here is the demand for a reconsideration of
such archaic notions in order for women to compete for government
positions at all levels.

The category of civil rights also reflects the concerns of women at
this historical juncture. In all Arab countries (except Tunisia) citizenship is passed on from the father to the children or wife. Women don't
have the right to pass their citizenship to their husband or their children. In 1989, after the declaration of independence was passed by
the Palestine National Council (PNC) and the leadership started is-
suing Palestinian passports (not valid as travel documents), women
petitioned the PLO leadership to give them the right to pass their nationality on to their husbands and children. This was because in the
diaspora many Palestinian women have married non-Palestinians but
they want to share their national identity with their offspring. The
leadership agreed, but no steps were taken to guarantee this right.

Also in this section women demand a woman's right to be protected
from family violence and granted the right to "express herself." The
right to "express oneself" could, of course, imply the right to choose
one's husband, although it might have been far more effective to state
that outright as is the case in the second draft. Interestingly, the document calls for compensation for chores conducted by women within
the house: "Motherhood should be looked upon as a social post.
House chores should be regarded as a task of social and economic
value." This constitutes a very progressive position, although to date
this demand has not been implemented by more progressive countries with more resources.

The section of the document on economic, social, and cultural
rights stresses equality in work opportunities and wages, in all securi-
ties and compensations, in training and promotion, and in women's
right to maternity leave and other services which enable women to
combine their family duties and work. Palestinian society in general is
not averse to seeing women in positions of power in the workplace.
However, because of the extreme shortage of jobs under occupation,
women anticipate that they will be elbowed out by men seeking em-

ployment in the coming phase under autonomy. Childbearing could be used as an excuse to keep women out of the job market. Palestinian society is very family oriented and bringing up the children is a very important consideration. Therefore, to enable women to work, there have to be excellent day-care facilities and a sufficiently long maternity leave to prevent critics from claiming that working women cause undue hardships to their children and their families.

Equality in educational opportunities is only hinted at. It is possible that women did not feel a sense of urgency in requesting this right, because institutions of higher education generally do not bar women who seek to be admitted. Palestinians have a near obsession with seeking an education, perhaps because with the loss of their land in 1948 the only source of income for the individual became through education. Many Palestinians were able to work in Gulf countries, underdeveloped at the time, and some amassed great fortunes due to their education. However, parents often have to choose between sending their sons or their daughters to school due to financial hardships.

While the final draft shows a more democratic and a more self-assured tone, the second Tunis draft is more direct in presenting the rights of women than the final document. It might have been better in the final draft to address separately each of the rights discussed in the third section, economic, social and cultural rights, since by lumping them together the text is sometimes confusing. However, as one of the authors of this document has said, the real achievement here is in having a majority of women's groups agree on a single document.

More difficult than all obstacles encountered in ratifying and drafting this document will be the process of incorporating it into a future constitution of the country. At the moment, the response of the leadership has been that the document will be incorporated as long as it does not contradict the *shari'a*. This is a political statement that leaves the issue up for interpretation, and a lot depends in this case on the resistance put forth by political Islam, and Hamas in particular.

17

The Women's Document: A Tool for Women's Empowerment and Struggle

An Interview with Eileen Kuttab*

Who was involved in initiating and preparing the women's rights document?

The process of preparing the document, in my view, passed through three stages. I can talk about them briefly and elaborate during the interview.

The first stage represented the different uncoordinated local initiatives of various human rights institutions like Al-Haq in Ramallah, the Women's Center for Legal Aid and Counselling in Jerusalem, and of other women's committees which are part of the constituency of the Women's Technical Committee, Women's Working Committee and Women's Action Committee (Fida). All of these different initiatives had a common understanding that a certain document of principles should be prepared at this stage to be presented to the Palestinian Authority to be included in the Palestinian constitution to protect women's rights, and to guarantee a democratic law that can protect all human rights including those of women.

During the same period, the executive board of the General Union of Palestinian Women from Tunis presented a proposed draft of a document on principles of women's rights asking "women" of the occupied territories to respond to it and present any required changes

* This interview was conducted by and first appeared in *News from Within* (Jerusalem), vol. 10, no. 9, Sept. 1994. Reprinted by permission.

that would accommodate the issue of women in occupied Palestine. The proposal, I think, has activated the work and institutionalized it in the Women's Technical Committee, at first.

The other women's committees and some developmental institutions which also represent women's concerns have not been formally part of the initiatives, as they were opposed to actual involvement with quasi-governmental organizations like the Women's Technical Committee. At the same time, they possessed doubts about the possibility of the autonomy to promote a Palestinian constitution, as it does not possess the legislative power to do so. This, in addition to the initial idea that the document will be presented to a legislative body to insure that there would be no discrimination in the constitution and hence the document would be used as a tool to pressure the autonomy, have marginalized the women in opposition and women's grassroots organizations.

Eventually, the different discussions and debates among women of all political affiliations in the different women's platforms like Palestinian Women's Advocacy Group (Task Force) — which consists of different professional and political points of view — clarified the position of the opposition that they will not be part of the initiative as long as the committee works in the context of the Women's Technical Committee; also, they said, they will not use it as a tool to pressure the Palestinian Authority. This discussion, in addition to the full awareness that a united women's position is required for such a document to be a powerful tool, urged some of the members of the Women's Document Committee to propose the idea of an independent unified committee that could represent all different political affiliations, in addition to the representation of different legal and human rights institutions. Hence, this idea was fruitful in unifying women in the drafting of the women's document and the formulation of the Women's Document Committee ended the second stage.

The third stage represented the process in which the opposition, especially the Union of Palestinian Women's Committees headed by Maha Nasser, proposed the idea of involving the General Union of Palestinian Women in the discussion of the document and to try and make them adopt it, as they are the legitimate representatives of women's NGOs and umbrellas: the union of the women voluntary organizations (charitable societies) and the women's committees. This initiative was successful, and it became a reality when the executive board of the General Union of Palestinian Women adopted it as their own document and the document committee became an ad hoc committee to the GUPW.

Is the United Council of Women still functional as it was during the intifada in organizing women's political work?

No, there are different new structures where women coordinate in addition to the still existing legitimate structure that represents the women's movement, which is the GUPW. The previous structure that represented unity collapsed after the signing of the Palestinian-Israeli agreement and new structures have emerged to address the priorities of the new political stage. For example, the Women's Technical Committee (mentioned above), which was one of the first to take the initiative to prepare the document, its core represents women from the Women's Working Committee, the Women's Social Work Committee (Fatah), and some "professional experts" who are defined as independent women. This platform is mainly concerned with gender issues and it is now in the process of becoming a formal appendage of the autonomy.

Another new structure is the Palestinian Women's Advocacy Group, which is both professional and representative. This group has two functions: it works as an advisory board of the UNDP (UN Development Program) on women's projects, and its representative nature enriches the discussion and debates and coordination of women in different issues that are of concern to women. They hold different workshops to facilitate the preparation of the Palestinian women's agenda, according to women's priorities.

And then the document would be presented for inclusion in a future Palestinian constitution?

Yes, that was the initial idea, that this document should be presented to the Palestinian Authority to be endorsed in the Palestinian constitution. This will be done by the different women's committees that have accepted the autonomy as a political resolution. For the opposition, the document is a tool for empowerment, as they think that the women's struggle should maintain its status at a non-governmental level as it is the only approach for building a democratic civil society. These institutions should not be coopted in the formal politics or in the autonomy governmental structure, as this broadens the gap between the leadership and the masses and hence the women's leadership becomes a group of alienated elites that don't represent the ambitions and priorities of the women masses.

The GUPW passed this document to all its chapters to discuss it and to endorse the changes that are relevant to their priorities, and this process, which is a democratic process led by Samiha Khalil (Um

Khalil), the president of the GUPW, was in a way empowering and consciousness raising. After ending this process some changes were proposed on the draft with the understanding that this document is a draft and will be presented by a conference in the near future.

What exactly do you mean when you say that the document should be used as a tool for empowerment?

For the opposition, the main objective is to use it as a tool for struggle, to empower women on a grassroots level to promote gender consciousness and awareness around social and political issues, which in turn will mobilize women to define a framework for action. In addition to that, this document should become like a thermometer for measuring the gender sensitivity of the NGO structure — mainly NGO institutions and political parties — as even the Left parties have maintained their patriarchal orientation and a movement should be organized to promote and adopt the different principles in their internal regulations.

Another tool which was proposed by the document committee was a petition that would highlight the main principles of the document, and one million signatures will be gathered to use as a tool to mobilize people around it. By adopting these principles, the community is choosing a democratic society that maintains human rights including women's rights. This activity means that the women's question becomes a societal one and the NGO structure is responsible to act on the one hand as a pressure structure on the Palestinian Authority to adopt human rights as a strategy, and on the other hand a support structure that can protect and mobilize the community.

So the document is a means and not an end in itself because in many different Western societies such principles have been adopted by governments but have never been implemented in their daily development policies, since the women's grassroots movement and the community itself have never been considered a tool for achieving democracy.

What were the main differences of opinion in the group which prepared the document?

There were different issues that created debate among the members of the document committee. One was how it was going to be used and to whom it should it be addressed. The end result or decision was that this should be presented to the PLO and the future Palestinian state that will achieve the national rights of the Palestinian people, namely the right of return and self-determination and an independent Palestinian state. In relation to the other issue of how this should be used, the final decision was to leave it up to each institution or women's committee to use it as they wish independently, in addition to formulating a unified action plan that can realize the execution of the different principles that govern the document.

The other issue that created an argument was that of family law. Are we going to adopt civil laws of a secular nature or are we going to surrender to the religious and traditional powers to govern the future women's status? The document has included only general principles and rights that can only be used to formulate the essence of the future laws. Different workshops have discussed this issue and to really be objective and realistic the women's movement is hesitant to launch this struggle now as the women's masses are not yet ready. Um Jihad (the minister of social affairs) and Arafat have announced that they will adopt the general principles of the women's document as long as they do not challenge Islamic law. Historically, political compromises have occurred at the expense of women's rights and it is not going to be any different here. However, women's future work should address this issue and should work on promoting awareness among women that the Islamic laws are not going to solve women's problems. The work in this context is still limited, and the only way for it to succeed is by the NGO institutions and hence the community through its different activities promoting such consciousness that will challenge the ideology of the autonomy in the future. Secularism as a concept should be introduced through the work of the different democratic women's platforms and NGOs. Pressure to translate it realistically is a dream at this stage. The time is not yet ripe for it.

What was the aim of the meeting at the National Palace?

At this conference a misunderstanding took place with the sudden appearance of the minister of social affairs, Um Jihad, which provoked the opposition in particular. There is an understanding by the women's movement that such activities should maintain the non-governmental nature and that there shouldn't be any hegemony over these activities by the government. The GUPW which adopted the document is an NGO organization and it becomes worrying for all civil and human rights activists to see these attempts by the Palestinian Authority to coopt the NGOs. I think this attempt will be challenged, as there is an awareness by the women of the NGO movement of the crucial role they can play to build a free and independent civil society. This challenge characterizes the new political phase of Palestinian politics.

Is the call for a unified Palestinian women's movement still on the agenda?

Organizational unity as a concept in Palestinian politics has always been an alienating slogan and decision, imposed from above without taking into consideration the real interests of the people. As we know, the women's movement is a political expression of different political parties with different national, political, and social agendas. Therefore, "unity" becomes a utopia. Moreover, multiplicity is more enriching for the process of democracy. However, there could be shared and similar positions on different gender issues so that unified positions become functional, like those in the document. In building this process the women's organizations should learn to accommodate each other and in certain instances political differences could be marginalized. As long as women are marginalized in the different political parties, such a unified position can never be achieved as male leaders tend to prioritize the political issues.

However, one should also understand that in promoting a social liberation struggle the class dimension becomes a crucial one. In the intifada, which expressed a national liberation struggle, unity and cohesiveness within the community were more feasible — but in a democratic struggle, gender issues are more closely interrelated to class which complicates the matter even more. New community coalitions can be promoted when different democratic approaches can work together on promoting a democratic society.

18

The Women's Movement on the West Bank

Rita Giacaman[*]

My sisters and I grew up in Bethlehem with a confused sense of patriotism and identity, and the closed-mindedness of a Christian minority. When we were young, we didn't know very much about our society, partly because we studied in foreign schools. I personally studied with nuns in a private French school.

My mother was a strong woman. She influenced my life the most; I loved her as much as I feared her strength and domination. I had an exceptional aunt. She was one of pioneers of the women's movement in Bethlehem and was a member of one of the women's organizations. She gave a lot to her community, despite the fact that she was raised in a traditional and repressed atmosphere. At fourteen she married a cousin and left with him for Nicaragua, but the marriage didn't work out and she returned with a son. Society made her lose confidence in herself and stay home to serve her mother. After my mother got married, strong ties developed between her and this sister. My mother encouraged her to apply to college in London and to study social services by correspondence, and then to live on her own. My mother took care of my grandmother so that my aunt could move away to have a career. My aunt did brilliantly. Thus my background contained two strong, influential women.

Political affiliation and political thought were not a part of the environment in which I grew up. At eighteen, I enrolled in Bir Zeit Uni-

* Dr. Rita Giacaman teaches Social Health and Women's Studies at Bir Zeit University on the West Bank. She describes herself as an independent; she is not affiliated to any political group. This interview was translated from the Arabic; it forms part of a collection of interviews with activist women conducted by Shaoun Al-Mara'a (Women's Affairs), the research center in Nablus on the West Bank.

versity and became immersed in the process of changing myself. Like all the rest of the so-called Kit-Kat girls (this name was given to girls with enough money to afford these candy bars and who were thought to have no social consciousness because of their privileged position), I isolated myself at first and was afraid of becoming part of this politically changing environment. At that time Bir Zeit University was beginning to change from an elite private school to a popular institution imbued with political fire. Slowly we began to become part of what was going on around us and take part in it. My sister was more active than I was. She fell in love with a young Muslim student from Nablus who led the protests at the university. When she confided in me about the news of her love and the political nature of her boyfriend's interests, I became very concerned. But she succeeded in convincing me to accompany them to the mosque for a sit-in, so I followed, and was surprised to find the place far from the tranquility I anticipated. The local population of Bir Zeit treated the politically involved students like heroes and brought us food at the mosque. I heard discussions and participated in chanting slogans, and I began to feel nationalistic sentiments I had never known existed within me.

From Bir Zeit I traveled to Beirut to finish my studies. The distance away from my parents made me self-reliant. I began to accept what I was, who I was, and what I wanted. I am an Arab woman, I like my people, and I want to give back to the people. What I know and what I am capable of achieving is for their sake. But I am a woman and in their consciousness an incomplete person. From Beirut I traveled to America. Because of my father's sudden financial problems, I learned how to be self-sufficient. I was liberated and learned the meaning of progressive thinking regarding social justice, based on my reality as a woman and as a Palestinian.

When I returned to Bir Zeit, I found the popular movement growing and people resisting, rising up, and trying to change their reality. The air was charged and individuals were encouraged to give and work together for their common goal. Real attempts were made to resist occupation on every level. In the area of health, I found three strategies operating at once:

1. A strategy that gives Israel control over health-care, which is in turn exploited by Israel for the purpose of carrying out its political policies.

2. A nationalist bourgeois strategy that hopes to control health-care without offering any revolutionary ideas that challenge the present socio-political situation. The opinion behind this strategy can be summarized as "Anything that can be taken from the government should

be considered profit." Basically, it works through legal means within the system and doesn't go beyond it. As a result, this strategy was unable to challenge the policies of the military government and it therefore didn't succeed in meeting people's health needs.

3. A revolutionary strategy that doesn't focus on medical treatment but on preventative medicine. This strategy aspires to establish health programs through cooperative committees that involve people in their own health-care program. Work on the mass level is emphasized and individual focus is rejected. As a result, this method leads to some form of confrontation with the military occupation.

In the beginning, I didn't know which path I would take. My experience and training in the U.S. prepared me for laboratory analysis in the American system. Frustrated, I considered returning to the U.S. Then, as a result of my increasing involvement in the women's committees and the medical aid committees, things started to crystallize, and I made two decisions: first, to remain in the country no matter what it took; second, to change my specialization from laboratory to pharmacological work, something our country really needs and which is related to the socio-political health situation we live in. Through the committees, I began to visit villages and see the reality of the health conditions facing women and children there. Female child mortality rates in some villages reached twice that of male child mortality because of the distinction made between males and females in traditional Palestinian society, where male children receive more attention. Also, women's health in general is worse than men's health for this same reason. This situation is compounded by the problems resulting from women's repeated pregnancies and childbirth. Working with the committees, we developed a feminist theory which views the health situation as directly related to our social and sexual reality; on one level, we wanted to deal with the health situation by developing women-oriented programs to make women aware of health problems specifically related to them and how they can treat them in the cheapest and easiest way. We also achieved our goals of completely undermining the military law and superseding its limitations and of reaching people's health needs in their villages instead of waiting for villagers to come to the clinics in the city.

When we observed, studied, and traveled, we saw that the people in the villages needed cleanliness and general health-care more than labs. Our health-care system is based on development of health services related to cleanliness and preventing illness, and on building an apparatus which doesn't rely on the resources of institutions or require the land of huge hospitals. The daily cost for a single bed in a conventional hospital equals the expenditures of an entire primary health-care center in any village, and 70 percent of the inhabitants of the occupied territories live in such villages.

SOME ISSUES PERTAINING TO FEMINIST CONSCIOUSNESS ON THE WEST BANK

In my opinion, the national liberation struggle contained the seeds of a growing consciousness among women about women's issues. This relationship between the national liberation struggle and the development of women's consciousness proved to be a mixed blessing: on the one hand, the national struggle forced women out of the domestic sphere and offered them a new political role outside the home, raising their consciousness to their own oppression as women; but, on the other hand, the struggle presented women's issues as a secondary front, the primary front being the liberation of the land. Yet the intifada could not have continued as it did if it was not for the emergence of a feminist consciousness. This feminist consciousness is an integral part of the general national consciousness, existing with it simultaneously in a constant dialectical exchange.

The social change resulting from the intifada has created new roles for women. The women's organizations and the committees taught women the skills needed to be politicians and strategists, and the intifada taught them how to be political leaders. The important movement of women into leadership roles in the male arena was necessitated by the mass imprisonment of male political leaders. This movement was coupled with women's emergence into the political as opposed to the domestic sphere in demonstrations, breaking up fights between the army and the youths. Very often the women who reached leadership positions were girls in their teens. Women also proved their capabilities in the Popular Committees, where they worked side by side with men. These changes widened the circle of women's concerns and contributed to their sense of belonging to the struggle. Whereas previously their sense of belonging was limited to the family, it was now extended to the neighborhood, the block, and even to the city as a whole. Their expanded horizons found them the focal point in the street and at the forefront of the struggle.

One fears that there will be regressions concerning women's roles and that women will go back into the home once the struggle is diminished or in the period after the national struggle is won, as is often the case. What makes me worry is the fact that this positive change did not have time to take roots. The demonstrations and confrontations in which women participated en masse are not enough to produce permanent change on the structural and cultural level of society. After the eruption of the intifada, small changes took place in the distribution of labor within the home, but women are still responsible for most of the work. They are single-handedly responsible for cooking, cleaning, washing the dishes, and bringing up the children. Women leaders still suffer from a split allegiance to their traditional role on the one hand and to their new revolutionary role on the other. For example, these women leaders, even during the most critical moments of the struggle, would suspend their political and organizational role in order to attend to duties at home, such as cooking dinner or caring for a sick child. The husband, by comparison, does not suspend his political duties to do housework. We must conclude from this that women's participation is not considered by society equal in importance to men's participation. As long as women do not challenge the traditional division of labor, no serious transformations will take place in the structure of society.

Despite all the turbulence and potential for change, the expected role of women has not changed. For example, women are encouraged to become secretaries, but not to become carpenters or study commerce, and women who are studying medicine are always encouraged to become nurses.

In my opinion, the most important weakness of the women's movement is that the four factions to which women's groups belong are not independent of male leadership, as they are part of the political ideologies of these factions. Because they are not independent, women's committees are not unified. The point that illustrates this weakness is the issue of democratic representation in the women's movement: the Higher Council for Women, a body that is supposed to make decisions that affect the lives of all Palestinian women, consists only of members of the four political factions and therefore represents only five percent of women. Is this democracy? I personally do not and never will belong to a political faction; this means that even though I am politically active, I belong to the 95 percent of women who are not politically organized or represented by the Higher Council for Women. Why is this Council incapable of full representation when it is one of the arms of our official leadership (the PLO), whose structure includes independents and insures their representation?

The third point of weakness is competition, which is a waste of time and effort. Before the intifada, the various factions used to compete with each other over who would establish child-care, workshops, etc. in a village, the same neighborhood, or even the same street. The intifada reduced the amount of competition but didn't stop it completely.

Despite the presence of these weaknesses, the strengths of the women's movement are clear and numerous. Most important of these, as I previously mentioned, is that the committees taught women roles outside the realm of the home as well as the art of politics and planning. Further, the intifada produced superb women leaders who have proven themselves through their abilities and effectiveness. Yet the Unified Leadership perceives women only as mothers and wives of martyrs. What about our female martyrs? What about our struggle in the streets and the camps and the schools and the hospitals? What about all the things we women gave? Why is it that the Unified Leadership sees only the contributions that women make through men, as mothers and wives? Why did they address all of the sectors by name (in the fliers or *bayanat*) except women? Why do they insist on treating us as if we are mouths without tongues, as if our opinions are only peripheral? This situation will not change unless women are part of the political leadership in decision-making positions.

SPECIFIC REQUESTS FROM THE WOMEN'S MOVEMENT

1. The most important request I'm making of the women's movement is that it unify women by representing independents in the Higher Council for Women, and choose representatives on the basis of their efforts, not their contacts or the contributions of their families.

2. A feminist thinking and strategy for women's liberation must be developed which is in accordance with the national ideology. National ideology is an important base but it must not rule out progressive social thinking; the internal social conflicts in our society will not be resolved through the liberation of the land. It has never happened before that the national solution brought about solutions to social problems. I am also asking that the women's movement create a balance between national rights, social rights, and economic rights.

3. I ask that the women's movement conduct more studies about the backward situation of women in our country, and that the findings of these studies should be used for the establishment of practical projects and programs to improve the condition of women. The projects should have political significance and not focus exclusively on nurseries, sewing centers, and illiteracy workshops.

4. I am asking for a change in all laws, from the *shari'a* to civil law code. I am Rita Giacaman, the doctor, the professor, the mother. I don't accept having a protector or a legal guardian to grant me per-

mission to travel or to prohibit me from it. I don't accept being married by a priest and then forbidden to get a divorce if need be, or having the priest prevent me from marrying a Muslim (my husband is a Muslim). Nor would I accept being married by a sheikh who lets my husband marry again or divorce me when he wants.

PART SEVEN

Women in Political Islam

19

Women in Islam: "The Mother of All Battles"

Yvonne Yazbeck Haddad and Jane I. Smith

Islamism, often called political Islam, has clearly placed the issue of the roles and rights of women at the center of its agenda. The rhetoric of Islamist teaching, speaking, and writing makes it abundantly clear that the ways in which women act, dress, and comport themselves are crucial in the reconstitution of a new and authentically Islamic society.[1] Much of the power of the Islamist position comes in its legitimate critique of autocratic regimes, the unequal economic power base in many Muslim societies, and the failure of imported prescriptions to cope with the prevalent problems of modernization and urbanization. Islamism is offered as the most effective solution to economic as well as political and social problems. Implicit (and often explicit) in this analysis is the importance of women's behavior and roles for the reconstruction of an appropriate and effective Islamic order.[2]

Secularist and liberal Muslims tend to agree with the Western perception that Islamist positions in regard to women are regressive and represent a significant loss of rights gained for women through the hard-fought battles of the twentieth century. Some Muslim women are angry about what they see as restrictions that have been thrust upon them in the name of Islam, and bitterly resent the perceived loss of freedom and often the loss of rights that they believe are legitimately theirs under Islam. They are repelled by what they understand to be the "political" nature of the Islamist stance toward women and the potential for violence and abuse that they believe it contains.[3]

But it is abundantly clear that for a great many Muslim women the Islamist platform represents an effective response to the challenges of modernity and one in which they are happy to play a role. And they are willing, sometimes with modifications, to play it according to Islamist rules.[4] Some of them seem to acquiesce agreeably to the expectations put upon them with no attempt to question or criticize. Others have given careful and thorough consideration to the implications of the Islamist position on women, like what they see, and believe that their carefully defined role in the movement is essential to the process which will renew and revitalize Islam and Muslim states.[5]

Absolutely basic to the Islamist discourse is the rejection of the West and the conviction that "freedoms" enjoyed by Western women are among the key factors in the moral and ethical disintegration of Western societies. The early platform of the Muslim Brotherhood in Egypt denounced the Western model for women as exploitative, based on the commercialization of sex and the sale of products designed to display the female body.[6] Islamist responses continue this critique, pointing to the process of "commodification" in which the perfect female body is marketed and held up as a constant although unnatural and thus unattainable goal for women. They thereby urge that by rejecting such myths and carefully defining the appropriate roles for women, as well as the appropriate ways for them to dress, they will be able to insure that Muslim societies do not fall into the same kind of degradation.

Islamist women are deeply convinced that Western women are not only used and misled, but that they have lost their sense of pride and dignity and despite their feminist protestations are not happy in their circumstances. From their perspective, even the highly touted Western freedoms for women render them not free at all but deprived of healthy familial relationships and subject to sexual and other forms of exploitation. These freedoms have not liberated Western women who are still subject to the chauvinism of the males in Western society; they have in fact turned them into sexual objects.[7] Many women have had the opportunity to study or travel in Western Europe or the United States, and eagerly share their perceptions of the ills of Western society and its mistreatment of women. Popular American-made television programs such as *Love Boat, Dallas,* and *Dynasty,* believed to accurately depict life in the United States, contribute to these perceptions.

Obviously the anti-Western rhetoric has a strong basis in Muslim responses to colonialism and Western imperialism.[8] In Iran, for example, the attempts to give women an Islamic identity are specifically seen as counteracting the militantly propagated Western image many Iranian women chose to emulate under the rule of the Pahlavis.[9] In general the colonial process brought Western critique of Muslim customs, particularly as they related to women. Christian missionaries and colonial bureaucrats set about persuading Muslims that the plight of their women was one of the prime reasons for the backwardness of their societies. It is not surprising, then, that as Muslims work to dissociate themselves from colonialist and imperialist influences they are quick to denounce the Westernizing and secularizing tendencies that they connect with increased freedoms for women and to redefine women's proper role in an indigenous Islam. In most Islamist platforms women are not understood to be the passive recipients of a newly defined identity, but active participants in the new culture and society that the Islamists are intent on bringing into being. Islamists have appropriated from the heritage of Islam various values for which they have found precedent and justification, assuring their audiences that the "new" values that are propagated are grounded in true Islam. The failure to uphold moral and ethical values in Western society is portrayed as having led to such deep societal ills as AIDS, pornography, a high rate of divorce, and abandoned wives and children. Muslim women who continue to wish to emulate their Western sisters therefore are depicted as outside of Islamic culture, misguided or even traitorous, bringing shame and dishonor on their families and their communities.

The new Islamist society, then, is one in which the role of women and the importance of the family are understood to be divinely prescribed, thus providing a bastion against the kind of anarchy that is seen to characterize Western society. The goals toward which Western women aspire are, Islamists point out, already available in the laws of Islam, such as legislation to force men to support their children, the right to domestic upkeep, and freedom from the fear of divorce in the polygynous marriage system. While Western feminists advocate gender equality in the division of labor, Islamists believe that by balancing roles and responsibilities women's interests are protected. They contrast the importance of family care and support for children in Islam with Western patterns of external child-care. Western approval of birth control and abortion is countered with the Islamist affirmation of the importance of children as the torchbearers of a new Islamic culture, as well as the Quranic proscription of the killing of children. Some even attest to the more sinister motives of Western advocacy of birth control for Muslims as a way of keeping down the Islamic world population. In that light, birth control programs propagated by Western authorities are seen as tantamount to genocide.[10]

Islamists make frequent reference to the Quranic affirmation that males and females are created from one soul, and have been charged with parallel responsibilities and duties. Nonetheless, basic to the Islamist understanding of women is the conviction that males and females have been created by God to have different natures and abilities. Thus, they argue, it is only reasonable that their roles and functions as members of communal units, whether those be families, societies, or nations, should be different. They have no use for Western feminist "unisex" ideas in which women aspire to play roles identical to men, in fact identifying those ideas with a new kind of male chauvinism.[11] Traditions are cited in which the Prophet Muhammad is said to have cursed women who dress or act like men, or that one of the signs of the imminence of the day of judgment is that women try to become like men, which is seen as going against the natural order. Islam, in contrast, advocates the equality of males and females, based on the clear affirmation of the Quran that both earthly responsibilies and the rewards or punishments of the hereafter are assured for both sexes. This equality, however, unlike Western notions, is not understood to mean identity but rather complementarity, in which roles are harmoniously balanced to assure the smooth functioning of the Islamic society.

Opponents of this ideology have argued that it is merely a ruse designed to limit women's opportunities and, most particularly, to keep them under the dominance of males. The accusation is made that by this kind of "equality but not identity" ideology women are duped into believing that theirs is a status with honor and distinction, while in fact they are so restricted in their activities that they have no real degree of emancipation.[12] Those who accept the Islamist arguments, however, believe that the inequities that are current in many Islamic societies will disappear when the true laws of Islam are initiated. Women will be affirmed and fulfilled in their roles as maintainers of the household, of the family life of the community, and of the standards and ideals of Islam.

There is, however, a great deal of discussion in current Islamist literature about exactly what equality for men and women under Islam really means. For many, differentiation of roles does not imply a hierarchy in value, although all are in agreement that Quran verses such as 4:34 do indeed mean that men have responsibility over women because they are to care for them from their financial means. Others are willing to say that the fact that the true natures of the two genders are in contrast really means that men are superior to women. A growing number of Islamist women who are educated in the Quran, tradition, and law believe firmly that the Islamic system is based on the justice of God, which affirms true equality between men and women and guarantees full rights to women based on a balance of roles and responsibilities. Women's rights that have been highlighted as Islamic within this century are the right to live, to own property, to have one's own business, to inherit, and to keep one's own name. More recently emphasis has been put on the right to assent to the choice of one's spouse (silence is taken to mean assent), to divorce (if it is specified in the marriage contract), and to conjugal relationships (divorce on the grounds of abandonment, for example, can be granted if a woman's husband does not visit her for a year).

The bottom line for understanding the Islamist position in regard to women seems unquestionably to be the crucial importance of modesty. While this is strongly encouraged for both sexes, it plays itself out in an ideology that focuses on women and the ways in which their roles are circumscribed by the essential understanding that they must maintain their modesty physically, emotionally, and socially. This is most evident in the key areas of current Islamist discussion, namely conservative Islamic dress for women, women's first and foremost responsibility to home and family, and issues of female education and employment. Underscoring all of the discussion for Islamists is the hope and intention that Muslim societies will be governed by Islamic law, establishing a divinely sanctioned social system based on appropriate roles for both genders. That women understand and assume those roles, with whatever implications they have for the curtailing of certain kinds of freedoms, is essential to the realization of this intention.

A great deal of attention has been given in the last decade or more to what is called the phenomenon of Islamic dress. While Islamist men also are increasingly attempting to dress in ways that acknowledge their Islamic identity, this distinctive attire is most apparent on the part of women. It is important to underscore that this dress (a) is often (though not always) the voluntary choice of the women involved; (b) often has deeply political overtones, as seen for example in its appearance in the Arab world after the 1967 Arab-Israeli war and manifesting itself more obviously as Muslims react to continuing instances of Western imperialism; and (c) is evidenced in a great variety of ways, from little more than simple covering of the hair (*hijab*) to adoption of clothing that covers one completely, including a *niqab* or full face-veil. Wearing some form of Islamic dress *(al-ziyy al-islami)* affirms that one is a good and modest woman who understands the importance of appropriate relations between the sexes, of confirming in this external way one's allegiance to Islam, and of comporting oneself in a manner that will contribute to achieving the goal of a truly Islamic society.[13]

Muslim women who dress Islamically profess to find this clothing comforting, protective, the object of deep personal pride, and helpful to the extent to which they need to participate in professional or social circumstances in which they interact with men. Many women believe that the Quran insists that they be fully covered;[14] others understand that such a command was only for the wives of the Prophet but choose to identify with those "mothers of the believers" in their own comportment. Increasingly, Islamist women think of those who expose themselves with bare arms and legs to the (probably lustful) eyes of men as exhibiting an essential immorality. Sherifa Zuhur insists in her study of veiled and unveiled Egyptian women: "The linkage of faith to modesty is essential to the Islamist argument."[15]

Conservative dress, of course, is not worn at home when one is with one's family, but adopted for social circumstances. Normally it is first put on either at puberty or at whatever point a woman feels that she is ready to make this obvious affirmation of her commitment to Islam. Many women who choose veiling indicate that they have been supported in this choice not only by their families but also by women friends who have gone through the sometimes difficult decision-making process. Most affirm that the choice, once made, is irrevocable. In some societies, notably Iranian and Saudi, dressing so as to leave nothing but the face and hands exposed is not optional for women.[16] In most other Muslim countries, adoption of some form of Islamic dress is more and more apparent on city streets and in public places. Beginning more specifically as a movement of the lower middle and middle classes, it is increasingly the costume of choice for women across class lines. Shops in Cairo and other major cities of the Middle East feature specially designed Islamic dress with matching accessories, causing some alarm among the *ulama* or religious teachers that fashion might take precedence over modesty. While it can serve a wide range of functions — psychological, political, revolutionary, economic, cultural, practical, domestic[17] — its primary justification for Islamist women is on religious grounds (as prescribed by God, *shar'i*) and is said to reflect an inner as well as an outward modesty. "Basically, Islamic dress is holy. If we are Muslims it is a religious law to wear *Al Shari* .... I would say that even if Islam didn't ask me to wear *Al Shari* I would have worn it anyway. I don't like to be treated as a female body ... "[18]

Many secularist women in the Islamic world have reacted extremely negatively to what they feel is another means of subjugating women by the imposition of inhibiting dress, and are convinced that there is a connection between the enforcement of such dress and continuing abuse of women by men.[19] For others, however, dressing Islamically has opened up a world of social activism. Feeling that they are appropriately modest, such women can not only move freely in the world outside the home but can insist that since women are living up to their responsibilities in such an obvious way it is incumbent upon the state to make sure that the equality and rights guaranteed to them are actually forthcoming.[20]

There is no question that in some countries Islamist women who are ideologically committed to the movement, and who feel that this is exhibited in their dress, mobilize and provide support for its advancement. But these same women are also fundamentally aware that a function of this kind of active support is the affirmation that their primary responsibility is to home and family. That the family in Muslim society has always played an extremely important role in the life of the community is undeniable, although as Judith Tucker has demonstrated, the characteristics of that family are not as constant as has often been portrayed.[21] In general it can be said that the women in the family have been clearly subordinate to the males, especially in their younger years. While some Muslim women see the strong Islamist emphasis on the role of the woman in the family to be yet another signal of a loss of many of the advances for women that have been achieved in this century, those who adopt the Islamist position argue that a woman's real power and authority are best realized precisely in her role as sustainer of the family and as the repository of true Muslim values.

Again the argument is frequently made that the Muslim understanding of family is far more adequate than the Western model, in which divorce is rampant, children are left unattended, and women are no longer guaranteed full provision. Islamists feel that with the Muslim model, based on extended family support (although in actuality that kind of support is often less available than in former days) and a de-emphasis on the rights of the individual, there is greater guarantee that decisions will be made that support the effective functioning of all members. The goal of social interdependence, to which Islam has a deep commitment, is much more immediately served than is the case in Western family life.[22]

Explicitly stated, the primary role of the woman in the home is to bear and rear children.[23] It is difficult to break from the traditions of a culture that has valued sons far more than daughters, but Islamist theory generally honors girls as much as boys as integral members of the community and Islamists point with pride to the Prophet's having abolished the practice of female infanticide.[24] Some one hundred verses in the Quran are cited as specifically defining the role of women and the Muslim family. Man and woman are created of one spirit to protect, support, and comfort each other. They are to relate to each other with mutuality and cordiality such that marriage can be a blessing to husband and wife. Chastity is required in both partners, and absolutely mandatory for the wife. (The theme of chastity, purity, and honor runs through all of the discussions of women's roles, from dress to marriage to education and work.)

Somewhat more complicated are the issues of obedience and authority. Some male Islamist writers stress that within the family unit the wife is to be absolutely obedient to her husband. And some even talk about his right to beat her in order to restore her to her senses if she is disobedient. Most writers, however, do not go to this extreme. And the majority of both men and women agree that husband and wife should share in shaping their lives together. The wife is even assigned responsibility for general decision-making within the home environment. Recent material from the Muslim Brotherhood emphasizes that *shura*, consultation, is the fundamental form of decision-making in Islam even in the home. If, however, there is disagreement and consensus cannot be reached, the husband is the final arbiter. It is acknowledged that every social unit needs a leader, and in the family this responsibility falls to the husband because the woman carries the task of giving birth and mothering. This reality seems not to bother Islamist women as much as give them a sense of order and security.

Islamist discourse, while building on the traditional concept of the extended family, has had to recognize that with modernization and urbanization the nuclear family is often now the primary unit. This has created enormous stress for many women, particularly those who not only fulfill their responsibilities within the family but for a variety of reasons also work outside the home. Some have argued that in fact the very strength of the Islamist movement is that it provides a vision of community that extends beyond one's own family and fills a need for a context of belonging to a larger group than the nuclear unit.[25] In countries such as Egypt, Tunisia, Kuwait, and Jordan, participation in Islamist support groups provides assistance in getting financial help, in finding jobs for either husband or wife, and in having access to social services that government bureaucracy has not been able to provide. Rural people immigrating into urban areas are particularly comforted by the kinds of support they find provided by these groups, as they try to cope with the stress of a new environment and new problems without the comfort of their extended families. Quran study circles, for example, provide important networking and help in individual problem-solving.

The Islamists use the fact of the double burdens put on women who do find employment outside of the home, and thus have to carry the equivalent of two full-time jobs, as additional arguments for the value of the woman remaining at home if at all possible. Many women who have suffered from trying to perform these double roles see the wisdom in these arguments. These issues feed directly into the more extreme Islamic discourse which supports the confinement of women completely to the home, based on such sayings attributed to the Prophet Muhammad as "The woman goes out of the house twice, once to the house of her husband and the other to the grave." From this perspective women are to devote themselves completely and exclusively to the service of their families, attending to the needs of the husband and to the raising of children.

Such an extreme position, however, does not represent the attitude of most Islamists in their attempts to reconfigure new roles for women as participants in Islamic society. In what is interpreted as a significantly new message in the Islamist discourse, women are portrayed not as diminutive and second-class members of a family unit, but as assuming the exceedingly important task of educating their children, especially their sons, to what it means to be informed and contributing citizens of the Islamic community or *ummah*. This responsibility means that in addition to providing for the physical and emotional needs of their children, mothers need to teach them about religion and also give them as broad-based a general education as possible to prepare them to become productive citizens. Here again is the emphasis on the importance of women as essential for the advancement of the Muslim state.

Zaynab al-Ghazali, founder of the Society of Muslim Sisters in the middle of this century, has been a particularly noteworthy example of an Islamist woman who understands the signal role that women are called on to play. "[Women] are the ones who build the kind of men that we need to fill the ranks of the Islamic call. So women must be well educated, cultured, knowing of the precepts of the Koran and Sunna, informed about world politics .... Islam does not forbid ... [a woman] from working, entering into politics, and expressing her opinion ... as long as that does not interfere with her first duty as a mother, the one who first trains her children in the Islamic call. So her first, holy, and most important mission is to be a mother and wife. She cannot ignore this priority."[26]

Ghazali, then, underscores both the essential nature of a woman's role at home and the importance of her receiving a sufficient education to be able to carry out her broader tasks. The general Islamist position is that a woman's education is actually the fulfillment of her Islamic duty rather than a distraction from it. Though there is a great deal of discussion as to exactly what kind of education is appropriate for women, and how it should be used, women for the most part are encouraged to become as well educated as possible. Recent studies of veiled women in Egypt indicate that the great majority of them are very much in favor of women's rights in both education and the workplace, although they insist that proper attire and conditions are requisite.[27]

Whether or not the education that women receive should be put to concrete use through their employment in the workplace is a subject of great controversy and discussion.[28] Some Islamists are firm that women should attend only to their responsibilities in the home, while others are equally persuaded that true Islam affirms opportunities for a woman to seek employment to the degree that she is prepared, wants to, and has the approval of her husband, as long as she does so above and beyond the fulfillment of her family duties. Some insist that having women in the workplace provides another example of the social nature of Islam, affording them opportunities to contribute to the betterment of society. The woman who is able to manage her family successfully probably has the skills to be successful in an outside job. Recent Muslim Brotherhood publications have urged that not only is it a woman's right to be employed outside the home, but it is her duty to work for the development of her country through the political process. The Islamic Front in Jordan now urges that women have the right to vote, to be elected members of parliament, and to assume office. There is, however, considerable disagreement as to the specificity of what kinds of jobs are appropriate for women. Many argue for traditionally "feminine" occupations such as teaching children, providing medical care to other women, and the like. As always, modesty is the key measure, although for some this means that women should not work at all in the company of men while for others it simply suggests appropriate attire and comportment.

Much of this kind of Islamist response to the issue of women and work comes in reaction to the kind of social and economic engineering that has been undertaken in various nation-states by providing education and employment opportunities for women when it serves the immediate good of the state. In Jordan during the 1970s, when Jordanian men were working in the Gulf states, women were needed in the workplace. Therefore work training programs and opportunities were provided for women. But when the demands for labor in the Gulf abated, the Jordanian government dismantled the apparatus by which women were brought to work and sent them home, citing Quran 4:34 that men are in charge of women because they provide for them. And an Egyptian writer suggests that if all women working in Egypt were sent home where they belong, there would be no problem of unemployment in Egypt since all men would have jobs. Many Islamists today, even those who might have supported such manipulation earlier, are affirming the ongoing responsibilities of women as contributors to the state.

For some women the new opportunity now afforded them to become more knowledgeable about matters of religion has extended beyond the role as educators of their children. Women are becoming involved in religious organizations outside of the home in ways that they never have before, playing out the Islamist agenda of channeling women's energies into religious and charitable activities that are designed to foster the common good. Women are studying at *shari'a* colleges in Kuwait, Tunisia, Morocco, Jordan, Egypt, Syria, and Qatar. A few are actually teaching Quran and *shari'a* to other women in major cities such as Cairo and Damascus. In Jordan and Indonesia some are training to become preachers.[29] In Iran, women are attending religious meetings in which interpretations of Quran and law are discussed and a *hozeh-ye Islami* or theological school training women in theology and law in Iran is open to women from a range of backgrounds.[30] Islamist groups that grew up in the 1970s and 1980s include large numbers of middle-class women who, supportive of the generally conservative agenda of their leaders, have been active in grassroots movements as well as in the general social and religious activities of Islamist mosques.[31]

If those women who are actively promoting the Islamist agenda are to be called "feminists" at all, which is debatable, it must be with a new understanding of feminism in an anti-Western, pro-Islamic mode that stresses women's participation in the building of Islamic society. Some feel that the term "feminist" is to be avoided because it bears the burden of Western elitism, and that perhaps a "womanist" interpretation stressing the complementarity of the sexes would be more appropriate.[32] Islamist women who do participate actively in promoting the rights and opportunities that they believe Islam truly accords them generally do so out of a position that speaks from within their own culture, consciously avoiding articulation that represents foreign ideologies or perspectives that seem to reflect Western feminism.[33]

Thus Islamist discourse refuses to identify the affirmation of the equality of men with women and of newly defined roles for women as having anything to do with liberation, as that term is defined in the West. Islam is seen as providing all of the rights and responsibilities appropriate for women. Islam is thus itself the liberating force that can be set in motion through the devoted adherence of both males and females. Islamism seeks liberation from alien values that are perceived to debase women and portray them as sex objects. It liberates men and women from bondage to Western constraints on their God-given roles, freeing women to enjoy the roles designed by God for their own happiness and well-being and ultimately for the redemption of the world.

Islamism, then, posits a view of women that is demonstrably different from both the traditional view of women's inferiority, insignificance, and inability to function on their own propagated by some in earlier centuries, and from the imported ideologies of the West that are perceived to threaten the fabric of both family and society. It is understood by its advocates to be the true interpretation of God's divine system for human life. It offers the right of full participation in society, albeit under certain clearly understood rules, for both men and women. It guarantees women rights in marriage and family matters, in inheritance and the management of their own money, in developing their full intellectual capacities, and in participating in the creation and maintenance of Islamic society. Perhaps most appealing, it puts the woman in a position of respect and responsibility as the purveyor of Islamic values to her children and even, in some cases, to her fellow Muslims. For an increasing number of women, such benefits make the accommodations that Islamists insist are mandated by God a small price to pay. For others, this adventure in recreating a wholesome Islamic order continues to be a burden that they want to shed.

Notes

1. For fatwas regarding minute details of women's proper dress and comportment, see: Muhammad Ibn Saleh al-'Uthaymin, *Al-Fatawa al-Nisa'iyya* (Beirut: Dar Maktabat al-Tarbiya, n.d.); cf. Khalid Mustafa 'Adil, *Al-Mar'a kama Yuriduha al-Islam* (Beirut: Dar Ibn Hazm, 1994); 'Atiyya Saqr, *S[ual] wa J[awab] li al-Mar'a kama al-Muslima* (Cairo: al-Dar al-'Asriyya li al-Kitab, 1988); Ibrahim Muhammad al-Jamal, *Kaba'ir al Nisa'wa Sagha'irihinna wa Hafawatihinna* (Cairo: Dar al-Bashir, 1989); Muhammad Sa'id Ramadan al-Buti, *Ila Kul Fatat Tu'min bi'llah* (Tunis: Maktabat al-Jadid, 1988); 'Abd Allah al-Talidi, *Al-Mar'a al-Mutabarrija wa Atharuha al-Sayyi'fi al-Ummah* (Beirut: Dar ibn Hazm, 1990).

2. "This attempt to relate gender inequality to other political and economic sources of global and national inequality is the key insight offered by this discourse." Mervat Hatem, "Toward the Development of Post-Islamist and Post-Nationalist Feminist Discourses in the Middle East,"

in *Arab Women: Old Boundaries, New Frontiers,* ed. Judith E. Tucker (Bloomington: Indiana University Press, 1993), p. 44. For background information on the Islamist agenda, see: Yvonne Yazbeck Haddad, "Islamic 'Awakening' in Egypt," *Arab Studies Quarterly* 9;3 (1987), pp. 234-59; cf. Yvonne Yazbeck Haddad, "Muslim Revivalist Thought in the Arab World: An Overview," *The Muslim World* 76;3-4 (1986).

3. Malika al-'Asimi, *Al-Mar'a wa Ishkaliyyat al-Dimuqratiyya* (Casablanca: Afiqia al-Sharq, 1991).

4. This situation, says Valentine M. Moghadam, has brought about a kind of ideological polarization of women in the Middle East. "Rhetorics and Rights of Identity in Islamist Movements," *Journal of World History* 4;2 (1993), p. 244. For aditional material, see: Laila Hassan Sa'd al-Din, *Al-Mar'a al-Muslima: Bintan. Zawjatan. Umman* (Tunis: Maktabat al-Jadid, n.d.); Mahdiya Shihada al-Zamili, *Libas al-Mar'a wa Zinatuha fi al-Fiqh al-Islami* (Amman: Dar al-Furqan, 1982); Fatima Bint 'Abd Allah, *Al-Moda fi al-Tasawwur al-Islam* (Cairo: Maktabat al-Sunna, 1991).

5. "Many of these women believe that the changes resulting from their participation in the fundamentalist movements are irreversible and form a part of the social advancement of women, and that above all their participation aids in the evolution of these movements in a favorable way to women, an 'entryist' position if any." Marie-Aimée Hélie-Lucas, "Women's Struggles and Strategies in the Rise of Fundamentalism in the Muslim World," in *Women in the Middle East: Perceptions, Realities and Struggles for Liberation,* ed. Haleh Afshar (New York: St. Martin's Press, 1993), p. 221. Cf. Amal 'Abd al-Qadir, *Hijab al-Mar'a al-Muslima* (Tunis: Maktabat al-Jadid, n.d.).

6. See, e.g., Leila Ahmad, *Women and Gender in Islam* (New Haven: Yale University Press, 1992), p. 194.

7. "And these sexually liberated women could in an instant turn into whores or prostitutes in men's eyes; their sexuality remains a potential source of shame and social disgrace and it is still the most accessible means men have of subjugating them." Bouthaina Sha'aban, quoting from a Palestinian women, in *Both Right and Left Handed: Arab Women Talk about Their Lives* (Bloomington: Indiana University Press, 1988), p. 164.

8. "The colonizers of the Islamic East are fully knowledgeable of this truth. They fear nothing as much as the rise of an Islamic movement that reconnects us with our history and joins us directly with our nature and inclinations and launches us to fulfil our duty in a manner that revives [the glory days of] Islamic civilization, the day we spat on Tartar ascendancy and turned off their lights and confronted the Crusader invasion and dismantled it and washed away its filth." Muhammad al-Ghazali, *Min Huna Na'lam* (Cairo: Dar al-Kitab al-Haditha, 1370H), p. 11.

9. See Nesta Ramazani, "Islamic Government Need Not Repress Women," in *Islam: Opposing Viewpoints,* ed. David Bender and Bruno Leone (San Diego: Greenhaven Press, 1995), p. 76. Cf. Moghadam, "Rhetorics and Rights," p. 245: "A term especially important in the Iranian context is *gharbzadegi.* Variously translated as 'Westoxication,' 'occidentosis,' 'Westitis,' or 'Euromania,' *gharbzadegi* is an illness, 'a plague from the West'...the embodiment of all that is wrong in contemporary Iranian society is the *gharbzadeh* woman. She represents all social ills: dependency on the West, cultural imperialism, and consumerism."

10. For additional information on the topic, see: Abul Ala Maududi, *Birth Control: Its Social, Political, Economic, Moral, and Religious Aspects* (Lahore: Islamic Publications, 1968).

11. See, e.g., Lamya' al-Faruqi, *Women, Muslim Society, and Islam* (Plainfield, IN: American Trust Publications, 1991/1994), pp. 25-26.

12. See "The Standpoint of Contemporary Muslim Fundamentalists," by Fouad Zakaria, an Egyptian liberal who is deeply opposed to Islamist ideology. In *Women of the Arab World,* ed. Nahia Toubia (London: Zed Books, 1988), pp. 27-44.

13. Other authors object strongly to veiling. "Wearing the veil, therefore, falls at the junction between the repudiation and denunciation of the body... and excessive concern for the body and the danger it could pose to the woman herself as well as to others... She is supposed to have an ascetic appearance, to be suspicious and aggressive towards others and their possible motives and to minimize mixing with men. At the same time, however, she is supposed to behave towards her husband as a wholly sexual female... A woman is expected to encompass both extreme chastity and lustful sexuality. She must constantly reverse her modest, even drab

appearance and prove to her husband that she is a desirable woman." Fouad Zakaria, "The Standpoint of Contemporary Muslim Fundamentalists," p. 32.

14. In fact the Quran only suggests modest clothing for both men and women.

15. *Revealing, Reveiling* (Albany: State University of New York Press, 1992), p. 90.

16. Ayatollah Khomeini, for example, reimposed Islamic dress, called *hijab*, on working women in government offices in March 1979, and later extended it to all women. See Halah Esfandari, "The Majles and Women's Issues in the Islamic Republic of Iran," in *In the Eye of the Storm: Women in Post-Revolutionary Iran*, ed. Mahnaz Afkhami and Erika Friedl (Syracuse: Syracuse University Press, 1994), pp. 63-64.

17. Yvonne Haddad, "Islam, Women and Revolution in Twentieth-Century Arab Thought," *The Muslim World* 74;3-4 (1984), p. 158.

18. Sha'abaan, *Both Right and Left Handed*, p. 95, quoting the testimony of a Lebanese woman.

19. "Most young [Algerian] women do not veil…and many who once wore the *hijab* [veil] at the zenith of legal FIS power in the early 1990s have stopped doing so. Wearing blue jeans has become an act of defiance, as has wearing one's hair short or remaining single." Karima Bennoune, "Islamic Fundamentalism Represses Women," cited in *Islam: Opposing Viewpoints*, *pp. 69-70*.

20. Ramazani, "Islamic Government Need Not Repress Women," p. 76.

21. "The Arab Family in History," in *Arab Women: Old Boundaries, New Frontiers*, pp. 195-207.

22. Al-Faruqi, *Women, Muslim Society, and Islam*, pp. 23-25.

23. Critics charge that the reproductive role has usurped the productive role, while Islamists counter that bearing children is *the* primary way in which women are productive.

24. Sayings attributed to the Prophet, such as "Whosoever has a daughter and does not favor his sons over her, God will cause him to enter into paradise…" are frequently cited.

25. See Andrea B. Rugh, "Reshaping Personal Relations in Egypt," in *Fundamentalisms and Society*, ed. Martin E. Marty and R. Scott Appleby (Chicago: University of Chicago Press, 1993), pp. 151-180.

26. Cited in Ahmad, *Women and Gender in Islam*, p. 199.

27. Ibid., p. 227. "Even though the majority agreed with the proposition that the purpose of educating women was to make them better wives, the sum of their responses on matters of women's roles and rights indicates that most were consistently *for* education…"

28. It should be noted, however, that this discussion relates exclusively to women in more urban contexts. In rural areas women are full participants in the production of food, planting, reaping, etc. We have not found a single Muslim author who explicitly says that rural women should not work. The issue of urban women working seems to center on the possibility that they will be forced to interact with men outside of their family units.

29. A new kind of literature advocating the role of the woman as a *da'iya*, one who calls to the path of righteousness, has appeared. For example, there is a weekly column in *Al-Mujtama'* magazine published by the Islamists for Kuwait that provides guidance for the woman who engages in *da'wa*. See for example: Najla' Ahmad al-Zahar, "al-Sabr fi al-Da'wa," *Al-Mujtama'*, 1140, February 28, 1995, p. 60. Cf. Muhammad Hasan Breighesh, *Al-Mar'a al-Muslima al-Da'iya* (Zerka, Jordan: Maktabat al-Manar, 1983).

30. Ramazani, "Islamic Government Need Not Repress Women," p. 76.

31. Hatem, "Toward the Development of Post-Islamist and Post-Nationalist Feminist Discourses," p. 41.

32. Sherifa Zuhur, "Women Can Embrace Islamic Gender Roles," cited in *Islam: Opposing Viewpoints*, pp. 92-93. Cf. Mahnaz Afkhami, "Women in Post-Revolutionary Iran: A Feminist Perspective," *In the Eye of the Storm*, pp. 17-18, who notes that the problems of Western women are often of a different order than those of Third World women: "Consequently, they appear alternately as self-righteous promoters of their own Western culture, when they advocate principles and rights that differ with the tenets of Third World societies, or as self-deprecating defenders of atrociously anti-feminist conditions, when they explain away oppressive behavior in the developing world on the grounds of cultural relativism."

33. Moghadam, "Rhetorics and Rights," pp. 251-52.

20

Women and Property Rights in Islam

Abla Amawi[*]

In recent years, there has been increasing concern voiced among feminists and supporters of democratic movements in the Middle East about the status of women. This has arisen largely due to the increasing strength of Islamic fundamentalism and the political victories it has scored in several countries. Indeed, when listening to the vigorous reform programs the Islamists advocate within the spheres of politics and economics, this question becomes all the more relevant, especially for those who consider that the development of women's potential is a criterion and prerequisite for modern civilization and national development. What are these movements' conceptions of the role of women in these processes? How can women contribute to these programs of "Islamic development," or are they destined to remain on the sidelines?

This paper cannot possibly discuss the matter in its entirety, so will instead focus on two aspects of the question of women in national Islamic development as they relate to debates within Islamists circles in Jordan today. The first deals with Islamist views on the role of women in politics, and the second deals with Islam, women, and property rights.

1. WOMEN AND POLITICS

The Quran embodies a complete economic, political, and social system. The governing laws are outlined in the *shari'a* (Islamic law)

---

* This paper was first presented at a conference entitled New Faces of Arab Women, held in Washington, D.C. in March 1992. The conference was sponsored by the Institute for Arab Women's Studies and the Middle East Institute. Reprinted by permission.

which refers to commands, prohibitions, guidance, and principles
that God has addressed and maintained pertaining to the conduct in
this world. Its texts are identified with divine revelations, and are generally understood to be indisputable. This stands in marked contrast
to other kinds of issues which are subject to interpretation by *figh* (jurisprudence).

Two main Islamic principles governing politics will be discussed
here: The right to participate in political elections *(wilaya khassa)* and
the right to a political office *(wilaya 'amma)*, which covers the responsibility over the community, legislating and executing laws.

A. THE RIGHT TO HOLD POLITICAL OFFICE

This right is governed by the concept of the *bay'a* or the Islamic term
for the procedure of nomination of the Caliph or the political leader
of the Muslim community. The *bay'a* is not identical with the Western
concept of elections. The candidate does not nominate him or herself
for office. He or she is chosen by knowledgeable representatives of the
community or granted office by the legal jurists and experts in public
life representing the *umma* (Islamic community) on the basis of the
Prophet's sayings: "He who seeks *wilaya* (rule) shall not get it."

Islamists consider the post of a citizen's representative as a crucial
one, especially in its role in legislation and control over the executive.
For women to run for a political office and assume a position of leadership was considered (by some Islamists) as contradictory to the
"standards of Islam" and consequently outlawed by al-Azhar, Islam's
premier institution of higher learning in Cairo, in 1952. The reasoning was that political office demands public male/female interaction,
traveling to other countries and relegating family life to second priority — issues which were felt to violate Islamic standards should they
be carried out by woman. But the real issue at stake was a woman's
alleged inability by nature to undertake the responsibility of the position fully. We will return to this idea shortly.

The ideas which have been put forward to criticize women's participation in the public sphere or to ban them altogether center on
what can be termed an "ideology of domesticity." This ideology is
based on several factors. The first is that the *shari'a* focuses on the significance of the family as the fundamental unit of society and the
main center of growth. Islam commands that males and females pursue knowledge and education equally. The Quran's message is equality of men and women in respect to rewards and punishments.
Although Islam stresses the equality of men and women in such ways,

their social roles are distinct. In Islamic ideology, women's duty requires that they concentrate on fulfilling their "real" task of taking care of their husband and children and that they allow the men to run the affairs of government.

Secondly, the ideology of domesticity is closely tied to the ideology of gender differences: whereby the physical, physiological, and biological differences between men and women are translated into universal and immutable differences in their social and intellectual capacities.

Thus, while women and men have equal rights in many spheres, they do not in others. In the sphere of marriage, for instance, men and women have different roles and expectations. This "differentness" is soon translated into a hierarchy, as in all spheres of life where a relationship of subordination/domination exists.

Thirdly, the concept of Islamic domesticity rests upon certain allegedly immutable female qualities which render women unsuitable for public office. The first is the actual inferiority of women, which is presumed on the basis of the Islamists' own construction of the reason/emotion dichotomy. A woman's ability to think rationally is considered more limited than a man's. Her emotional nature also makes her more easily influenced by others' views and propaganda. These themes of gender difference (in fact, gender inequality) and the need for female domesticity are linked to another theme — that of the danger inherent in the female nature. Some Islamist writers dwell on the theme of female sexuality and enticement. A woman running for office may use her physical attributes of beauty and so forth to gain more votes. Many Islamic ideologues consider men eminently susceptible to female lures, resulting in reduced productivity by men. Therefore the focus is on stressing the role of women as benevolent wife/mother and destructive sexual creature.

Consequently, Islamic movements wish to formulate constitutions on the basis of *shari'a* as the law of the land in which all laws and regulations concerning civil, criminal, financial, economic, administrative, cultural, and military affairs be based on Islamic standards. In this standard, the approach to women and gender relations is straightforward: the rights and responsibilities of men and women are not equal. The woman's role is to be a wife and mother, and the man's to be a breadwinner and fighter.

Interestingly enough, Islamic movements found themselves in a dilemma when they decided to take part in the democratization wave which is sweeping the Middle East. To increase their votes and their seats in parliament, they had to lure women electors. How they dealt with that is discussed in the next section.

B. THE RIGHT TO PARTICIPATE IN ELECTIONS

The right of a Muslim woman to elect someone to represent her and defend her rights was seen as compatible with Islam by some scholars. They argued that there is nothing in Islamic texts which prohibits a woman from voicing her wishes as to who rules over her. Historical precedent indicates that women did in fact participate on many occasions in decision-making during the time of the Prophet, took part in battles and were consulted on important issues. Consequently, women were granted their right to vote in the Middle East at various points after the Second World War (Syria in 1949, Iran in the early 1960s, and Jordan in the 1980s).

Al-Azhar issued a *fatwa* (Islamic opinion) in 1952 against women's right to participate in elections on the basis that the approval of the means (election) may lead to acceptability of the end (women in a ruling position).

But the main obstacle in granting women the right to vote was seen in the actual mechanism of voting which was not based on "Islamic standards." Islamists' election policies reinforce patriarchy in its Islamic variant, the defining feature of which is gender segregation.

How one could segregate women yet have them participate fully in the elections was the issue for several Islamist movements. These movements had to make conciliatory comments regarding women's status and had to concede certain things to women, stressing equality of men and women in Islam. This manifested itself in Muslim Brotherhood campaign literature in Jordan, where election pamphlets addressed the reader as *akhi al-nakhib, ukhti al-nakhiba* (brother voter and sister voter). These movements also claim that every person has the right to pursue the occupation and education he or she chooses, but encourage women to return to the home and to insure that they remain there. One Islamist in Jordan even suggested firing women and returning them to their homes as a way to improve male unemployment in the country.

While stressing equality to win women's hearts, the Islamist movement also organized to get women's votes. In some districts in Jordan, women were personally registered by Islamists to enable them to vote. They also organized separate polling places for men and women during the 1989 parliamentary elections and during voting for one of the professional associations in Jordan.

It is important to note that Islamic scholars are still divided over the issue of the compatibility of women's participation in politics, whether as candidates for office or as electors. The Muslim Brotherhood approves of women's role in voting as long as the principle of segregation is upheld, but they disapprove of women running for office. Hizb Allah (the Party of God) in Lebanon used the slogan that "two factors make a man — a woman and the Quran," which placed women on the same level as the Quran to indicate her high esteem. Most importantly, to encourage her to enroll in their party, women enlisters in the party were paid twice as much as men enlisters.

However, some see no contradiction between Islam and women's role in politics. They find no evidence of any text in Islam which prohibits women's participation in politics and see many examples in Islamic history of women in politics. Many of them use the same texts cited by their anti-women opponents to refute them.

Yet even among these radicals there is the belief that although there is no religious obstacle to women's participation in politics, a woman's nature (biological and psychological), social conditions, and her role in life preclude her running for office. So a woman's ability to lead the country toward political and economic development is in question.

II. WOMEN AND PROPERTY

The *shari'a* emphasized that contractual agreements must be fulfilled, that one should not abuse someone else's property, and it upheld the right to engage in the market of selling and buying except through usury.

The economic provisions in Islam covering women were considered very progressive since they gave women rights to inheritance, equal rights in contracts, rights to enterprise, and to earn and to possess property independently of men. Moreover, women were also granted a non-alterable percentage of transferable property which is inherited by all living relatives. This percentage is lower than that granted to men, however.

A woman is also allowed to keep her own personal property after divorce; any property belonging to her when she enters the contractual relation remains hers after the marriage is terminated. In discussing the laws governing property rights in the *shari'a*, texts which deal with property rights are considered clear and unequivocal *(qat'i)* texts. A definitive text has only one meaning and admits no other interpretations. An example is the entitlement of a husband to half of his deceased wife's estate. These definitive laws covering shares in inheritance are considered essentials to the faith. Their validity may not be disputed. Everyone is bound to follow them and they are basically not open to interpretation, or *ijtihad*.

The property rights laws were made on the basis that the husband is solely responsible for the complete maintenance of his wife, his family, and the needy relatives. The wife may work and she may keep anything that she earns if the husband grants her permission.

This paper will focus on the specific issue of a woman's right to inherit land, as this has recently become an issue among Islamists in Jordan.

Women's legal rights to inherit property are enshrined in both religious and secular law in Jordan. The state and the religious courts hold authority over different types of land, harking back to the legal distinction between *mulk* (private property) and *miri* (crown lands) in Ottoman law and the different laws of inheritance which relate to each.

The first type of land is *mulk*. According to the 1858 Ottoman Land Code, *mulk* is pure free private property to which the state claimed no rights except taxation. The Land Code recognized four types of *mulk*, but the most important category historically were small areas such as gardens and built-up areas within the borders of towns and villages, as well as houses, wells, etc.

The second type of land is *miri*. According to the 1858 Land Code, *miri* lands were the ultimate property of the state, which granted rights to usufruct *(tasarruf)* in them in return for a fee.

Throughout the late nineteenth and twentieth centuries, *miri* came to be indistinguishable from *mulk*, for the right of usufruct could be bought, sold, and inherited just like *mulk*. *Miri* includes all agricultural land in the country and covers a much larger area.

The significance of distinguishing between these two types of lands is the distinction between them in terms of inheritance. The inheritance of *mulk* land is governed by *shari'a* and so gives male heirs a larger share than female heirs. Unlike *mulk*, the 1858 Land Code (which became the Jordanian land law) dictates that male and female children inherit rights to *miri* land equally, and placed them first on the list of those having the right of inheritance (incidentally, wives of the deceased originally appeared seventh on the list, although this was improved later).

Despite numerous changes in the Jordanian land law carried out during the 1930s and 1940s and the erasing of virtually all distinctions between *miri* and *mulk* land for all practical purposes except inheritence, the state never relinquished its title to *miri* lands. Until today, the state still technically possesses title to most of Jordan's land, and women inherit an equal share with men. We will shortly return to this point.

THE ROLE OF CUSTOM IN DEPRIVING WOMEN OF THEIR PROPERTY RIGHTS

One must always keep in mind the difference between law and custom when dealing with women in Islam, for often Islam grants them rights which social custom strips away.

During Ottoman and mandate times, women could and did own land in Transjordan in keeping with secular and religious law. Lists of landowners drawn up during Transjordan's general registration of land title carried out during the 1930s and 1940s confirmed that women did not own very much land. Since they should have been inheriting land equally with men, what was going on?

The *shari'a* gives a woman the right to inherit property once a male relative (for instance, her father) dies, but she may be disinherited by all sorts of devices prior to his death (gifts to male members of the family, the establishment of family *waqf*, or trust, etc.). It still remains custom in some rural areas today for fathers to distribute their land to their male heirs before their deaths, to avoid dividing it and giving shares to female heirs.

These tricks keep the land from being inherited by women, which men feared would lead to the loss of the land to the family (because a woman's share of the inherited property would go to her children after her death, and her children were not considered part of her family but as part of her husband's family).

Moreover, when females do inherit land, they are pressured to give up their shares to male relatives in return for a cash settlement and/or a pledge that the men will take care of them.

It is interesting to note that women were not secluded in such economic enterprises. They appeared freely before the court, sued people and were sued by others. They even sued members of their own family, including their fathers and brothers. Women sometimes pressed their claim to inherited land. During the general land registration campaigns of the 1930s and 1940s, it was not unusual for women to come forward and complain that land which their male relatives were trying to register in their own names had been unlawfully taken away from them.

Officials from the land department and the courts often sided with the women, citing their legal rights to inheritance under Islamic and secular Jordanian law, and forced the male relatives to share the land or buy out the women's share. Moreover, Jordanian law provides that heirs cannot give up their rights until they reach the age of 18, so such settlements must wait until that time.

The government also upheld a woman's right to land given to her as *mahr* (dowry). If the husband's father could not afford to pay the *mahr* in cash, he sometimes gave land or pledged it as a guarantee against eventual payment of the money. It is interesting to note that in rural areas Christians charged *mahr* as well as Muslims.

Where this leaves us today is that, as we mentioned, all of Jordan's land which lies outside of the towns and villages technically remains *miri* land, even though the state stopped exercising its rights as the ultimate owner of the land decades ago. But in 1990, the Muslim Brotherhood raised a new issue. Why couldn't the state, in its technical role as the ultimate owner of most land in Jordan, pass legislation requiring the application of Islamic inheritance laws to *miri* land, as they applied to *mulk*? This would give male heirs a larger share of inherited rural properties. This demand by the Islamists may strike us as odd, since women generally do not own much rural land (*miri*) anyway, since in many cases they are disinherited. But even if symbolic, such a gesture represents an attempt by the Muslim Brotherhood to use Islamic law joined with local customs to deprive women of their rights to land, and in this way sets a potentially serious precedent.

This paper ends with no definite prescription. It is doubtful that there is any at this historical juncture. The Islamist tide is increasing. To alienate them is a no-win solution. Perhaps the best policy is to strengthen a dialogue with the Islamists to seek reform from within these movements. If there are reformed-minded fundamentalists, are they our hope?

21

Feminism Comes of Age in Islam

Fadwa El Guindi[*]

It is difficult to demonstrate the existence of a discourse, a movement, a consciousness such as Islamic feminism in a climate that assumes the universal supremacy of Western feminism. It is even more difficult to argue for the combination of Islam and feminism in such a climate, which assumes a natural incompatibility between the two.

Western feminism is, of course, grounded in Western thought, ideology, and values, which are in some fundamental ways different from those of Islam or Arab tradition. Thus resistance to feminism in the Islamic or Arab world might in essence be a resistance, conscious or not, to cultural conversion. If we are to understand and appreciate alternative feminist forms, we will have to release Western women's claim on feminism — or, to put it differently, to free feminism from a Western hold on it.

Non-Western feminist struggles around the world have tended to be grounded in larger movements, mostly nationalistic and anti-colonialist, which function to strengthen and empower women rather than overshadow their feminist goals. In Egypt and parts of the Arab East, movements against foreign domination have provided an ideological framework that sustains the struggle for women's issues and allows women to participate in a process of liberating systems within which they are seeking complementary space with men. This is now happening among Palestinians under occupation.

The early 1970s saw an Islamic reawakening throughout the Arab and Islamic East, with a strong women's activist presence. The

* This article first appeared in the *Los Angeles Times*, Feb. 17, 1992. Copyright © 1992 by Fadwa El Guindi. Reprinted by permission.

women assertively identifying with the movement tend to come from urban middle and even upper classes, young, college-educated, and career-oriented, in professional fields requiring certification by national examinations in which both sexes compete. In other words, there has been a concentration of Islamic activism among the highest achievers. This belies the superficial image of the Islamic movement as necessarily conservative and its activists as essentially regressive. While many educated women are choosing the modesty of Islamic dress, their visibility is increasingly in the workforce and in public life, including the mosques.

After the early days of Islam — in seventh-century Arabia, when women did have a central role in the birth and spread of the faith — Muslim women gradually turned inward, giving up their right and obligation to have an active public role in religious life. Distanced from scriptural information and first-hand knowledge of Islam, they became dependent on men for guidance on spiritual and practical issues of immediate concern in their lives.

As part of the 1970s movement, women began acquiring literacy in Islamic matters, which fostered their interest in Islam's original sources and the interpretive process. For many women, this became an avenue of legitimate access to the force previously inaccessible to them, an opportunity for the first time in a millennium to have a dynamic role in the Islamic process. These women, in their knowledge of an adherence to Islamic principles, released men from the role of authority over them in Islamic matters.

The young activists posed a challenge to traditional structures at the beginning of the movement, especially in Egypt. Mothers were alarmed and objected to their daughters' taking the veil of the new modesty. Today, those same mothers have themselves acquired a secularized version of modesty. In fact, gradually a general mood of conservatism has stabilized in Egypt outside the Islamic movement.

The activists also posed a challenge to the Islamic establishment. Change is expected to move from authority downward, not the other way around. By adopting Islamic modesty, college women put on the defensive al-Azhar, the male-dominated seat of Islamic teaching, interpretation, and legislation. When al-Azhar remained silent in the 1970s on Islamic dress for women in secular coeducational universities, it was accepting the young activists' initiative. When al-Azhar enforced the Islamic dress of the movement in the 1980s in identical form (style, fabric, colors) in its own women's college, it was legitimizing the activists' pioneering role in determining the public image of Muslim women.

By choice, the young college women initiated a movement and defined its premises and its symbols. By presenting themselves publicly in a modest way, they asserted their place in society's traditional structures. They were, simultaneously, living models of Islamic morality and progressive participants in education, employment, and the professions. They evoked a hierarchy separate from the men's in which they became leaders in the university and in the mosque. Ideologues emerged among them who published on Muslim women's issues and lectured widely in the Islamic East.

This is a legitimate participation in the traditional sphere that is most vital for Muslim women's concerns. It is a feminism true to its society's traditions; these are women who chose to define their identity in Islamic terms and developed a consciousness that is Islamic in character. Their Islamic dress, so mystifying and misunderstood in the West, is in fact an anti-consumerist claim for their right to modesty, to control of their own bodies, to sexual space and moral privacy.

This Islamic reawakening is in its third decade. It has witnessed the Islamic Revolution in Iran, the ascent of a Muslim woman to high political office in Pakistan, a merging with nationalism in Palestinian territories, and a liberation from the secular communist hold on Islamic republics in the former Soviet Union. It has tasted political victory for Islamic "parties" within the democratic process, such as in Egypt (as a coalition with another party), in Jordan, and most strongly in Algeria (where it is now suffering anti-democratic political repression).

The Islamic East once again felt the force of foreign dominance in its most violent form in the Gulf War. It was a lesson, perhaps, for keeping feminism, democracy, and nationalism embedded in the larger Islamic movement so that women and men both are empowered as their nations are liberated.

Until the West chooses a non-confrontational, non-divisive path in its Middle East policy, one based on respect for the people and their tradition, I can only foresee the intensity of the Islamic awakening becoming increasingly defiant to the West.

22

Muslim Women and Fundamentalism

Fatima Mernissi[*]

When analyzing the dynamics of the Muslim world, one has to discriminate between two distinct dimensions: what people actually do, the decisions they make, the aspirations they secretly entertain or display through their patterns of consumption, and the discourses they develop about themselves, more specifically the ones they use to articulate their political claims. The first dimension is about reality and its harsh time-bound laws, and how people adapt to pitilessly rapid change; the second is about self-presentation and identity building. And you know as well as I do that whenever one has to define oneself to others, whenever one has to define one's identity, one is on the shaky ground of self-indulging justifications. For example, the need for Muslims to claim so vehemently that they are traditional, and that their women miraculously escape social change and the erosion of time, has to be understood in terms of their need for self-representation and must be classified not as a statement about daily behavioral practices, but rather as a psychological need to maintain a minimal sense of identity in a confusing and shifting reality.

To familiarize you with the present-day Muslim world and how women fit into the conflicting political forces (including religion), the best way is not to overwhelm you with data. On the contrary, what is most needed is some kind of special illumination of the structural dissymmetry that runs all through and conditions the entire fabric of

* This article was first published in *Middle East Report*, July-August 1988. It was adapted from the introduction of the revised edition of Fatima Mernissi's *Beyond the Veil: Male-Female Dynamics in Modern Muslim Society* (Bloomington and Indianapolis: Indiana University Press, 1987). Reprinted with the permission of MERIP/Middle East Report, 1500 Massachusetts Avenue, N.W., #119, Washington, D.C. 20005.

social and individual life — the split between acting and reflecting on one's actions. The split between what one does and how one speaks about oneself. The first has to do with the realm of reality; the second has to do with the realm of the psychological elaborations that sustain human beings' indispensable sense of identity. Individuals die of physical sickness, but societies die of loss of identity; that is, a disturbance in the guiding system of representations of oneself as fitting into a universe that is specifically ordered so as to make life meaningful.

Why do we need our lives to make sense? Because that's where power is. A sense of identity is a sense that one's life is meaningful, that, as fragile as a person may be, she or he can still have an impact on her or his limited surroundings. The fundamentalist wave in Muslim societies is a statement about identity. And that is why their call for the veil for women has to be looked at in the light of the painful but necessary and prodigious reshuffling of identity that Muslims are going through in these often confusing but always fascinating times.

The split in the Muslim individual between what one does, confronted by rapid, totally uncontrolled changes in daily life, and the discourse about the unchangeable religious tradition that one feels psychologically compelled to elaborate in order to keep a minimal sense of identity — this, as far as I am concerned, is the key point to focus on in order to understand the dynamics of contemporary Muslim life.

If fundamentalists are calling for the return of the veil, it must be because women have been taking off the veil. We are definitely in a situation where fundamentalist men and non-fundamentalist women have conflicts of interest. We have to identify who the fundamentalist men are, and who are the non-fundamentalist women who have opted to discard the veil. Class conflicts do sometimes express themselves in acute sex-focused dissent. Contemporary Islam is a good example of this because, beyond the strong obsession with religion, the violent confrontations going on in the Muslim world are about two eminently materialistic pleasures: exercise of political power and consumerism.

Fundamentalists and unveiled women are the two groups that have merged with concrete, conflicting claims and aspirations in the postcolonial era. Both have the same age range — youth — and the same educational privilege — a recent access to formalized institutions of knowledge. But while the men seeking power through religion and its revivification are mostly from newly urbanized middle- and lower middle-class backgrounds, unveiled women, by contrast, are predominantly of middle-class, urban backgrounds.

As a symptom, the call for the veil tells us one thing. Telling us another thing is the specific conjuncture of the forces calling for it — that is, the conservative forces and movements, their own quest, and how they position themselves within the social movements dominating the national and international scene.

TRESPASSING

Islam is definitely one of the modern political forces competing for power around the globe. At least that is how many of us experience it. How can a "medieval religion," ask Western students raised in a secular culture, be so alive, so challenging to the effects of time, so renewable in energy? How can it be meaningful to educated youth? One of the characteristics of fundamentalism is the attraction Islam has for high achievers among young people. In Cairo, Lahore, Jakarta, and Casablanca, Islam makes sense because it speaks about power and self-empowerment. As a matter of fact, worldly self-enhancement is so important for Islam that the meaning of spirituality itself has to be seriously reconsidered.

What was not clear for me in the early 1970s was that all the problems faced in recent decades are more or less boundary problems, from colonization (trespassing by a foreign power on Muslim community space and decision-making) to contemporary human rights issues (the political boundaries circumscribing the ruler's space and the freedoms of the government). The issue of technology is a boundary problem: how can we integrate Western technological information, the recent Western scientific memory, without deluging our own Muslim heritage? International economic dependency is, of course, eminently a problem of boundaries: the International Monetary Fund's intervention in fixing the price of our bread does not help us keep a sense of distinct national identity. What are the boundaries of the sovereignty of the Muslim state vis-à-vis voracious, aggressive transnational corporations? These are some of the components of the crisis that is tearing the Muslim world apart, along, of course, definite class lines.

Naive and serious as only a dutiful student can be, I did not know in 1975 that women's claims were disturbing to Muslim societies not because they threatened the past but because they argued and symbolized what the future and its conflicts are about: the inescapability of renegotiating new sexual, political, economic, and cultural boundaries, thresholds, and limits. Invasion of physical territory by alien hostile nations (Afghanistan and Lebanon); invasions of national television by *Dallas* and *Dynasty*; invasion of children's desires by

Coca-Cola and special brands of walking shoes — these are some of the political and cultural boundary problems facing the Muslim world today.

However, we have to remember that societies do not reject and resist changes indiscriminately. Muslim societies integrated and digested quite well technological innovations: the engine, electricity, the telephone, the transistor radio, sophisticated machinery, and arms, all without much resistance. But the social fabric seems to have trouble absorbing anything having to do with changing authority thresholds: freely competing unveiled women; freely competing political parties; freely elected parliaments; and, of course, freely elected heads of state who do not necessarily get 99 percent of the votes. Whenever an innovation has to do with free choice of the partners involved, the social fabric seems to suffer some terrible tear. Women's unveiling seems to belong to this realm. For the last one hundred years, whenever women tried or wanted to discard the veil, some men, always holding up the sacred as justification, screamed that it was unbearable, that the society's fabric would dissolve if the mask were dropped. I do not believe that men, Muslim or not, scream unless they are hurt. Those calling for the reimposition of the veil surely have reason. What is it that Muslim society needs to mask so badly?

The idea one hears about fundamentalism is that it is an archaic phenomenon, a desire to return to medieval thinking. It is frequently presented as a revivalist movement: bring back the past. And the call for the veil for women furthers this kind of misleading simplification. If we take the Egyptian city of Asyut as an example, we have to admit that it is a modern town with a totally new cultural feature that Muslim society never knew before: mass access to knowledge. In our history, universities and knowledge were privileges of the elite. The man of knowledge enjoyed a high respect precisely because he was a repository of highly valued and aristocratically gained information. Acquisition of knowledge took years, and often included a period of initiation that compelled the student to roam through Muslim capitals from Asia to Spain for decades. Mass access to universities, therefore, constitutes a total shift in the accumulation, distribution, management, and utilization of knowledge and information. And we know that knowledge is power. One of the reasons the fundamentalist will be preoccupied by women is that state universities are not open just for traditionally marginalized and deprived male rural migrants, but for women as well.

Persons under 15 years of age constitute 39 percent of Egypt's and 45 percent of Iran's total population.[1] The natural annual population increase in Egypt and Iran is 3.1 percent.[2] The time span for doubling the population is 22 years for Egypt and 23 for Iran. Secondary school enrollment in Iran is 35 percent for women and 54 percent for men. In Egypt, 39 percent of women of secondary school age are in fact there, as compared to 64 percent of men.[3] The same trend is to be found in other Muslim societies.

Centuries of women's exclusion from knowledge have resulted in femininity being confused with illiteracy until a few decades ago. But things have progressed so rapidly in our Muslim countries that we women today take literacy and access to schools and universities for granted. Illiteracy was such a certain fate for women that my grandmother would not believe that women's education was a serious state undertaking. For years she kept waking my sister and me at dawn to get us ready for school. We would explain that school started exactly three hours after her first dawn prayer, and that we needed only five minutes to get there. But she would mumble, while handing us our morning tea: "You better get yourself there and stare at the wonderful gate of that school for hours. Only God knows how long it is going to last." She had an obsessive dream: to see us read the Quran and master mathematics. "I want you to read every word of that Quran and I want you to answer my questions when I demand an explanation of a verse. That is how the *qadis* [Muslim judges] get all their power. But knowing the Quran is not enough to make a woman happy. She has to learn how to do sums. The winners are the ones who master mathematics." The political dimension of education was evident to our grandmothers' generation.

While a few decades ago the majority of women married before the age of 20, today only 22 percent of that age group in Egypt and 38.4 percent in Iran are married.[4] To get an idea of how perturbing it is for Iranian society to deal with an army of unmarried adolescents, one has only to remember that the legal age for marriage of females in Iran is 13 and for males 15.[5] The idea of an adolescent unmarried woman is a completely new idea in the Muslim world, where previously you had only a female child and a menstruating woman who had to be married off immediately so as to prevent dishonorable engagement in premarital sex. The whole concept of patriarchal honor was build around the idea of virginity, which reduced a woman's role to its sexual dimension: to reproduction within early marriage. The concept of an adolescent woman, menstruating and unmarried, is so alien to the entire Muslim family system that it is either unimaginable or necessarily linked to *fitna* (social disorder). The Arab countries are a good example of this demographic revolution in sex roles.

SPACE AND SEX ROLES

Young men faced with job insecurity, or failure of the diploma to guarantee access to the desired job, postpone marriage. Women, faced with the pragmatic necessity to count on themselves instead of relying on the dream of a rich husband, see themselves forced to concentrate on getting an education. The average age at marriage for women and men in most Arab countries has registered a spectacular increase. In Egypt and Tunisia, the average age at marriage for women is 22 and for men 27. In Algeria, the average age at marriage is 18 for women and 24 for men. In Morocco, Libya, and Sudan, women marry at around 19 and men at around 25. The oil countries, known for their conservatism, have witnessed an incredible increase of unmarried youth: age at marriage for women is 20 and for men is 27. And of course nuptiality patterns are influenced by urbanization. The more urbanized youth marry later. In 1980, in metropolitan areas of Egypt the mean age at marriage was 29.7 for males and 23.6 for females. In the urban areas of Upper Egypt, where the fundamentalist movement is strong, the mean age at marriage was 28.3 for men and 22.8 for women.[6]

The conservative wave against women in the Muslim world, far from being a regressive trend, is on the contrary a defense mechanism against profound changes in both sex roles and the touchy subject of sexual identity. The most accurate interpretation of this relapse into "archaic behaviors," such as conservatism on the part of men and resort to magic and superstitious rituals on the part of women, is as anxiety-reducing mechanisms in a world of shifting, volatile sexual identity.

Fundamentalists are right in saying that education for women has destroyed the traditional boundaries and definitions of space and sex roles. Schooling has dissolved traditional arrangements of space segregation, even in oil-rich countries where education is segregated by sex: simply to go to school women have to cross the street! Streets are spaces of sin and temptation because they are both public and sex-mixed. And that is the definition of *fitna*: disorder!

Fundamentalists are right when they talk about the dissolution of women's traditional function as defined by family ethics; postponed age of marriage forces women to turn pragmatically toward education as a means for self-enhancement. If one looks at some of the education statistics, one understands why newly urbanized and educated rural youth single out university women as enemies of Islam, with its tradition of exclusion from knowledge and decision-making. The percentage of women teaching in Egyptian universities was 25 percent in 1981. To get an idea of how fast change is occurring there, one only has to remember that in 1980 the percentage of women teaching in American universities was 24 percent and it was 25 percent in East Germany.[7] Even in conservative Saudi Arabia, women have invaded sexually segregated academic space: they are 22 percent of the university faculty there. Women are 18 percent of the university faculty in Morocco, 16 percent in Iraq, and 12 percent in Qatar.

What dismays the fundamentalists is that the area of independence did not create an all-male new class. Women are taking part in the public feast. And that is a definite revolution in the Islamic concept of both the state's relation to women and women's relation to the institutionalized distribution of knowledge.

Notes

1. *1983 World Population Data Sheet* (Washington, D.C.: Population Reference Bureau).

2. Ibid.

3. "People's Wallchart," *People's Magazine* vol. 12 (1985).

4. Ibid.

5. Ibid.

6. *World Fertility Survey* no. 42: "The Egyptian Survey," November 1983.

7. *Annuaire statistique* (Paris: UNESCO, 1980).

PART EIGHT

Women, the State, Civil Society, and Kinship Ties: "Private" and "Public" Space

23

Economic and Political Liberalization in Egypt and the Demise of State Feminism

Mervat F. Hatem[*]

In the late 1950s and the 1960s, an Egyptian welfare state was developed to provide the economic basis of a new social contract between the Nasser regime and its key class allies. Its main beneficiaries were the men and women of both the middle class and the labor aristocracy, who were to staff and run its expanding state sector. For Egyptian women, who were scorned by the pre-1952 state, the new welfare state offered explicit commitment to public equality for women. It contributed to the development of state feminism as a legal, economic, and ideological strategy to introduce changes to Egyptian society and its gender relations. In its own turn, state feminism contributed to the political legitimacy of Gamal Abdel Nasser's regime and its progressive credentials.

The adoption of the policies of economic and political liberalization by the regimes of Anwar Sadat and Hosni Mubarak redefined women's relationship to the state and the role they were to play in society. These policies were identified with the development of conservative social, economic, and political systems that were hostile to state activism, in general, and state support of women's public equality, in particular. The social and economic retreat of the state and the consequent demise of state feminism in the 1980s undermined the prospects of lower-middle-class and working-class women. They benefited a small group of bourgeois and upper-middle-class women. The over-

* This essay was first published in the *International Journal of Middle East Studies*, vol. 24, no. 2 (1992), pp. 231-51. Reprinted with the permission of Cambridge University Press.

all effect of these changes was to introduce pronounced economic, social, and ideological divisions among Egyptian women that make it increasingly difficult to develop a single organization and/or a program for action that can represent their conflicting needs and aspirations.

STATE FEMINISM AS A STRATEGY AND THE QUEST FOR WOMEN'S LIBERATION

It is important not to trivialize the concept of state feminism by using it to describe the formal (legal and ideological) state commitment to women's rights. More appropriately, it refers to ambitious state programs that introduce important changes in the reproductive and productive roles of women. The concept of state feminism was coined and used in this way by the students of the welfare state in Scandinavian society. It referred to government efforts to remove the structural basis of gender inequality by making reproduction a public — not a private — concern and the employing of increasing numbers of women in the state sector. To those who believe in the reformist character of the state, the Scandinavian welfare states provided an example of how patriarchy, as a system of structural relationships used to subordinate women, could be reversed. More recently, Scandinavian feminist critics have pointed out that state feminism represented a conservative top-down strategy to women's issues that did not solve the problems of underrepresentation, discrimination, and subordination. These continued under new conditions.[1] Still, state attention to women's reproductive and productive concerns increases the public resources available to them and improves their options economically and politically. The social and economic retreat of the state represents a step backwards, because it leads to a return to women's economic and social dependence on patriarchal families and the market's fluctuating demand for women's labor.

The accomplishments of Egyptian state feminism in the areas of production were impressive by the standards of the 1950s and the 1960s. State commitment to providing equality of opportunity to all Egyptians was unequivocally stated in the 1956 constitution and was reaffirmed in the slightly revised one adopted in 1963. They declared all Egyptians equal under the law and forbade discrimination on the basis of gender, racial origin, language, religion, or belief. This commitment to public equality was operationalized by law number 14 of 1964, which guaranteed jobs in the state sector for all holders of intermediate school diplomas and college degrees irrespective of gender. Labor laws were changed to insure and protect women's equal standing in the labor force. This entitled women to 50 days of paid maternity leave, and it obligated employers to provide day-care services where 100 or more women were employed. Finally, it forbade employers to fire pregnant women while on maternity leave. In this way, it made reproduction of public concern for state and private employers, not just the personal concern of the family. As a result, social attitudes toward women's education and employment changed, and their presence in those areas multiplied. In addition, women were given the vote in 1956, a victory for the older generation of suffragists that included Duriya Sahfiq and Ceza Nabarawi. All these achievements gave a new generation of women novel definitions of their productive and reproductive roles.

Paradoxically, this progressive framework also accommodated more conservative social outlooks to women's positions in the family and in the political system, which were left unchallenged. For example, the personal status laws passed in the 1920s and the 1930s continued to be upheld. These laws defined women as the economic dependents of men, unstable emotional beings that could not be trusted with the right to divorce, and unable to leave a husband without his consent and/or in cases where he was incurably ill or impotent. The right to suffrage aside, the state demobilized Egyptian feminist organizations. As a result, women's political representation in parliament and in other political institutions remained erratic.[2] In short, state feminism under the Nasser regime produced women who were economically independent of their families, but dependent on the state for employment, important social services like education, health- and day-care, and political representation. While state feminism created and organized a system of public patriarchy, it did not challenge the personal and familial views of women's dependency on men that were institutionalized by the personal status laws and the political system.

THE IMPACT OF ECONOMIC LIBERALIZATION ON WOMEN

The contraction and retreat of the state sector as a part of the shift to a market economy where Egyptian, regional, and international capital played the leading developmental role had serious consequences for state feminism. With the retreat of the state as a social and economic agent of change, many official commitments to gender equality were either ignored or abandoned within and outside the state sector. This created an ideological and economic vacuum that was filled by the Islamist entrepreneurs, local and international capitalist enterprise, and/or institutions like USAID. None of these local and international actors was interested in the goals of state feminism. On the contrary, each proved to be hostile, in different ways, to the quest of economic and social equality for women. Labor migration to the Gulf economies was the 1970s solution to the economic woes of the middle and working classes, and it had numerous negative effects on women and their families. It is the young lower-middle-class and working-class women who have borne the brunt of these painful economic and social adjustments.

From the very beginning, the Sadat regime (1970-81) was plagued by a heightened awareness of an impending economic crisis. The younger generation of men and women seemed particularly sensitive to the impact that this would have on them as the newest members of the labor force. In the 1972 student uprising, college students expressed a clear concern over the differential impact that the war economy had on different classes. They asked that each class "make proportional sacrifices based on its ability to contribute."[3] Students were conscious of the increasing gap between the different classes on campus and those outside it. As a result, they demanded that the "highest income should not exceed a multiple of ten times the lowest incomes."[4] For many students, who sought employment in the state sector after graduation, the downgrading of state salaries threatened their economic prospects and social status. College women were equally concerned because the public sector had emerged in the previous decades as the largest employer of women.[5]

It is this young, urban lower segment of the middle class, whose status seemed most precarious, that was simultaneously attracted to and targeted by the Islamists on college campuses. In the early 1970s, the Islamists were supported by the regime in their challenge of the Nasserite student leadership in different elections. The Islamist platforms offered a voluntarist and individualist development vision, which they claimed could address the mushrooming social and economic problems facing the young members of the middle class. Their message was focused on self-help solutions that were compatible with the privatization ideals of the new open-door system. It suggested ways in which individuals could cope with declining incomes. For example, modest modes of dress were seen as respectable alternatives to the ideal of the expensively dressed college students. At their inception, the Islamic modes of dress accommodated the individual's need for both comfort and thriftiness. It implied the religious devotion of the woman who was wearing it and thus deterred the young men who habitually engaged in the sexual harassment of women in the streets and in public transportation.

The modestly dressed college women were presented as desirable marriage mates. Not only were they well behaved and trustworthy, but they were also not likely to tax the income of new college graduates. The Islamist message encouraged women to do without the financially cumbersome obligation that discouraged men from entering into marriage. They argued in favor of symbolic dowries *(mahr)* and shared dwellings, usually with one's in-laws.

The Islamist views of women's education and employment have been destructive to the accomplishments of state feminism. Zaynab Radwan's study of young, veiled college women showed new conservative perspectives on both. While the Islamists supported women's education, they saw it primarily as a means of preparing them to be good wives and mothers. They were quite ambivalent about women's work. Only one-third of the sample (33.2 percent) supported the unqualified right of women to work. Another third (33.7 percent) stated that women should only work if they needed to. Another 20.9 percent only approved of women's work in traditional female occupations like teaching, medicine, and social work. Finally, 12.2 percent of veiled women were totally opposed to women's work.[6]

The lack of interest in paid work by veiled women may have been a response to the already substantial high rate of female unemployment among literate women. In 1960, men's unemployment rate was 1.9 percent while women's unemployment rate was 5.8 percent. In 1976, when economic liberalization started, total unemployment shot up to 7.7 percent: 5.5 percent for men and 29.8 percent for women. By 1986, the overall unemployment rates had doubled to 14.7 percent: with 10 percent for men and 40.7 percent for women. While in 1960, the women's unemployment rate was three times as high as that of men, in the 1980s this rate rose further to four times that of men. Not surprisingly, the late 1970s witnessed heated public debates on the desirability of women in the workforce. Governmental studies were conducted to assess the economic and social feasibility of women working. The state's position on this issue was in line with the conservative social climate it helped create. It offered its women employees numerous incentives to take a leave of absence without pay to raise their children and/or work on a part-time basis. Secular and religious opponents of women's employment stressed the adverse effects that it had on the family and children. They also blamed working women for crowded transportation and lower productivity. Despite the public pressures put on working women to stay at home, most continued to work. Most government studies concluded that spiraling inflation had made two incomes an economic necessity for most families.[7]

For upper-middle-class women, the changes have been equally complicated. Among the young college women from comfortable socio-economic backgrounds, whether defined by family income, the father's profession, or the parents' education, the proportion of those choosing the veil was still high: 43 percent, 47.7 percent, and 48.2 percent, respectively.[8] Unfortunately, Radwan does not address herself to this aspect of her study because it complicates her main thesis regarding the lower-middle-class roots of the veiled college students. Some possible answers can be suggested, however. Among the veiled women, 23.2 percent said they were the only ones who were veiled in their families. When veiled women were asked as a group how their families reacted to their decisions, 71.2 percent indicated that their families agreed with their decision, 12.8 percent said that their families had no opinion, and 15.5 percent said that their families were opposed to it. When asked about how they reacted to this opposition, 60.5 percent said that they tried to reason with their families, 26.3 percent ignored their opposition, and another 13.2 percent said they asked God to show their families the right path.[9] Within this group, the break with one's parents' beliefs and lifestyles seems to be part of the life-cycle changes brought on by adolescence and the ways a new generation distinguishes itself from the older one. In response to a question on whether they solicited the assistance of others to convince their parents, not a single one answered in the affirmative,[10] indicating a strong need for self-assertion and autonomy.

In other words, a socio-economic perspective on veiling offers only one explanation of a complex phenomenon. It is clear, for instance, that most veiled women, regardless of their class background, shared a strong sense of religiosity, which spread in the 1970s and the 1980s. When veiled women were asked about their reasons for adopting the veil, they cited (a) their conviction that this mode of dress brought them closer to God (40.8 percent); (b) their religious consciousness and the fact that this was compatible with the *shari'a* (33.2 percent); (c) fear of going to hell and the desire to go to heaven (20.6 percent); (d) deep interest in religious teachings (10.1 percent); (e) having very religious families (3 percent); and (f) peer pressure (2 percent). Clearly, veiling is a socio-economic and social phenomenon as well as an ideological one. While all of those veiled young college women shared a strong sense of religiosity, the decision to veil took on different meanings depending on their class backgrounds. Because some veiled upper-class women faced opposition from their families (18.6 percent), they draw on attention to the generational dimension. A decision to veil served to distinguish the values of a conservative younger generation from those of the one that preceded it. It also helped young women going through adolescence to assert themselves within their own families using existing cultural modes of expressions and values.[11]

The social and economic changes brought about by the open-door system had different effects on older upper-middle-class and upper-class women. College graduates with knowledge of foreign languages found lucrative jobs in international enterprises.[12] Unfortunately, however, these well paid positions tended to be concentrated in clerical ranks with very limited prospects for professional advancement. In addition, those jobs required longer work hours without all the occupational and/or social security benefits available in the state sector. Many of these companies also had an unwritten policy of not hiring veiled women because they did not fit the image these companies wanted to project.

Upper-class women with capital of their own have joined the entrepreneurial ranks. Many of the businesses they own are small boutiques and motels. Others own large subsidiaries of international firms. These entrepreneurs report that they feel they have to work harder to get the recognition that is automatically awarded to their male competitors.[13]

For some older upper-middle-class women, improving the family income required migration with their husbands to the Gulf. These represented, however, a small percentage of the women of that class. In many cases the mothers with older children, most stayed behind to avoid disrupting the education of their children. In both cases, working women either quit their own jobs or took leaves of absence without pay to care for their families. In some of these comfortable families with an absent husband, many women expressed unwillingness to work for the low salaries in the state sector. The attitude that this group of upper-middle-class women had toward work represented a return to the older ideal that viewed women's public work as an indicator of economic need and not as part of women's contribution to society. It signaled a return of the economic stigma associated with women in the workforce. While the remittances sent by the husbands working in the Gulf allowed them to continue to live comfortable lives, many women complained of loneliness.[14]

Finally, there was still a group of older professional middle-class women who, despite their complaints about the deteriorating work conditions in the state sector, clung to their work roles as a means of self-realization and as symbol of the gains made by women of their generation. These tended to be feminists active in women's groups whose key task was to defend the rights women gained in the 1950s and the 1960s that were now under attack by the conservative Islamists.[15]

By contrast with middle- and upper-class women's retreat from the workforce, the inflation and migration that were products of the open-door system served to push urban and rural working-class women into the labor force. The feminization of the urban and rural workforce began in the mid-1970s. It manifested itself first in the industrial companies of the public sector. While most male workers were interested in the better paying jobs of the private sector and/or of the Gulf economies, in order to deal with spiraling prices, women workers preferred employment in the public sector because it offered such benefits as subsidized transportation, child-care, and maternity leave.[16] Even though factory managers were increasingly having to depend on women workers as part of a more stable workforce, they continued to consider them as poor employment risks because of their need for maternity leave and child-care.[17] The cost of both made their labor expensive. Managers held on to this view even though many had to pay incentive bonuses to retain some of the skilled male workers.[18]

These stereotypical attitudes toward women's industrial work explained why some managers chose to replace male workers with machines and not women workers.[19] Some USAID projects followed the same policy as well.[20] Clearly, local and international industrial enterprises shared the same prejudices regarding the unsuitability of women for industrial work.

Finally, as evidence of the regime's increasing lack of social and economic commitment to women in the workforce, the minister of industry passed a measure in March 1987 to stop hiring women (workers and professionals) in the textile industry. It cited women's health (pregnancy and breast feeding) as the reason why they were barred from this type of polluted work. Another reason it stated was that they leave work in search for subsidized goods.[21] In response to an extremely angry reaction from numerous women's groups, the minister denied that any such measure was approved. He also argued that the intent of the ministry was misunderstood. This decision was made in the middle of intense discussions regarding the dramatic return of many male migrant workers from the Gulf states and the desire to rehire them.

Those employed in the service sector as beauticians and boutique saleswomen faced different dilemmas. They improved their earning power, but complained of work conditions, especially the long hours. For these women, the open-door system improved their incomes but not the conditions under which they worked and/or the condescending social attitudes toward their work.

Urban and rural working-class women were less likely than middle- and upper-middle-class women to accompany their migrant husbands to the Gulf. Urban working-class wives, who were left behind by their migrant husbands in search of better incomes, were either forced to quit their jobs to take care of their added family responsibilities or to take new jobs in the informal sector to support their families until the remittances started to come in. While the flow of remittances from the Gulf states improved the living standards of many urban working-class families, the migration of a husband had demoralizing social and emotional effects on working-class women and their children. Young working-class wives and their children were very often expected to move back with their in-laws or their own families. This return to the extended family coincided with the re-emergence of the authoritarian control of the brother (or brother-in-law) or the mother-in-law over these young women and their children. The freedom and autonomy these women experienced in the nuclear family was undermined in the extended family. Very often they did not receive or control the way the remittances sent by their husbands were spent. The husband either sent instructions about how the money should be spent or delegated that authority to one of his male kin.[22]

While older women continued to live in their own homes and to retain their own autonomy, they now had to handle numerous responsibilities within and outside the household. Assuming the roles of mother and father strained their relations with their children. Their social lives became restricted. In some instances, they were afraid of socializing with others lest their reputations suffer. This contributed to their seclusion and isolation. On the whole, the urban working-class women viewed male migration negatively and saw themselves as having lost on most social and familial fronts.[23]

If one looks at the rural picture, one is struck by the simultaneously overlapping and contrasting effects of the migration of husbands on working-class women and their families. In Qabbabat and Dahshur in lower Egypt, for instance, both young and older women experienced an increase of their work loads due to the absence of the husband, but while older women remained free of the control of their in-laws, younger women returned to the authoritarian control of their mother-in-law in extended households.[24] If the wife was young, rural husbands tended to send the remittances as well as instructions regarding how to spend them to the older male in his family. Older women were more likely to receive the remittances directly.[25]

When husbands sent remittances to their wives, these women assumed responsibilities often associated with men, such as managing the land and dealing with village cooperatives and other public officials. In terms of setting expenditure priorities outside of agriculture, women emphasized the importance of house improvements that would make their lives and those of their children more comfortable. Women were also more inclined to be sensitive to the health and the educational needs of their daughters, which rural working-class fathers habitually ignored. Important decisions, like the marriage of a family member and/or the purchase of important consumer items, were, however, left until the husband returned.[26]

Rural women who migrated with their families to land reclamation settlements like Tahadi experienced the many positive effects of the move. They escaped the strong grip of the in-laws and participated with their husbands in making important decisions concerning the land, the house, the children, and the community.[27] They also reported having better incomes and working conditions. Interestingly enough, the improvement of the family income seemed to contribute to marital instability because husbands could, and sometimes did, take a second wife. Taking a second wife was described by a husband as a means of disciplining the first one. Another stated the need for more children to work on the land as the reason for taking another wife.[28]

In another study, of the small community of Izbat al-Warda, improvement of working-class family income has meant the seclusion of previously active peasant women. It seems clear that work in the fields was, and continues to be, associated with poverty. The middle-class ideal in the countryside puts value on simply being a housewife and views women's public presence as a shameful act.[29] Despite the conservative implications of this social ideal, which restricts and controls women's movement, it reduces women's workloads and explains why the ideal is popular among peasant working-class women.

The study of Izbat al-Warda also showed that the feminization of agriculture did not necessarily contribute to the empowerment of women. Most of the men in the village chose either to migrate or take jobs in the service and state sectors. They worked as taxi or tractor drivers, took clerical government jobs, became construction workers, or enlisted in the army, where they learned to be truck drivers, wall painters, plumbers, or construction workers. These had become the most attractive male occupations and/or sources of income. As a result, women have since taken over most of the agricultural tasks previously done by men, through reliance on other women and their cooperation networks *(muzamala)*. Because child and female labor on the land has increased significantly, agriculture has been devalued as an activity that is largely handled by women.[30]

To sum up, state adoption of economic liberalization as a policy orientation has created new forms of economic management that have affected the demand for the labor of women, the type of employment open to them, and the conditions under which they work. It has effectively undermined economic state feminism, which stressed the importance of women's integration in the economy by making women's productive and reproductive roles a concern to public policy. By declining to hire women on the grounds that the provisions of maternity leave and child-care, stipulated by the law, made their labor expensive, employers in both the state and private sectors have made economic liberalization identified with inequality of opportunity in the labor force. While the progressive laws of the 1950s and the 1960s, which were designed to provide women of different classes with equal opportunity in the workplace, still stand, the rise in unemployment has neutralized women's capacity to achieve economic equality.

In terms of its effect on women of different classes, economic liberalization has had an uneven record. It seriously diminished the economic and social prospects of upper-class and upper-middle-class women as a result of the large-scale unemployment among their young members. The widespread support this group of young women has given to the Islamists should be seen as a sign of protest against their declining economic fortunes. The Islamist ideologies have also provided this group with a means to rationalize the very harsh reality of female unemployment and the difficult economic decision of returning to the home. In stark contrast, economic liberalization has enhanced the prospects of upper-class and upper-middle-class women. It has provided them with jobs in international enterprises and with investment opportunities. It supplied their migrant husbands with external opportunities to maintain their comfortable family income. Migration, as a means of maintaining a comfortable middle-class status and improving the prospects of working-class families, has turned out to be a mixed blessing. Very specifically, the migration of husbands to the Gulf provided some economic reprieve, but at the expense of the social and emotional needs of women and children. The decision to keep families intact usually meant economic hardships.

Finally, the present generation of young men and women of different classes, who are making the serious sacrifices required for the transition to a new economic system, have only the most limited employment prospects. Most have to delay marriage plans and to accept support from their families in the case of migration. It is this system of gender, class, and generational inequalities that has become identified with economic liberalization in Egypt. It explains the very pessimistic outlook shared by the majority of Egyptian men and women of the middle and working classes regarding their economic future.

POLITICAL LIBERALIZATION FROM THE TOP, AND STATE CONTROL OF THE GENDER AGENDA

In a parallel way, the move away from the authoritarian one-party system and the introduction of some degree of political liberalization in Egypt did not result in greater participation for women of different classes. The Sadat regime's decision to liberalize the political process (i.e., to open it up to competing political parties and groups) in 1976 signaled its willingness to share power, but without significantly retreating from this arena. The result was a political system that used the rhetoric of democracy, but accommodated a state that specified for the public which political groups it was and was not willing to tolerate. In the early 1970s, the regime allied itself to the Islamist groups (represented in the mid-1970s by the Muslim Brotherhood and its journal *Al-Da'wa*) and allowed them to reach and organize their supporters. It harassed the radical and secular political parties (represented by the Unionist Progressive Party and its newspaper *Al-Ahali*) with repeated shutdowns and arrests. This strategy of simultaneously including and excluding particular groups in the political process was and continues to be a key characteristic of the process of limited political liberalization from the top that the Sadat and Mubarak regimes described as democratization.

Lacking independent representative organizations of their own, women remained captives of the state's political needs. More importantly, gender issues were used by the state, and by its foes and its allies, to distinguish themselves from one another and to score ideological and political victories. State policies concerning women, including the presidential decrees passed in 1979, which introduced changes in the personal status laws and women's representation in parliament, were designed to distinguish the social agenda of the regime from that of its political opponents. This resort to presidential decrees as a means of bypassing parliamentary opposition cast the shadow of authoritarianism on women's rights. It created dissonance among women of different political persuasions and mobilized opposition against the regime and the cause of women's rights. The resulting public and constitutional backlash signaled the political demise of state feminism as an acceptable political strategy for women's rights. Still, the Mubarak regime used the passage of an amended version of the 1985 personal status law to placate the Islamists and the active women and to preserve its positive international image at the end of the UN Decade for Women. Finally, liberalization contributed to the proliferation of new forms of women's formal and informal groups and associations but reproduced the organizational problems of limited democratization that prevailed in the Egyptian political system within these new institutions.

THE SADAT REGIME

From the very beginning, the Sadat regime instituted a pattern of strengthening its control of active middle-class women who were identified with state feminism in parliament and the executive branch. It used them to serve the changing national and international agendas of the regime. Following the coup (1971) against the radical elements within the Arab Socialist Union (ASU), Egypt's only political party, the president instructed the general secretary of the party to create separate youth and women's organizations that owed their allegiance to him personally.[31] In addition, the president opined that the new women's secretariat should be headed by *"Imra'a rajul"* (a woman who is like a man).[32] In other words, while the regime was clearly interested in mobilizing women through a new organization, it was opposed to the idea of developing an organization that was feminist in orientation for fear that it might have a competing and/or an independent (gendered) agenda. Karima al-Sa'id, a pioneering technocrat who became the under-secretary of the Ministry of Education in 1966, was the first president of this new domesticated secretariat (1971). Under her leadership, the organization obliged the regime by operating within the limits set for it. For example, it did not challenge the new social and political qualifications introduced by the 1971 constitution with regard to the state's commitments to women's public equality. Very specifically, rule 11 of the constitution reiterated the familiar "commitment of the state to providing the means to reconcile the obligations women have in the family, their work in society, and their equality to men in the political, social, and cultural arenas," but added the important qualifications "provided that [the above] did not infringe on the rules of Islamic *shari'a*."[33] This new constitutional stipulation represented a significant political departure from the secular discourses of the 1960s. It also constituted an important overture to the Islamist groups, who had been prosecuted by the Nasser regime and were to become important allies of the new regime. As a reward for the silence and/or compliance of the women's secretariat regarding the change discussed above, seven women were elected to the 1971 people's assembly and the president appointed two more, bringing the total number of women in parliament to nine: triple the number of women represented in the Assembly in 1969.

With the advent of the UN Decade for Women in 1975, the regime created a larger Egyptian Women's Organization, as part of the political reorganization of the ASU, and a National Commission for Women, which brought together women in key positions within the executive branch who dealt with women's issues. According to Mrs. Sadat's speech to the First Intentional Women's Conference held in Mexico City, the two organizations were delegated the task of "ending the last traces of discrimination that obstructed the spirit of our legislation regarding family life and the position of women."[34] In practice, the two organizations concerned themselves with family planning, the care of mothers and their children, and female illiteracy.[35] These were the national tasks handled by these organizations during this period. They were technocratic preoccupations that did not involve any discussion of the politically sensitive issues of Islam's attitude to birth control and/or the need to change the personal status law to discourage polygyny.

The confrontation between the regime and the Islamists, following a long period of cooperation and coexistence (1971-77), started with the assassination of Shaykh al-Dabi, the minister of religious affairs, in 1977. In response to the Islamist challenge of the authority and power of the state, Mrs. Sadat began a campaign during that same year to reform the personal status laws that dealt with marriage, divorce, and the custody of children. Politically, the change of the law offered a way of undermining the power and the legitimacy of the Islamist groups among women, who represented a large constituency within the movement. Through it, the state also hoped to distinguish its social character from that of the Islamists and to begin the mobilization of a district internal and international base of support.[36] It hoped to build a secular anti-Islamic bloc (of men and women) in a new coalition with the state. Internationally, the law would enhance the positive image of the regime as it asked for economic and political support, especially from the United States.[37]

The following were some of the suggested changes introduced by the law. First, it required the notification of the first wife that her husband had taken another. Second, it considered the husband's decision to take a second wife to be a source of "harm" to the first wife and, therefore, entitled her to file for divorce if she chose to. Finally, a divorced wife with children was entitled to keep the family until her children were grown up. These were not exactly radical changes. They did not outlaw polygyny or give women the unqualified right to divorce. They just regulated the former and specified additional cases where the latter would be allowed.

Still, the Islamist groups succeeded in mobilizing the public against the law. First, they discredited Jehan Sadat, who was the dominant force behind the campaign, and the feminists who supported her, as imitating Western women.[38] The Islamists argued that this group of women was different from the average devout Muslim woman who recognized the religious wisdom behind the gender asymmetry between men and women in the family and sanctioned by the Quran. They argued that the suggested changes that regulated men's right to take a second wife were in violation of the *shari'a* and thus represented the views of atheists who were engaged in subverting Islamic rules. Next, the Islamists tapped the latent male opposition to their diminishing monopoly of power in matters relating to marriage and divorce by presenting the new laws as denying them the right to take more than one wife. Since the new law was to give a wife and her children the right to the family home, it was described as being unfair to men, considering Egypt's chronic housing shortages. This strategy simultaneously divided women and unified men — the old and the young, the religiously minded and the secularists, the right and the poor — against the law.[39]

To complicate matters politically, the state responded to criticism by the opposition to the Camp David Accords in April 1979, by denying some political elements (especially the communists and the secularists of the New Wafd Party) the right to participate in the political process.[40] By eliminating and discrediting these potential allies in the battle for the law, the state transformed the reform of the personal status laws from a means of organizing a new base of support into a political liability. To overcome its political isolation, the new law was passed by presidential decree in June 1979 along with another decree that gave Egyptian women thirty seats in the Assembly and 20 percent of all seats in the local People's Councils.

Some argue that the two presidential decrees passed in 1979 enhanced women's personal and political rights and that they were,
therefore, examples of the survival of state feminism into the 1970s.
This argument is very difficult to accept, given the lack of a coherent
state program on gender issues during this period. As was made clear
in the first section, the state had abdicated the defense of women's
rights in the economic arena in the attempt to accelerate the drive to
economic liberalization. The state's move to introduce changes in
gender relations within the family and in the political arena had less
to do with either its commitment to the rights of women or its desire
for political liberalization. It was a question of how it defined its political interests at the time. Unfortunately, the state's desire to continue to dictate social and political policy made a mockery of official
rhetoric regarding political liberalization and further undermined its
legitimacy. It made the Sadat regime doubly inadequate. Not only did
it fail to provide economically for its own citizens, but in addition it
continued to be politically authoritarian. The economic retreat by the
state made such political interventions (especially in gender relations
where there was no social consensus) less tolerable.

THE MUBARAK REGIME

The assassination of President Sadat, following the crackdown by the
state on all sections of the opposition (the left, the right, Islamic, Cop-
tic, old, young men, and women) contributed to expanded public debates on how to correct the problems that contributed to the collapse
of the political order. During the early 1980s, a broad consensus
emerged regarding the state's need to share power as part of the process of political liberalization. In practice, this process depended for its
success on the emergence of a strong judiciary and legalized Islamist
political presence. The judiciary asserted its independence through
correcting the abuses of political power by the executive branch and
its intervention in the legislature. For example, the council of state reversed the state's decision to outlaw the New Wafd Party, thus allowing it to join the political process, and it struck down the 1979
personal status law that was passed by presidential decree. It also can-
celed the 1979 electoral law that entitled women to more seats in the
Assembly in 1987 because it constituted preferential treatment for
women. Finally, it ruled in favor of the right of radicals and Islamists
interned and accused by the state.[41]

Secondly, the recurring Islamist rebellion in Upper Egypt and in
Cairo pressured the state into allowing the Islamists to work within

the system and in this way split them politically. In the 1984 elections, the Islamists formed an alliance within the New Wafd Party, and in the 1987 elections they allied themselves to the Labor Party. In both instances, these electoral coalitions allowed them to emerge as part of the opposition in the Assembly. This made the legislature very conservative on social issues and further discouraged the state from supporting women's issues and/or the election of women representatives.

These two developments had significant institutional effects on women. They now faced an unsympathetic judiciary and a hostile legislature unwilling to support their agendas. The decision to strike down the 1979 personal status laws and the repeal of the reserved parliamentary seats for women in 1987 offer enlightening accounts of the way political power began to be shared unequally by the executive, legislative, and the judiciary branches under a system of limited liberalization. This diminished the social and political prospects for women.

The striking down of the personal status law caused an uproar among different groups of women: in the Assembly, in the executive branch, in non-governmental associations, as well as the mass of unaffiliated women. A committee for the Defense of the Rights of Women and the Family was quickly formed to lobby for the passage of a new law that would respond to the social needs addressed by the 1979 law.[42] During this period, the state was engaged in a tense confrontation with the Islamists over the implementation of the *shari'a* in different areas of public life. It also faced the embarrassing prospects of going to the International Women's Conference in Nairobi, marking the end of the UN Decade for Women, after having struck down a law that gave women new rights. Instead of allowing a confrontation to develop between the Islamists and women, which would have been disastrous both nationally and internationally, the state took the lead in suggesting a new watered-down personal status law to the People's Assembly that would appease both.

The new law, approved hastily on July 2, 1985, showed the state to be on the defensive, retreating from the task of pushing for change in gender relations. The state chose to rely on the conservative social views of the judges to interpret the minor gains given to women by the 1979 law and in this way dilute them. Under the 1985 law, "a wife whose husband takes a second wife may file for a divorce if she suffers from material or non-material harm [*darar ma'nawi*] that makes smooth marital relations within that class [*bayna amthaliha*] difficult. A judge determines whether or not such harm has occurred and tries to reconcile the couple, and only when he fails does he grant her a divorce."[43] In assuming that the meaning of harm differs from one class to another, the law gives the judge more latitude in assessing the claims of women who file for divorce on these grounds.

As for the right of a divorced mother to the family home, the new law required that a man, within at least three months, provide his ex-wife and the children with suitable separate housing. If he is unable to do so, the woman and her children will continue to occupy the home where they lived before the divorce. A judge will also ask the woman to choose between keeping the place where she has been residing and asking the judge to assign other adequate housing for her and the children. In this particular area, the new law retreated from a statement of the unequivocal right of mother and children to their family home in favor of giving the ex-husband a choice in the matter. The judge again emerges as an arbiter in the process, not just an executor of the law.

Finally, the High Constitutional Court decided to void the law that established reserved seating for women.[44] The court argued that the law undermined the constitutional principle of gender equality in its preferential treatment of women. The ruling explicitly challenged the acceptability of state intervention on behalf of women to deepen gender equality that had been a key pillar of the state feminism of bygone eras. The court chose to interpret the principle of gender equality as requiring a "hands off" policy by the state even where inequality in political representation existed.

The state welcomed this ruling for a number of different reasons. It allowed the state to solidify its peace with the moderate Islamist groups, who again joined the parliamentary opposition in 1987. It also made it possible for the state to rid itself of the feminist mantle that was increasingly being questioned by women in the many formal and informal groups. Recognizing this new level of feminist consciousness, President Mubarak declared that women were now ready to compete with men on an equal basis on the different party lists.[45] The immediate results of both the new ruling and this new attitude by the NDP (New Democratic Party) were negative. Whereas in the 1984 elections women held 33 out of a total of 448 seats in the People's Assembly, the 1987 elections brought only 18 women to the Assembly; 14 women were elected and four were appointed. In the 1990 elections, the number of women elected to the Assembly dropped even further to ten: seven were elected and three were appointed.

The state's diminishing support for the political representation of women encouraged middle-class women to organize themselves into autonomous and semi-autonomous formal and informal groups. The Islamists were the first to successfully mobilize and organize their supporters. In view of their impressive popularity among college men and women,[46] they encouraged women on campuses to organize themselves into groups that provided the members with social support and social services (e.g. free transportation, mimeographed lecture notes, and medical care). The *"amirs"* (leaders) of these groups of college women were always men.[47] Women were excluded from the leadership of their own groups on the grounds that male leaders know more about Islam than women. In other words, despite the visibility of women in the Islamist movement, they were largely represented at the lowest levels. The formation of gender-segregated groups did not necessarily propel women into leadership positions. Leadership continued to be the sole preserve of men even in women's groups.

The only female figure who occupied a national leadership position in an Islamist organization was Zaynab al-Ghazali. Her political history showed the ambitions some women had in joining the movement and the difficult road to national leadership. As founder and president of the Association of Young Muslim Women (Jam'iyyat al-Shabbat al-Muslimat), she saw herself and the association as establishing an Islamic alternative to Huda Sha'arawi's Feminist Union.[48] Al-Ghazali used the association as an independent base of power within the Muslim Brotherhood. It is for this reason that she refused an invitation by Hasan al- Banna (the political and spiritual leader of the Muslim Brotherhood in the 1930s and the 1940s) to dissolve her association and join the subordinate al-Akhawat al-Muslimat (Muslim Sisterhood) which al-Banna was trying to strengthen. She only decided to join the Brotherhood when it became clear that they were going to attempt to take over power in 1948.[49] Al-Ghazali's imprisonment and torture, under the Nasser regime, established her as a revered figure in the movement.

Even though her political reputation developed in relation to the Young Women's Muslim Association, al-Ghazali condemns the secular organizations of women and their feminist demands for the change of the *shari'a* laws on the grounds that Islam gave women their rights. She argues that the Islamic ideal of womanhood, which relegates them to the household, does not deny them their economic rights and their right to eduction. Through the family they can also participate in the affairs of their society and express their views and opinions. While women were supposed to exercise their power through the household, closer scrutiny shows that they only had power over their children and that men were the leaders of both the women and the children within and outside the family.[50] The complementary Islamic ideal does not allow women to aspire to leadership roles even in their own separate domain, whether that is the family and/or the sexually segregated groups identified with the movement. Instead, it is horizontally defined so that women's participation is restricted to the lowest political and domestic levels, with men monopolizing leadership positions at all levels. This hierarchical model of participation supported by the Islamists mirrored women's limited political participation at the top in the regimes of Nasser, Sadat, and Mubarak. Aside from the few token women present in the Ministry of Social Affairs and the Assembly, the change from political authoritarianism to liberalization did not include a challenge of the legitimacy of this horizontal political model of participation and representation for women.

In response to the ideological and organizational successes of the Islamists, secular and feminist women of the middle class started to form their own formal and informal groups and organizations. The Women's Committee within the Reporters Union was formed in 1979. The Federation for Progressive Women, affiliated with the Marxist National Progressive and Unionist party, was established in 1982. Finally the Permanent Committee on the Conditions of Women of the Arab Lawyers Federation joined these other affiliated groups in 1984. In this same year, the first unaffiliated and non-governmental organization, Bint al-Arad (Daughter of the Land), made its appearance in Mansura, a town in Lower Egypt. Despite the importance of this organization, whose formation showed the initiative and feminist awareness of women outside of Cairo, and despite the popular perspectives and diverse activities carried out by Bint al-Arad and the other organizations mentioned above, which made them more representative of Egyptian feminism at the present stage, they have been overshadowed by Tadamun al-Mar'at al-Arabiyya (The Solidarity of Arab Women's Association), founded by the charismatic Nawal el-Sa'adawi in 1985. Western support (including international funding of its activities and selecting it as the true representative of Egyptian feminism) has also contributed to its powerful institutional presence in the Egyptian scene.

Organizationally, this new secular and/or feminist organization did not offer its members greater opportunities for participation at all levels. As one Egyptian critic put it, Tadamun operates as a family enterprise. For example, Nawal el-Sa'adawi is the editor of the association's magazine, *Nun*. Her daughter is the assistant editor and her husband is the managing editor. They are also the ones who represent the association in Arab and international conferences.[51] This family monopoly of all positions of power in the association and its resources casts serious doubts about the organization's success in opening up leadership ranks for its women members, who are denied these opportunities elsewhere, in both Islamist and state institutions.

Tadamun's agenda, and/or the approaches it uses to analyze the important issues, is superimposed on the Egyptian social map from the outside. For instance, there is more than one article that questions the marriage institution. One discusses why women are happier in love, but not in marriage, another discusses the desire to become mothers outside the marriage institution, and a third equates marriage to slavery.[52] While the critique of the marriage institution is not new in Egyptian women's writing, the idea of abàndoning marriage to become single mothers and/or free women does not sound very Egyptian. If these are the ideas and the feelings of a minority of Egyptian upper-middle-class and upper-class women, who have the means to raise a child by themselves and avoid the censure of their peers, they are not the primary aspirations of most Egyptian women. And they are not the burning issues around which one can mobilize Egyptian women.

The same is true of the large space allotted to the critical discussion of cosmetics and fashion as alienated self-expression. Considering that the majority of women in the urban areas have elected to veil to escape both, this represents undue attention to an issue that only concerns a minority of Westernized women. The arguments used to discourage women from using cosmetics (i.e., the freshness of natural beauty, the idea that cosmetics hurt the skin and only benefit the cosmetic companies) are not new and remind one of those used by American feminists in the 1960s, which they no longer hold.[53]

Finally, there are numerous condescending attacks on the veil and veiled women who do not understand the connotations of their actions and how it reinforces women's inferiority. They are accused of not distinguishing between what is and what is not important in Islam. El-Sa'adawi even describes them as suffering from "false consciousness."[54] These Westernized views and concerns distinguish upper-middle-class and upper-class women from their counterparts who belong to the lower middle classes. Their ideologically polarized positions make coalition building extremely difficult at best. It confronts these different organizations with the serious challenge of political fragmentation.

CONCLUSION

Economic and political liberalization did not enhance the equality or the liberty of Egyptian women that state feminism had delivered in the 1950s and the 1960s. On the contrary, they have introduced new forms of gender inequality in the economic and political arenas. This does not lead one to support the return to women's dependence on the state, which was the fatal flaw in state feminism as a strategy for improving the economic and political prospects for women. As Egyptian citizens, women have continued to pressure the state to respond to their needs and demands. They do not do that, however, from a position of strength. They need to develop their own representative organizations, which can exert political influence in support of their gendered agendas. Given the ideological and social class divisions that economic and political liberalization have introduced among women, there is a need for plural organizations as part of the effort to create a new social consensus that incorporates the interests of different classes and generations of women.

Notes

1. Harriet Holter, "Women's Research and Social Theory," in Holter (ed.), *Patriarchy in the Welfare Society* (London: Global Books Resources Ltd., 1984), pp. 18-24; Helga Maria Hernes, *Welfare State and Women Power: Essays in State Feminism* (Oslo: Norwegian University Press, 1987), chap. 2.

2. Mervat Hatem, *The Demise of Egyptian State Feminism and the Politics of Transition (1980-1991)*. Working Paper no. 3 (Fall 1991), Los Angeles: G. Evon Grunebaum Center for Near Eastern Studies, UCLA.

3. Ahmed Abdalla, *The Student Movement and National Politics in Egypt* (London: al-Saqi Books, 1985), p. 191.

4. Ibid.

5. Hanna Papanek and Barbara Ibrahim, "Economic Participation of Egyptian Women: Implications for Labor Force Creation and Industrial Policy," unpublished report of USAID, 1982, p. 52.

6. Zaynab Radwan, *Bahth zahirat al-hijab bayn al-jam'iyya* (Cairo: al-Markas al-Qawmi li-al-Buhuth al-Ijtima'iyya wa-al-Jina'iyya, 1982), pp. 15-16, 99, 101.

7. Ahmad Nasr al-Din, "Hal ta'ud al-mar'a al-'amila ila al-bayt?" *Al-Ahram*, August 30, 1982, p. 3.

8. Radwan, *Bahth*, pp. 44, 42, 40, 37. These are my calculations using the data Radwan reports but does not analyze.

9. Ibid., pp. 81, 138.

10. Ibid.

11. Ibid., p. 138; Theodora Lurie, "Feminists Are Dismayed as Egyptian College Girls Turn to Orthodox Islam," *Globe and Mail*, December 13, 1979, p. T6.

12. Judith Gran, "Impact of the World Market on Egyptian Women," *Middle East Report* (June 1977), p. 6.

13. Earl Sullivan, *Women in Egyptian Public Life* (Syracuse, N.Y.: Syracuse, University Press, 1986), p. 144.

14. Malak Zaalouk, "The Impact of Male Labor Migration on the Structure of the Family and the Women Left Behind in the City of Cairo," paper presented to the First International Conference on Arab and African Women, Cairo, February 25-28, 1985, p. 13.

15. Mervat Hatem, "Egypt's Middle Class in Crisis: The Sexual Division of Labor," *Middle East Journal* 42;3 (Summer 1988), pp. 420-21.

16. Papanek and Ibrahim, "Economic Participation of Egyptian Women," p. 52.

17. Ibid., p. 63.

18. Ibid., p. 64.

19. Ibid., pp. 50, 57-58, 64-65.

20. Ibid., p. 59.

21. Zaynab Sadiq, "Al-Harb al-khafiyya 'ala al-nisa," *Sabah al-khayr,* April 2, 1987, p. 27.

22. Zaalouk, "The Impact of Male Labor Migration," pp. 10-11, 13.

23. Ibid., p. 18.

24. Elizabeth Taylor, "Egyptian Migration and Peasant Wives," *MERIP Reports* 14;5 (June 1984), p. 8; Fatma Khafagy, "One Village in Egypt," *MERIP Reports* 14;5 (June 1984), p. 18.

25. Taylor, "Egyptian Migration," p. 9.

26. Ibid., pp. 9-10; Khafagy, "One Village," pp. 18-20.

27. Soheir Sukkary-Stolba, "Roles of Women in Egypt's Newly Reclaimed Lands," *Anthropological Quarterly* 58;4 (October 1985), pp. 182, 188.

28. Ibid., pp. 185-86.

29. Mona Abaza, "The Changing Image of Women in Rural Egypt," *Cairo Papers in Social Science* 10;3 (Fall 1987), pp. 66, 77.

30. Ibid., pp. 185-86.

31. *Mudhakkirat Muhammad 'Abd al-Salam al-Zayyat* (Cairo: Kitab al-Ahali, 1989), pp. 243-44.

32. Ibid.

33. Ahmad Taha Muhammad, *Al-mar'a al-misriyya* (Cairo: Matba'at Dar al-Ta'lif, 1979), p. 75.

34. Qizarat al-Ta'lim al-'Ali, *Al-mar'a fi misr* (Cairo: Al-Matabaa al-'Alamiyya, 1975), p. 71.

35. Ibid., p. 17.

36. Jehan Sadat, *A Woman of Egypt* (New York: Simon and Schuster, 1987), pp. 353, 356-57.

37. Ibid., p. 363.

38. Ibid., p. 360.

39. Ibid., pp. 358-61.

40. Abdel Monem Said Aly, "Democratization in Egypt," *American-Arab Affairs* 22 (Fall 1987), p. 16.

41. Ibid., p. 17.

42. Amary Kamal el-Dinn, Enid Hill, and Sarah Graham-Brown, "After Jihar's Law: A New Battle Over Women's Rights," *Middle East Magazine* (June 1985), p. 17.

43. *Al-Ahram,* July 1, 1985, p. 1.

44. *Al-Ahram,* January 1, 1988, p. 11.

45. Nadia Amine, "Women out of Power," *Middle East Magazine* (July 1987), p. 35.

46. Lurie, "Feminists Are Dismayed," p. T6.

47. Alia'a Redah Rafee, "The Student Islamic Movement: A Study of the Veil (the Hijab)" (Masters thesis, American University in Cairo, 1983), p. 99.

48. Valerie J. Hoffman, "Interview with Zaynab al-Ghazali," in Elizabeth Fernea (ed.), *Women and Family in the Middle East* (Austin: Texas University Press, 1985), pp. 234-35, 237-38.

49. Zaynab al-Ghazzali, *Ayyam min Hayati* (Cairo: Dar al-Sharq, 1987), pp. 23-24.

50. Ibn al-Hashimi, *Al-da'ya zaynab al-ghazzali: Masirat Jihad wa-hadith min al-dhikrayat* (Cairo: Dar al-I'tisam, 1989), pp. 55-56.

51. Ahmad Hashim al-Sharif, "Mushkilat Nawal al-Sa'adawi," *Sabah al-Khayr,* January 25, 1990, p. 12.

52. "Li-madha tas'ad al-mar'a bi-al-hubb wa tashqa bi-al-zawaj," *Nun* 1 (May 1989), pp. 6-8; "Arid al-amuma wa-la arid al rajul," *Nun* 1 (May 1989), p. 9; Muna Hilmi, "Mas'ibi al-thalath," *Nun* 3 (November 1989), pp. 54-55.

53. "Ubudiyyat al-jamal al-masnu'a," *Nun* 1 (May 1989), p. 16; Salwa Bakr, "Bayda'... Shaqra,'" ibid., p. 17; 'Azza Abu Shama, "Al-moda wa-la'bat al-wahm," *Nun* 2 (August 1989), pp. 18-19; Muna Hilmi, "Kayfa taz'harin al-taja'id," ibid., p. 39.

54. Sharif Hitata, "Al-hijab wa-al-khitan fi al-islam," *Nun* 1 (May 1989), pp. 22-23; Muhammad Nur al-Din Afaya, "Hijab al-mar'a kashf al-rajul," ibid., pp. 42-43; Nawal el-Sa'adawi, "Raj'al-hijab 'an al-mar'a," *Nun* 3 (November 1989), pp. 4-5.

24

Gender and Family in the Arab World

Suad Joseph[*]

The Arab world is a mix of social classes, racial and ethnic groups, religious affiliations, nationalities, and linguistic communities. People live in cities, provincial towns, and rural villages. Migrations of peoples from Africa, Europe, and Asia have brought about movements of ideas, values, and structures, and a crossbreeding of peoples and cultures. The past century has been a period of intense upheaval, escalated change, and revolutionary transformation. There is no moment from the past that we can point to as a time in which Arab culture was fixed.

Given this historical social and cultural fluidity and tremendous diversity, we have to be very careful before generalizing about gender and family systems, or assuming that they are the same across ethnic, religious, racial, national, regional, or linguistic groupings in this complex region. With this caveat in mind, it is possible to suggest a framework within which to understand broad patterns of gender and family dynamics in the Arab world, without ascertaining that they all apply everywhere. In addition, with few exceptions, most of the patterns described here are not uniquely Arab.

CORE UNIT

For Arabs, the family lies at the core of society — in political, economic, social, and religious terms. This privileged position is enshrined in the constitutions of many Arab states (which assert that the family is the basic unit of society), and is reproduced at almost every level of political life. Arab economies recognize the centrality of the family in many ways, including through worker recruitment and discipline, wages and benefits. Religious institutions consider themselves the guardians of family integrity and hold families responsible for safeguarding religious sanctity. People are keenly aware of each other's family memberships, identities, and status. Access to institutions, jobs, and government services is often through family connections.

I experienced this vividly the first time I returned to Lebanon, in 1968.[1] While carrying out a research project for the YMCA in the southern town of Marjayoun, I was confronted by a suspicious local teacher. "Who are you?" he asked, even though we had already been introduced by mutual friends. He wanted to know my family origins. I told him I was from the Awwad family. "Are you related to As'ad Awwad?" he asked. "He is *ibn 'ammi* [my father's brother's son]," "Oh, I had heard that *bint 'am* [father's brother's daughter] of As'ad Awwad was coming here," he observed. "Welcome to you!" Once he realized that I came from a known and reputable family, he supported my research and paved the way for me to meet with numerous other people.

The centrality of family in the Arab world has profound implications for gender relations, since Arab families are generally highly patriarchal. It was not incidental, for example, that the teacher asked me about my relationship to a man in my family. My answer indicated that I had family males to protect me. A woman's patrilineal male cousin can have considerable authority over her, superseded only by her father, uncles, and brothers.

The gender system in the Arab world is shaped by and works through the institutions of patriarchy which affect much of the social order. Some Arab scholars have even argued that patriarchy is a — or the — core obstacle to equality and democracy in the Arab world.[2]

PATRIARCHY

Patriarchy privileges males and elders (including elder women in the Arab world), and justifies this privilege in kinship terms. Females are generally taught to respect and defer to their fathers, brothers, grandparents, uncles, and, at times, male cousins. Young people are taught to respect and defer to their older kin. In turn, males are taught to take responsibility for their female kin, and elders are taught to protect and take responsibility for those younger than themselves.

Gender and age privilege generally enhance the power and authority of elder males, although elder women also come to have a degree of authority over those younger than themselves. Once males reach adulthood, they generally have more authority and power than even elder females.

These patriarchal rules are widely observed in Arab families, but like all social rules, there are many exceptions and many interpretations. A younger brother can come to have more authority than an older brother, for example, if the younger is more financially or politically successful. A sister can exert authority over her brothers if she acquires independent wealth or influence. The authority of paternal uncles can readily be challenged when unsupported by economic, political, or social resources. And if elderly fathers falter in health or wealth, they can lose authority to their sons.

Patriarchy has generally fostered patrilineality, patrilocality, and endogamy. Patrilineality means that descent is established through the father. Lineage membership is passed down through sons who bear the responsibility of not only reproducing the kin group, but also of protecting its members. In the cultural ideal, a married woman remains attached to her father's lineages, rather than her husband's.

The reality is more complex. At times, maternal relatives are more important than paternal relatives as sources of political clout, social status, or emotional support. Paternal kin sometimes do not fulfill the duties of the cultural ideal. As a result of global economic and political pressures of the past century, the extended patrilineal family ideal has been transformed in many parts of the Arab world (particularly urban areas) into joint, nuclear, single-parent, or other family arrangements. So while the patrilineal cultural ideal is upheld, in fact there are numerous family patterns in the Arab world today.

The patriarchal privileging of males and seniors, combined with patrilineality, enhances the power of male elders in the father's kin group. A father's brothers can have authority over their nieces and nephews, and male cousins can have authority over their female counterparts. The intersection of patriarchy and patrilineality increases the range of men with authority nested in kinship terms.

After a couple marries, it is preferred that they live near the male's family (patrilocality). In the contemporary world, most Arabs would perhaps not volunteer patrilocality as an ideal. Post-marital residence patterns today tend to conform more to local economic and sociological pressures than to patrilocality. Patrilocality, when practiced, can enhance the power of men over women. When combined with endogamy, it can also counterbalance the power of husbands over women by locating women near their birth families.

Endogamy refers to a cultural preference to marry within the father's kin group, and therefore one's own religious, ethnic, and national group. Endogamy, when practiced and when combined with patrilocality, means that both husband and wives have their families nearby and are part of the same lineage. Family elders, male and female, can exercise considerable authority over the couple. Women in this situation are subject to greater control from both families, but also have greater protection from possible in-law excesses.

Arranged marriages are still common, although much less so in urban areas and among educated, middle and upper classes. Arranged marriages are a vehicle to establish or reinforce relationships between families rather than just between couples.

Marriage patterns, in reality, vary greatly. Non-kin marriages outnumber kin marriages almost everywhere in the Arab world. In addition, inter-ethnic and inter-religious marriages are relatively common. Marriages among Arabs of different nationalities and between Arabs and non-Arabs have been common throughout the twentieth century. Patrilineal parallel cousin marriages, the ideal marriage, account for less than ten percent of marriages in any Arab country. Marriage to matrilineal extended relatives seems to be at least as common.

FAMILY RESOURCE

In most Arab countries, families generally feel obligated to take care of their members financially. Given the lack or inadequacy of government programs for unemployment compensation, health insurance, and retirement benefits, most people must look to their families for those assurances. In addition, family members often work together in the same businesses, help each other find work, own shops or land together, lend each other money, and share other economic resources.

The importance of family as the primary source of economic security has given weight to the patriarchal structuring of the family. The authority of men and elders has economic consequences for women and juniors. Many women, for example, never inherit their share of their patrimony, even through state law and Islamic custom entitles them to a share.[3] Some women choose to leave their inheritance with their brothers as insurance, so that they can return to their birth families if their marriages dissolve.

Family is also a key political resource in most Arab countries. This is in part because of the frequent inadequacy of government social service programs, and partly because Arab governments privilege family relationships in offering access to governmental resources.

Family provides a person with his or her basic political network: family contacts are usually the starting place if one needs access to a government agency. Political leaders, in turn, want to know of a person's family connections and whether family members support them.

Politicians and administrators often allocate resources to persons through heads of family, and privilege their own families in the process. This constant emphasis on family in the state arena turns family relationships into powerful political tools. And since family is patriarchal, politics also privileges patriarchy.

These political uses of family create kinship continuities between the state (the public sphere), civil society (the sphere of private organizations), and the family (the domestic sphere). Some have argued that for democracy to develop, civil society must be separate and autonomous from the state. This model of democracy and civil society is based on the (somewhat idealized) experiences of Western states. In Arab countries, there are often greater continuities between public, private, and domestic spheres that are linked to the centrality of the patriarchal family.

For women, these continuities between family, civil society, and state mean that they confront patriarchy in every sphere. Patriarchy is thus reproduced in multiple sites — a phenomenon not unique to Arab societies. The outcome is that women and juniors must be embedded in familial relationships to make the most effective use of the institutions in these spheres, and are therefore subject to patriarchal norms and relationships even in public spaces. Yet most women in the Arab world would argue for retention of these familial relationships because these ties also provide support.

With the exception of Tunisia, family and religion are legally intertwined. Most Arab countries defer personal status laws (also called family law) to religious institutions. Laws concerning marriage, divorce, inheritance, and child custody are under the aegis of legally recognized religious institutions. There is no civil recourse for marriage, divorce, or inheritance rules. Marriages between persons of different religions require the conversion of one of the partners, usually the wife, and the permission of the clergy performing the rites. Needless to say, this acts as an impediment to intersectarian marriage, although not a total barrier since agreeable clerics can usually be found.

By placing family law in the domain of religion, most Arab states have given over control of issues that dramatically affect women to institutions that are gender-biased. Clerics in the Arab world — Muslim, Christian, or Jewish — are all male, and their hierarchy is quite patriarchal. Arab feminist activists in a number of Arab countries have lobbied for years to change family law. Though there have been small successes in countries such as Iraq and Yemen, and for a while in Egypt, activists have seen these governments retreat in recent years in the face of conservative or radical religious mobilization to undo family law reforms.

GENDER AND FAMILY VALUES

Family values in the Arab world are diverse, but certain patterns are widely shared. Among these are concepts of generosity, hospitality, reciprocity, pride, dignity, valor, strength, emotional openness, indirect communication, conflict-avoidance, honor, and the use of mediators to negotiate relationships.

Perhaps the value most widely known outside the region is that of honor, which is crucial in the Arab world and Mediterranean societies more generally. Family honor implies that one's sense of dignity, identity, status, and self, as well as public esteem, are linked to the regard with which one's family is held by the community at large. The cultural assumption has been that a person's actions reflect on her or his family as a whole, and the reputation of the family as a whole is borne by each of its members. Children are taught that the good of the family comes before personal good. Sacrifice by individual family members to benefit the family as a whole is expected. Family members are supposed to be responsible to and for each other.

It is the historic centrality of the family to social, political, and economic security that accords family honor a role in controlling the behavior of family members. Just as honor has offered a measure of protection to family members, it has also been a means of controlling behavior, especially women's. The notion of family honor facilitates patriarchal power by circumscribing women's sexuality, movement in social arenas, and, to some degree, economic opportunities. It enhances the power of fathers, grandfathers, uncles, brothers, and male cousins over women.

Though these cultural beliefs generally prevail across most of the Arab world, enactments of family honor vary considerably. In the past few decades, extended kin, particularly in urban areas and in middle and upper classes, have been less able to use honor to control the behavior of distant relatives. Even the hold of nuclear families on their members had become equivocal in certain social strata.

Much of the scholarship on personhood and family in the Arab world has been divided into two camps. Some scholars argue that the Arab world is highly individualistic, with persons strategizing for individual gain and committed to little beyond self interest. Others argue that the person is totally submerged in families and communities.

While neither view captures the totality, both capture aspects of the relationship between personhood and family. Generally, socialization practices do not support individualism — the creation of autonomous, separate selves — but neither do they entirely conflate the person with the family. Rather, persons are encouraged to view themselves as always linked with, reciprocally shaped by, and mutually responsive to family and relatives.

This relational construct of self is encouraged in both men and women. The implications for women, however, are somewhat different. Women, more than men, are expected to put others before themselves and to see their interests as embedded in those of others, especially family members. In practice, this means that women are particularly encouraged to see their interests linked to those of their male kin. This often has the effect of reinforcing patriarchal hierarchy.

As in any society, family members can be and are quite competitive with each other. Siblings, especially brothers, can compete for status or affirmation from parents or extended kin. Yet brothers and sisters are generally socialized to love, support, and sacrifice for each other. It is in the tension between competition and generosity, between love and power, that the dynamics of family are often played out. The tension provides spaces for negotiation, maneuvering, direct and indirect empowerment. While women negotiate and maneuver as much as men, they, more often than men, find themselves in the subordinate position.

FAMILY AS IDIOM

The centrality of family in Arab society is often expressed through the use of idiomatic kinship — acting as if a person is a relative even when they are not socially recognized kin. In using family idioms, people call up the expectations and morality of kinship.

Once embraced as idiomatic kin, persons tend to be accepted by each other's families as part of the extended family. If my brother calls a friend his brother, I tend to see that man as my brother as well: I can call on him to do things for me that a brother might. For example, while I was doing fieldwork in the 1970s, a neighbor came to ask if I would help him obtain the government residency papers he needed. He began the conversation by calling me *"ikti"* (my sister), thus paving the way to making the claims of a brother. To help him, I recruited several friends with whom I had idiomatic sister and niece relations.

They in turn called upon real and idiomatic kin of theirs. In this manner, a network of *wasta* (brokerage connections) was created, mostly legitimated in kinship terms, that eventually got the job done. The use of idiomatic kinship is important not only in intimate circles, but also in political and economic spheres. Political leaders at times put themselves in the position of being family patriarchs. They expect to be treated as heads of families, with the deference and loyalties due to family elders. They use family idioms to justify the power relationships between themselves and their clients or followers. People who need each other's services for political mediation, brokerage, or gaining access to resources will often use kin terms to identify themselves.

Idiomatic kin relationships are often found in the economy as well. Owners of businesses, particularly owners of small businesses, often use kinship terminology to create a relationship with their workers. Workers then come to expect their employers to treat them with kin-like concern.

Women as well as men use idiomatic kinship to create effective and instrumental relationships. They, like men, create short- and long-term bonds by assimilating people into the moral domain of family. For women, however, there are other consequences. In evoking kinship, women intentionally or unintentionally also call forth the values and institutional arrangements associated with patriarchy. In so far as idiomatic kinship is successful, it reinforces patriarchy in public and private arenas of social life.

The gender and family systems in Arab societies, like all aspects of social life, are continually shifting in response to dynamic transformations in culture and society, locally and globally. The diverse family patterns in the Arab world are shaped by class, ethnic, racial, religious, national, and linguistic dynamics. Yet certain patterns tend to be reproduced. Key to these patterns is the centrality of family, in its multiple forms, to one's notion of self, social position, economic security, and political possibilities. Family relationships tend to be supported in most arenas of social life in the Arab world, including religious institutions.

Given the centrality of family, its patriarchal structure is crucial in understanding gender relationships in the Arab world. Family both supports and suppresses women. This paradox of support and suppression, love and power, generosity and competition compels both attachment to and struggle within families. Many features of these gender and family systems are found in many non-Arab cultures as well. Yet the combination expresses dynamics that are culturally and historically part and parcel of Arab societies.

Notes

1. I was born in Lebanon and moved with my family to the United States as a child. Much of my extended family remained in Lebanon.

2. See, in particular, Halim Barakat, *The Arab World: Society, Culture and State* (Berkeley: University of California Press, 1993); and Hisham Sharabi, *Neopatriarchy: A Theory of Distorted Change in Arab Society* (New York: Oxford University Press, 1988).

3. Islamic custom usually entitles daughters to half the share of sons. Many Arab states have overridden this custom with laws requiring equal distribution to both. However, the laws are not always applied.

25

Gender and Civil Society: An Interview with Suad Joseph

Joe Stork[*]

What questions does the idea of civil society raise concerning women?

The Western construct of nation-state, which became the compulsory political form for the rest of the world, is based on citizens as detached from communities, as individuals. In fact — in the Arab world, the Third World, and much of the West — persons are deeply embedded in communities, in families, in ethnic, racial, or other social groupings.

The Western construct of citizen — that of contract-making individual — implies a degree of detachment and autonomy that is not universal. The capacity to make contracts emerges from the fact that this individualized self is conceived as a property owner, first of all as owner of himself. I use "him" consciously here.

Why "himself"?

The Western liberal notion of citizen implies a masculinized construct. Males were the property-owners. Carole Pateman argues that the contemporary state is in fact a fraternal patriarchy. In the discourse that established the philosophical basis of liberal bourgeois society, the idiom is that of brothers. The social contract is entered into by free men who constitute themselves as a civil fraternity. It's an as-

* This interview was first published in *Middle East Report*, no. 183, July-August 1993. Reprinted with the permission of MERIP/Middle East Report, 1500 Massachusetts Avenue, N.W., #119, Washington, D.C. 20005.

sociation of autonomous, individualized, contract-making persons, and contract-making is possible only if you are a property owner, if you own yourself. The series of assertions that underlies this philosophical base are assertions of exclusion. Women and many minorities are not contract-making persons, because they are not property-owners. Civil society is a fraternity, not a sorority, and not a family.

If we move beyond the gender-bound language of these paradigms, and if women become more equal as property-owners to men, what keeps the state masculine? Is this still a problem?

In liberal feminist thought, with its goal of integrating women into and not challenging the basic structure of the state, the problem starts to get resolved. Marxist feminists argue that this only resolves the problem for elite women. Class, race, patriarchy, and other forms of exclusion are still operating.

But isn't that just saying that the integration is not inclusive enough? Is it a critique of the model of the state itself?

There's no way that you could have enough inclusions without transforming the class-based structure of society. The very existence of classes is a demarcation of exclusion. Ultimately what gets reorganized and restructured are class boundaries. If you're going to use inclusion as the avenue of resolving the problem, that can happen only if class itself is challenged.

It still strikes me as more Marxist than feminist, in that the locus of the problem is class. What's more difficult to reconcile — class or patriarchy?

There are feminists who would argue that class and patriarchy are dual systems that operate autonomously of each other; you have to fight them on different grounds. Others argue that they are woven into each other and your strategy of organizing has to take account of the fact that class already has patriarchy built into it. There isn't a single feminist answer as to the primary source of oppression — gender, class, or race.

The question we want to examine is: What has the imposition of the nation-state, with its gendered concepts of citizenship and civil society, meant in those countries where it has been imposed?

There was patriarchy in the Arab world prior to colonization. What is interesting to investigate is the intersections of the pre-colonial and post-colonial patriarchy in the attempts to construct the contemporary nation-state. My sense is that there was much greater fluidity to the patriarchy that existed in the Arab world in the seventeenth, eighteenth, nineteenth centuries. Judith Tucker's recent work on Nablus courts, dealing with issues such as custody and divorce and child support cases in the eighteenth and nineteenth centuries, indicates that women made use of the courts effectively and actively, and across class lines. Women were very assertive in claiming their rights within what might be considered a public domain in Palestine. There's interesting work from medieval Egypt up to the nineteenth century which shows that women were active property-owners. Julia Clancy's work on colonial Algeria indicates that women were active in religious movements, were looked up to and sought out as saintly figures. The point that comes out of all this is that there was a lot more fluidity in the pre-colonial period than we had previously imagined in terms of gender hierarchy.

Contemporary representations of the Arab world often depict more rigid gender hierarchies — greater exclusion of women from public domains, to an extreme degree in some states. Hisham Sharabi argues that what he calls neo-patriarchy is a post-colonial phenomenon: it's not that there wasn't patriarchy before, but contemporary patriarchy is a product of the intersection between the colonial and indigenous domains.

Is this in any way similar to what's happened in other societies?

There are some parallels — although we have to situate gender/state dynamics culturally and historically in each society. I'm particularly interested in comparing the Arab world to India and China, for a couple of reasons. One is that all three are areas with very long histories of state formation, and then periods of colonial control, and then of attempted "modernization." In all three societies, the literature seems to indicate a consolidation of gender domination for women in the contemporary period: increasing control by men, families, communities, and the state. There's evidence that the contemporary period in some ways has created new controls over women that were much more fluid in earlier periods.

Is this owing to the gendered character of capitalism per se, or also to the reactions to capitalism?

Both, and I think it's also related to the particular construct of the nation-state that these societies have attempted to erect.

But it's also a class construct of "the citizen."

Absolutely. Recall here Edward Said's argument in *Orientalism* that the East is feminized in relationship to the West. Many scholars subsequently argued that not only is the Orient feminized, but that the oppressed, the subordinate, the minority is feminized. Hierarchy has tended to genderize in contemporary nation-states: those in the superordinate position are masculinized, and subordinates are feminized. So constructs of class and citizenship have been imbued with gendered meanings.

And this is peculiarly modern?

The individual citizen, as an autonomous, contract-making self, is a peculiarly modern and Western discourse, a discourse that's becoming hegemonic. It is important to look at what these notions of civil society and citizenship are based on in Western discourse, and the problems created by their uncritical application to Third World societies.

I was struck years ago by an article by Rola Sharara, a Lebanese feminist, in *Khamsin*, in which she argued that women in Lebanon, as in many Arab states, cannot feel the impact of the state in their lives. They felt the impact of their communities, and in particular the men of their communities. I think Lebanon was an extreme example of this, where citizenship was mainly experienced through communities. That is, ethnic, religious, kin-based communities exerted considerable authority and claimed the loyalties of their members. In some societies, such communities were competitive with state authority. Women may at times feel the oppression of the patriarchy of their communities more directly than that of the state. Elsewhere, perhaps Iraq is an example, people have often experienced communities as a source of protection from a repressive state. Local women's movements will take different forms as a result. My political stance is one of critical support — to support local forms of resistance, but to engage in a critical dialogue based on the historical experiences of other countries. But I do not think the control of women by communities is independent of state control.

That's part of the paradigm of modernization.

That's what many of these states, notably Iraq and Syria, were attempting to do by undermining these communities in order to claim the control and the loyalties of their citizenry.

We have to be careful not to romanticize the control that does or did exist at the communal level.

Yes, it's coercive, particularly for women. It's not a question of preserving these ethnic, religious, tribal communities, or of the state saving women from these communities. States and communities can be competitive or collaborative forms of domination. These communities are organized though patriarchal idioms, moralities, and structures of domination. For women, in those states where communities are the primary vehicle through which they experience their membership in contemporary societies, these relations are mediated through patriarchy. In societies in which the state is more keenly felt, state forms of patriarchy penetrate more effectively into local communities. There are new, complex, shifting forms of gender domination. Insofar as the state is experienced as more repressive than the communities, then women often secure themselves in their communities, where they receive some protection from a repressive state. But to gain that protection they must submit to the control of the men of their community.

Western liberal philosophers have advanced civil society as the solution to the problem of state authoritarianism or despotism. If civil society consists of voluntary autonomous organizations capable of resisting arbitrary exercises of state power, let's look at who or what are these voluntary organizations. In contemporary societies, they would be professional associations, unions, political action groups, chambers of commerce, even religious fraternities. All are in the "public domain." They are the kinds of associations nearly always associated with men. Civil society is already identified or defined in a site from which women are thought to be excluded — the public domain. And it's characterized by sets of associations that are linked with male activity. If you go back to how it is that this came to be, the construct of civil society assumes from the very beginning a split between public and private domains. It's based on an assumed three-way distinction between that which is kin-based and non-voluntary, that which is non-kin-based, public, and voluntary — civil society — and that which is non-kin, public, and semi-voluntary — the state.

That definition of what constitutes civil society is based on a gendered distinction between the public and private domains. The civil society construct, a Western construct, is now being challenged in the West by feminists and people of color. Its uncritical application to Third World countries and the uncritical use of the relative existence of components of civil society as measures of "modernity" or progress are highly problematic.

What does this mean in terms of the Arab world?

The distinction between what is public and what is private, and therefore the dichotomy that the concept of civil society rests upon, is even
more problematical in the Arab world than in the West. In many Third
World countries, Arab ones included, kinship and community are
crucial organizers of social life. I don't see state institutions or civil society operating independently of kin-based and communal relations.
A person in a position of power in government office or a voluntary
organization brings with him or her the obligations, networks, and
rights of kin and community, and acts accordingly. Those claims of
kin and community are operating for people in those positions. The
people themselves don't separate public and private.

The boundaries between this triangulation of state, civil society,
and kinship or private domain are highly fluid. People's commitments
remain grounded in kin and community, and they carry those commitments with them, whether in the civil or state spheres. Men in
Lebanon are no less identified with kinship, and therefore private
communities and obligations, than women are.

But it's patriarchal.

What's crucial for understanding the gendering of these relationships
is not the split between public and private, say, or between civil society and state, or civil society and the domestic, but how gender hierarchy operates. In Lebanon, patriarchy privileges males and elders,
including elder women. Numerous other variables affect the opera-
tion of patriarchy — class, ethnicity, region.

*What does this mean for the stance we take on these questions of civil society
and human rights?*

Because men are very nested in familial and highly patriarchal communities, as nested as women, and insofar as states are often seen as
repressive and external, it is in these communal-based relationships
that both men and women find security. For many progressive Muslims in the Middle East, gender issues are secondary; familial bonds
are seen as sources of support and security against what is perceived
as an even greater oppression — the state. That isn't to say that there
aren't women and movements in the Middle East who argue that
gender oppression is as virulent as class or colonialism.

If one's rights are experienced as emerging from being part of these
familial, ethnic, sectarian communities to a greater degree than

emerging from being citizens of a state, then you can see the problem for women, because these communities are highly patriarchal. The control of these communities over women's lives has in fact been reinforced by the states, with Tunisia and Turkey being partial exceptions.

When the state intervenes actively to provide alternative arenas, at least in legal or administrative domains, for women's participation in society, it creates space for maneuvering and negotiating and, over the long run, for mobilization.

This sense of space is implicit in the argument for civil society. Some would argue that the components of civil society work as much to help the state exercise social control as to hinder it.

I agree. We have assumed that the hegemonic discourse in the West actually describes the empirical reality of the West. Then we say what's wrong with these Third World societies is that they're not coming up to the standard that in fact is not the reality even in the West. We have assumed distinctions between state and civil society, between civil society and the private sphere, and between the state and the private sphere. Both in the West and the Third World they're not so separate. The problem of the exclusion of women from the state has been accentuated by the attempt to separate these domains. The attempt to separate state, civil society, and kinship weds women to the private domain and excludes them from the sphere of civil society and from the state. Saudi Arabia may be an extreme example of that. But that's a modern phenomenon.

The whole argument about whether we have a weak state or a strong state, a weak society or a strong society, in a way is a specious argument, linked to an Orientalist perspective which sees other societies as seamless webs, whereas the West is articulated and differentiated. I don't see the West as being as articulated and differentiated as the West presents itself to be.

But formerly colonized societies to some extent have bought into the nation-state as the mode and vehicle of liberation.

The contemporary exclusion of women is in part — but not exclusively — the outcome of this compulsory model of the nation-state, a model which has built into it the marginalization of females and female activity.

The point I'm leading to is that people do not perceive themselves as having rights as a result of their being citizens of a state. They perceive themselves as having rights because they are embedded in com-

munities. And insofar as those communities are hierarchical and patriarchal, then the rights that they perceive will be organized around
those hierarchical and patriarchal structures of domination. When we
speak of human rights, we assume that we all know what we mean by
that term. But we've universalized human rights by glossing over the
diversity in the ways in which rights are understood. Our construct of
rights was premised on the construct of the autonomous, detached,
contract-making, individualized, and masculinized person that
emerged out of liberal bourgeois thought.

*We don't want to dismiss human rights as bourgeois constructs, as if they
don't matter.*

What I'm struggling to develop is a construct of rights, personal
rights, human rights, that is not embedded in a specific construct of
personhood. I don't have the answer to that now. The problem of the
construct of human rights is very linked to this concept of the individualized citizen. If we have a construct of citizen that is wedded to
a particular concept of self, it allows us to dismiss the rights of persons who don't share that sense of self. The way we construct the notion of civil society, and the way we construct the notion of a
nation-state — when you break out of those constructs, it not only allows for the possibility of the inclusion of women and other excluded
groups, but it shows us that the ways in which men and women operate, act out their lives, maneuver and negotiate are not inherently so
fundamentally different from each other. We constructed a difference,
which insofar as it became compulsory, became internalized. Gender
difference is historically and culturally constructed and reproduced
through complex moralities, idioms, and structures of power. Feminist discourse attempts to destabilize the hegemony of these constructs and by so doing create space for experiments in alternate
forms of relationships.

26

"Hassiba Ben Bouali, If You Could See Our Algeria": Women and Public Space in Algeria

Susan Slyomovics[*]

On January 2, 1992, Algerian feminists demonstrated against the Islamic Salvation Front (FIS) and their victory in the national elections of December 26, 1991. Their target was the Islamist assault on women's rights and the threat of violence against women. One of their posters addressed a martyred sister, a *moudjahida*, killed by the French during the battle of Algiers in 1956-57: "Hassiba Ben Bouali, If You Could See Our Algeria." At the same time, women marching in Oran waved a similar slogan: "Hassiba Ben Bouali, We Will Not Betray You."

In Gillo Pontecorvo's 1967 film, *The Battle of Algiers*, a famous scene shows three Algerian women — one of them represents Ben Bouali — in the act of donning alien European dress in order to pass freely through the French military cordon around the walled casbah. They enter the French colonial city and leave guns or bombs for Algerian freedom fighters. In the published script, each of the women

> stand[s] in front of a large mirror. [Hassiba] removes the veil from her face. Her glance is hard and intense. Her face is expressionless. The mirror reflects a large part of the room: it is a bedroom ... Every action is performed precisely and carefully. They are like three actresses preparing for the stage. But there is no

* This article first appeared in *Middle East Report,* January-February 1995. Reprinted with the permission of MERIP/Middle East Report, 1500 Massachusetts Avenue, N.W., #119, Washington, D.C. 20005.

211

gaiety; no one is speaking. Only silence emphasizes the detailed rhythm of their transformation. Her blouse and short skirt to her knees ... make-up, lipstick, high-heeled shoes, silk stockings ... [1]

The camera follows Hassiba as she crosses boundaries: from interior domestic space to the exterior public street, from Arab casbah to French *nouvelle ville*, from "native" to "colonial" space. The language of the film makes clear that her journey is not only real but highly symbolic, from what Western anthropologists of the Maghrib would call the secretive, cloistered, domestic, female world to its binary opposite, the male and public exterior domain. Domestic space has traditionally defined and reproduced social relations between Algerian men and women; but space outside the home, from which women have been traditionally excluded and in which male ambitions have always been produced and played out, becomes, with Hassiba's journey, the arena not only for a national but also for a gender struggle.

During the Algerian war for independence, women militants often discarded the veil, the traditional North African *haik*, to overcome the spatial segregation that reinforced prevailing values of Algerian men and French society. The absent veil confounded the one unifying perception of what defines the Algerian woman, characterized by Frantz Fanon as "she who hides behind a veil."[2] Most Algerian women did not follow Hassiba's example: they neither discarded the veil nor placed bombs. Even before the war of independence, during the colonial administration, according to Fanon, the veil became "the bone of contention" in a battle between colonizer and colonized, and the subjects for colonialism "displayed a surprising force of inertia." But if women at that time were not able to join in a political discourse still conducted in French by both sides, they were nevertheless visible in their silence. Marnia Lazreg's important work, *The Eloquence of Silence*, describes how Algerian women, primarily Arabophone and illiterate, were structurally marginalized by both colonial and native societies, yet used the weight of their silent physical presence to play an important role in the revolution.[3] Women participated in numerous anti-French marches and strikes, their thoughts and intentions as unknown and as unknowable as their physical appearance — a choking protrusion of a necessarily private world into the public and political domain.

SPACE AND STATUS

The interplay between society's spatial arrangements and the status of women reveals much about the ideological underpinnings of the Algerian state since independence. The violent deaths of women that are now being reported can be understood as a consequence of specific policies of National Liberation Front (FLN) rule since independence, namely its emphasis on education and industrialization. This entailed state encouragement of women's presence in two new arenas of public space, the school and the factory, a shocking innovation to Muslim traditionalists. In religious terms, women's presence is deemed illegitimate. Socially, they are perceived as intruders into masculine space, disturbing the equilibrium of a regulated, single-sex, urban milieu.

The short history of working women in Algeria has therefore been a troubled one. Even within factory spaces, the possibility of men and women working together has been avoided. The interior space of the factory workplace is socially constructed to be the same as the outside world. The daily activities and individual behavior of women workers are shaped by structures that insure men's exercise of power over women. Statistics from Tlemcen's state-run factories show that working outside the home is generally a temporary phase in women's lives. Most women factory workers are unmarried and from 20 to 30 years old. They work to augment family finances or to prepare financially for their own marriages, and tend to quit after marriage.[4] Thus, for complex historical, economic, and religious reasons, both women and men subscribe to economic and spatial arrangements that reinforce the legitimacy of women's lower status.

The presence and deportment of women in the workplace has continued to be controversial, subject to the ebb and flow of ideological tides. At this moment, the burning issue is the pressure being laid upon women to conform to norms of Islamic dress, and to wear the veil even in indoor workplaces. In Islamist quarters, parallels are often drawn between women in the labor force and the unauthorized presence of women in the street: both in the factory and on the street women are considered to be transgressively visible in exterior space. Women themselves resent this pressure but conform out of fear. "None of us wants to wear the veil," said Fatima B. (a pseudonymous 22-year-old junior manager in a Tlemcen factory), "but fear is stronger than our convictions or our will to be free. Fear is all around us. Our parents, our brothers, are unanimous: 'Wear the veil and stay alive. This will pass.' "[5]

SANCTUARY AND VEIL

In Algeria today, the "veil" under discussion is not the traditional North African *haik* but rather the *hijab*, an article of clothing imported from the Arab East. *Hijab*, a word with many meanings, is now often used as a synonym for modest Islamic dress for women. In Iran and Afghanistan, this may mean a *chador*, a head-to-toe cloak that envelops the female form; in Algeria, it means a headscarf, often worn with a loose gown.

Opposition to the veil is not universal among women who hope to leave traditional constraints behind. In a series of interviews among women students at the University of Algiers, Laetitia Bucaille discovered that Islamist students believed that the *hijab* forces rearrangement of the male public sphere to make room for the presence of women. It is a badge of religious and political allegiance, but the students also claimed that women who wear the *hijab* escape the male gaze and are therefore exempted from the dominant male group's ability to control social space by means of sexual harassment or sexual objectification of females. It was precisely their protective veiling, these women insisted, that allowed them to escape the traditional female roles of mother and wife in order to pursue professional, educational, and social lives necessarily conducted in public. "I have six brothers and I am the only girl and the youngest," said one student. "Before, everyone used to say: 'Where were you? Where are you going?' Now I am more free, I go to the mosque, even at night during Ramadan. They allow me everything."[6]

In other words, Islamist university women, an elite group, have built on the precedent set by the veiled women of the revolution. Indiscriminate mixing of the sexes in public places is an obstacle to the emergence of women in public space, they insist. Instead, they have articulated for themselves an image of the veiled woman — active in the social order and even on the street — as equivalent to the female body covered and protected within the home. For women to become knowledgeable, they must make their journey from the inside to the outside based on an intellectual sleight-of-hand that defines the two opposing areas, female interior verses male exterior, as equivalent only if the woman is veiled.

If it is the women of the Islamist movements and not the men who have constructed a new Muslim identity whose core is gender segregation, as Bucaille contends, then a different set of cultural, religious, and ideological justifications of gender segregation has emerged, profoundly altering the relationship between gender stratification and spatial institutions.[7] The views of these Islamist women, however, find little support among the FIS leadership. A FIS leader, Ali Ben Hadj, stated in a widely-quoted interview in 1989 that the natural place of expression for women is the home. If she must go out, there are conditions: not to be near men and that her work is located in an exclusively feminine milieu. In our institutions and universities is it admissible to authorize mixing? It is contrary to Islamic morality. It is necessary to separate girls and boys and consecrate establishments for each sex ... In a real Islamic society, the woman is not destined to work and the head of state must provide her with remunerations. In this way, she will not leave her home and consecrate herself to the education of men. The woman is a producer of men, she produces no material goods but this essential thing which is the Muslim.[8]

The spirit of Ben Hadj's statement is congruent with that of the laws enshrined in Algeria's Family Code promulgated by the FLN five years earlier, in 1984.[9] These laws reduced women to the status of minors, subject to the law of father or husband, and presaged the remarkable mixture of nationalism and Islamism (an intellectual FIS-FLN accord) that secularists described much later as "*le fascisme vert*" (green fascism). Feminists protested the family code from the very beginning. On March 4, 1985, a group of women rallied in the casbah of Algiers on the site where Hassiba Ben Bouali had been killed.

SOCIAL ORDER

Since 1991, institutional violence by the state has been matched by Islamist groups committed to the overthrow of the regime. Emerging armed factions (*jama'at al-musallaha*) such as the Groupe Islamique Armé (GIA) have specifically targeted women. Many women have also died in the violence directed against the intellectual elite (journalists, doctors, professors, writers, or actors), foreign nationals, the police, the military, and government officials.

Women are also assassinated simply because they are women — working women, unveiled women, and women active in social and political associations, categories that frequently overlap. In March 1994, a FIS/GIA communiqué warned that any women on the streets without the veil could be assassinated; on March 30, two women students, Raziqa Meloudjemi, 18, and Naima Kar Ali, 19, were killed by gunmen on motorcycles while standing at an Algiers bus station.[10] In May, travel by train was forbidden because men and women shared compartments; shortly afterward, the night train between Bejaia and Algiers was attacked and torched. At the beginning of the 1994 school year, the GIA threatened death to the 7 million primary and high school students and their 320,000 teachers unless the norms of Islamic education were followed — the separation of boys and girls, the veiling of women professors and girl students, and the elimination of gymnastics. Earlier, Amnesty International condemned the killing of Katia Bengana, a 17-year-old high school student in Blida, shot on February 28 after receiving threats that she would die unless she wore the *hijab*.

Operating as mirror image to the Islamist violence against women are the activities of a lesser-known vigilante group, the Organization of Free Young Algerians, OJAL (L'Organisation des Jeunes Algeriens Libres), which has ties to the government and claims to represent the secularism of the FLN regime. For them, too, women's spatial boundaries are at issue. They warn women against wearing the *hijab*, and in retaliation for Islamist killings of unveiled women they have killed at least two veiled women. They have called for reopening public places where women have traditionally congregated, such as beauty salons and public baths, places ordered closed by the Islamists.

Secularists and Islamist groups are attempting to define and promote diametrically opposed positions by using similar strategies. One of these is to control women's access to resources or knowledge by controlling space. To be male in the midst of Algeria's political turmoil means to express a logic of power relations according to which the dominant group, whatever its political ideology, can and must constrain women's movement and actions. What we see unfolding in Algeria is the competition of two very similar demarcations of the spaces that women are permitted to enter or traverse. Secularists allow women a modicum of movement outside the home, especially at beauty salons or baths. These spaces are precisely those not shared by the two sexes. They may encourage female sociability and solidarity that would not be permissible if women never left their homes. Islamists view even so limited a use of public space by women as a threat to the social order. But women are allowed to go to the mosques, interior spaces controlled by the FIS, free of unsupervised and potentially subversive socializing.

Islamist gender segregation extends beyond actual occasions where the sexes might mix in public life; it aims to eliminate even the possibility of such an occurrence. Municipal governments run by the FIS have banned concerts, cinemas, public dancing, wedding ceremonies in hotels, women on the beaches, and women in the municipal cultural centers and recreation halls that they fund and control.

Women in public places, veiled or unveiled, die for the interpretations secular or religious fanatics attach to their presence and appearance. Their dangerous and circumscribed situation is described in a letter from a friend who teaches at the University of Oran. In practical and symbolic ways, she finds that women have become prisoners in their own homes:

> As for us, we have become accustomed to this situation: here a death announcement, and there, the fear. The daily count of assassinations no longer frightens; we hardly pay any attention. This is, of course, true only on the surface. In reality we have all become anguished, sick, and neurotic. Faces are gray, conversations morbid. Laughter has deserted our country. We stay in spite of it all. All this gives us the feeling of being new *"mougahidine"* and the satisfaction of serving something — even if it means being stupid victims of blind terrorism. We lead a dull life. Work, home, with nothing extra because one must be shut in inside one's home. Even the rare cultural and social events at the university are gone; at least they used to allow us to see each other. As for me, I am like the rest. I take care of my daughters, my job, and my house. My job allows me to hold on. I can escape the problems of Algeria in speaking of the medieval age of Spain. In fact, everything is ruined in Algeria: political life, social life, and even family life. Terrorism has installed itself at every level, even in the family unit. We head towards barbarism.

Some women cooperate with the system of stratification out of religious beliefs. "Knowing that I have a message as an educated Muslim woman, I have two choices," Leila, 21, told Bucaille. "The first is to have a family. God created me in order to accomplish a certain mission and one of them is to have a family, have children, and transmit this message so that they too could transmit it to others."[11] Others see no alternative and do so out of fear. Still other women struggle against attacks on their rights.

ISLAMIST APPEAL

Hasiba Ben Bouali is one of a long list of women activists, *moudjahidat* and *chahidat*, who fought for Algerian independence against the French colonial system. There were others: Myrien Ben Miloud, Djamila Bouhired, Djamila Boupacha, Zohra Driff, Bahia Hocine, Samia Lakhdari, and Zhor Zerari (as well as many women whose anonymous lives and deaths were the subject of Assia Djebar's 1978 documentary, *Nouba des femmes de Chenoua*). They operated clandestinely, often forced to renounce home and family. In a chilling reprise, one of the prominent feminist leaders, Khalida Messaoudi, of the Mouvement pour la Republique (MPR), has gone underground in Algiers, forced to abandon her apartment and her work as a mathematics professor. In a recent interview she announced her readiness to take up arms:

> Unless the MPR to which I belong decides otherwise, for my part, I am ready to take up weapons. Let no one say that I call for civil war. We who kill no one and defend the values of secularism and equality are the victims of violence. Concerning women, what is going on at this moment in Algeria is not a confrontation between a majority and an opposition, but a war between the blueprints for society, one that appeals to the Enlightenment and human rights, the other marking a return to obscurantism and religious fanaticism. The coming of an Islamist state would be the negation of citizenship and Algerian identity.[12]

Like many feminists throughout the Arab world, Messaoudi understands that restrictions imposed in the name of Islam disguise patriarchal structures intent on seizing or maintaining political and military power. "I think I understand why the fundamentalists *(integristes)* are powerful," she says:

> The FLN had destroyed all the traditionally valued places, the places of the inside *(le lieux dedans)*, but without proposing others: only 4.2 percent of women work in Algeria. The Family Code came and aggravated the situation. The FIS, for those who agree to wear the veil, offers them all "some places outside" *(des lieux dehors)*: for example, the mosque. There, they are allowed what even the FLN denies them: a political voice. FIS women's "cells" debate every subject all over Algeria. This way they have the impression of acquiring a certain power and power that interests them.[13]

The FIS has reversed stereotypical value judgments about women's spaces. It has accorded women two things. First, it has assigned a higher status to the feminine knowledge associated with the home and child-raising, to the extent that the Islamists have raised even the value of women's home life above the status of women working in sexually segregated workplaces. Second, they have found room for women's study groups, monitored within FIS-controlled mosques. Islamist women can therefore argue that spatial segregation works to women's advantage by allowing them to develop networks and power independently of men.

Messaoudi, of MPR, when asked what secularists of her movement have to offer women that might counter the appeal of the Islamists, replied that "it is very difficult, because we democrats have only in exchange a major transgression to propose: that of the street. The political street, to which one must descend to confront the single party or the religious party; the cultural street, that marks the sexual division of space in the Muslim world."[14] To move women from the female to the male side of what has been defined as the proper place of each is to challenge the FIS's religious notions of how space is divided and delimited; it is to commit a sin. To segregate women within the workplace is to insure gender differences in earnings and positions. To restrict women forcibly to the home is to remove women from knowledge, action, and political power.

SOCIAL RESISTANCE

How do we interpret feminists demonstrating in the name of Hassiba Ben Bouali? In the Algerian war of independence, some women rejected both colonial status and the subservient roles traditionally assigned to women in Algerian society — Ben Bouali is only the best known. Most Algerian women played a less assertive role. Nevertheless, their veiled and silent participation in demonstrations and other forms of resistance marked a departure from the traditional confinement of women to the domestic sphere. Education and new social and economic opportunities for women have been part of the new order introduced by the FLN since independence. But these innovations were timid and tentative, and women's limited gains have been subject to continual challenge.

Today, many women in the social and intellectual elite, such as university students, profess fervent Muslim faith but reinterpret Islam's idea of women. It is precisely the protected status symbolized by the veil that encourages them to believe that they will be able to compete in the male public world. They are following in the footsteps of the veiled women of the revolution, not those of Ben Bouali. But these new and supposedly Islamic conceptions of women's roles are not supported by the FIS. More remarkably, the Islamist leadership's attitudes conform to legislation put in place after independence by the FLN. In other words, the factions now struggling for power in Algeria are in fundamental ideological agreement that women's social freedom must be severely restricted.

The FIS victory at the polls and the subsequent coup by the FLN have created an atmosphere in which women have the distinction of being targeted for abuse and even assassination no matter what they do. The threat to women's lives, and to their aspirations for the future, has produced an embryonic underground on the model of women militants in the war of independence. Messaoudi, unlike Ben Bouali, possesses no bombs or weapons. She has frequently called on an international community of democrats and human rights activists to denounce violations directed specifically against Algerian women. Most radical of all, the site of the domicile and domesticity is not where female resistance and subversion are located. According to Messaoudi, the point, as it was before against the French, is to take to the streets against tyranny or face death.

Notes

1. Piernico Solinas (ed.), *Gillo Pontecorvo's "The Battle of Algiers"* (New York: Charles Scribner, 1973), pp. 66-67.

2. Frantz Fanon, *A Dying Colonialism* (New York: Grove Press, 1965), p. 36.

3. Marnia Lazreg, *The Eloquence of Silence: Algerian Women in Question* (New York: Routledge, 1994), p. 96. Whatever the power of silence may be, revolutionaries and feminists seem to be ready to turn it in for social equality with men.

4. Rabia Bekkar cites statistics of women workers in a Tlemcen state-run factory: 81 percent single, 8 percent married, and 11 percent widows or divorced. "Territoires des femmes à Tlemcen: Pratiques et representation," *Maghreb/Machrek* (1994), p. 133.

5. *Los Angeles Times*, April 1, 1994.

6. Laetitia Bucaille, "L'engagement islamiste des femmes en Algerie," 144 (1994), p. 111.

7. Ibid., p. 117.

8. Quoted by Elisabeth Shemla, "L'Islam et les femmes," *Le Nouvel Observateur*, September 22-28, 1994.

9. Ministry of Justice, *Code de la Famille (Quanun al-Usra)* (Algiers: Office des Publications Universitaires, 1986).

10. *New York Times*, March 31, 1994, p. A3.

11. Bucaille, "L'engagement islamiste," p. 111.

12. Khalida Messaoudi, "Le voile, c'est notre étoile jaune," *Le Nouvel Observateur*, September 22-28, 1994.

13. Ibid.

14. Ibid.

27

State and Gender
in the Maghrib

Mounira Charrad[*]

Tunisia, Algeria, and Morocco constitute a geo-cultural entity. They all went through a period of French colonization and they became independent during roughly the same period in the late 1950s and early 1960s. Despite the similarities, however, the three countries engaged in markedly different policies in regard to family law and women's rights from the time of national independence to the mid-1980s. Tunisia adopted the most far-reaching changes, whereas Morocco remained most faithful to the prevailing Islamic legislation, and Algeria followed an ambivalent course.

The differences are made especially intriguing by the fact that it is neither the most industrialized country (Algeria), nor the most socialist and revolutionary regime (Algeria again), nor the society exposed to the French culture for the longest period (Algeria still) that made the most radical changes. Neither level of industrialization nor official socialist ideology accounts for the variations in state policies among the three Maghribi countries.

Most explanations of changes in women's status emphasize factors such as economic development or revolutionary ideology. Here, though, an approach that takes the state as a key variable is more useful. In explaining changes in women's rights, it is necessary to consider the process of state formation and to relate state and gender. State interventions are not only responses to economic or class-based demands. They are also shaped by the political requirements of state

* This article first appeared in *Middle East Report*, no. 163, April-March 1990. Reprinted with the permission of MERIP/Middle East Report, 1500 Massachusetts Avenue, N.W., #119, Washington, D.C. 20005.

stability or consolidation. At given historical moments, the state engages in actions to further its own interests of domination: and hegemony.[1] The state is an institution of domination, with its own structure, history, and pattern of conflict.

A common denominator of many newly independent countries is that they are "old societies," but relatively "new states."[2] Even where existing ruling dynasties go back to the nineteenth century or even earlier, the pre-colonial state effectively controlled only a fraction of the population with respect to taxation, military service, and law and order.[3] Colonial rule frequently weakened existing indigenous political institutions. A national state had to be either formed or consolidated in the wake of colonization.

In many new nation-states, the existing social structure at the time of independence is characterized by social segmentation. Collectivities — ethnic, caste or kinship-based, tribal, religious, or linguistic — retain a degree of separate identity and need to be integrated into the nation. The establishment or extension of state domination therefore entails a rearrangement of the nexus of social solidarities.

In the Maghrib, the ties binding local communities have historically been grounded in kinship. Members of a community thought of themselves as relatives issued from a common ancestor. Family and kinship served as the bases for social formations striving to remain autonomous from the state. They also offered a unifying principle for contesting state power. In the case of the Maghrib, the national state in formation had to take resources previously embedded in kin-based networks of obligation and redirected them toward national goals.

Germaine Tillion captures the character of Maghribi kin groupings with her metaphor of the many "republics of cousins."[4] Many kin groupings survived as cohesive entities until the period of national independence. As an integral part of this process, they kept tight control over their women, jealously saving them for the men in the "republic of cousins," or orchestrating collectively useful marriage alliances with outsiders.[5] Whatever the particular pattern governing marriage ties, the control of women was necessary for the maintenance of community cohesion. Women were key resources for the alternative centers of power resisting the state.

State formation affects the position of women in society in several ways. In particular, the state mediates gender relations through the law. Legislation is a key element in the panoply of strategies available to the state in its attempt to foster or inhibit social change, to maintain existing arrangements or to promote greater equality for women in the family and the society at large. Insofar as it regulates marriage, divorce, individual rights and responsibilities, and the transmission of property through inheritance, family law is a prime example of state policy affecting women.[6]

There is no single route to nation-building and state formation. The possibilities are several: the state can directly threaten and break tribal or kinship ties; it may tolerate them and only timidly chip away at tribal cohesion; or it may actively encourage the existence of tribes and lineages as part of the divide-and-rule stratagem. In all cases, the status of women is affected. Whatever its pattern, the process of state formation is likely to have consequences for gender relations.

ISLAMIC LAW AND WOMEN'S LEGAL STATUS

Islamic law, especially in its Maleki version that has historically predominated in the Maghrib, gives male members of the kin group extensive control over key decisions affecting women's lives. For instance, a woman need not give her consent to marriage during the marriage ceremony. It is the consent of the woman's guardian, her father or the next male in the kinship line, that makes the marriage valid. There is no legal minimum age for marriage.

Like other schools of Islamic law, Maleki law gives the husband the privilege of breaking the marital bond at will, while it specifies — and restricts — the circumstances to be considered legitimate grounds on which a woman may be granted a divorce. If a man chooses to repudiate his wife, the woman has no legal recourse. A man has the legal right to marry as many as four wives. No more than a small minority of men can afford more than one wife at a time, but the legality of polygyny threatens women, and pressures them to comply with their husband's wishes.

Maleki laws define precisely who is to inherit under various conditions. A woman receives half as much as would a man in a similar situation. Under many circumstances, the laws favor distant male relatives on the man's side of the family over the wife or female descendants.

Regulations on marriage encourage kin control of marriage ties and thus facilitate both marriages within the lineage and collectively useful outside alliances. Laws on divorce define the conjugal bond as fragile and easily breakable. The absence of community of property between husband and wife implies that the patrimony of each may remain untouched by marriage. By favoring males and kin on the male side, inheritance laws solidify ties within the extended patrilineal kin group.

The "message" of Maleki family law is that the conjugal unit may be shortlived, whereas the ties with male kin are enduring. Maleki law defines the kin group rather than the nuclear family unit as the significant locus of solidarity. It thus has implications for the broader social structure, at the same time as it subordinates women.

WOMEN'S RIGHTS AFTER INDEPENDENCE

What is the "message" of the laws promulgated in each Maghribi country in the wake of independence? What type of relationships do the new laws define as enduring, and what kind of family structure do they sanction?

When Morocco and Tunisia became independent states in 1956, and Algeria in 1962, the previous homogeneity in family law throughout the Maghrib came to an end. Morocco and Tunisia each equipped themselves with a Code of Personal Status and Algeria with a Family Code. All three national codes consist of a body of legislation on individual rights and responsibilities in the family, but they differ significantly.[7]

The Moroccan Code essentially reiterates Maleki family law in a more concise and codified manner. Consent to marriage is not expressed by the bride, but by her father or male guardian. The bride need not be present at the marriage ceremony for the marriage to be valid. Compulsory marriages remain a very real possibility. The procedure for divorce remains the same, except that repudiation, which could previously be a private act, must now be observed by two witnesses who record it in writing. Polygyny remains legal. Even fewer modifications have been brought to the law on inheritance.

Algeria's attitude toward family law and personal status oscillated for over 20 years. From the time of independence in 1962 until 1984, there were several attempts to reform the law, but the plans were aborted because of disagreement in the working committees or conflicts between liberal and conservative tendencies. Some of the slight modifications to Maleki law introduced by the French colonial regime were reconfirmed and a few new laws were passed, but for 22 years Algerians lived without an overall, comprehensive family law. Legislation consisted of a perplexing mismatch of Maleki law and secular codes. On June 9, 1984, the government finally adopted a long-awaited Family Code.

In the new Algerian Family Code, the legal prerogatives of husbands and unequal inheritance between women and men remain essentially unchanged. Polygyny continues to be legal. The principle of the matrimonial guardian is reconfirmed. An innovation is that if the father dies, the mother now becomes automatically the children's guardian. The term "divorce" has replaced "repudiation" and a divorce must occur in court, but the husband's will to terminate the marriage is still a sufficient and legitimate reason for divorce. For over two decades, Algerian leaders repeatedly expressed their interest in changing family law so as to increase women's rights. But they have not delivered on those promises. The codification of family law in sovereign Algeria remains faithful to Maleki legal principles.

Tunisian women saw their legal status change significantly when the Code of Personal Status was promulgated in 1956 and supplemented by additional laws thereafter. The bride must now attend her own marriage for it to be legally valid. Divorce can take place only in court, and husband and wife are equally entitled to file for divorce. Polygyny is abolished outright. It is punishable with imprisonment and a fine. Although the new laws of inheritance maintain that the share of women is worth half that of a man, daughters and granddaughters may, under certain circumstances, now receive the entire property to the detriment of distant male kin.[8] The law also ends the legal guardianship of man over women and redefines the rights and obligations of husband and wife so as to make them more equal.

THE IDEAL FAMILY

One of the key functions of a legal system is to present a summation of objectives for the society at large. The law provides a basis for social control and is meant to imprint on social dynamics a given rhythm and direction. The legislation that has emerged from the reforms in each Maghribi country contains an image of the ideal family as envisioned by the national state.

The Tunisian Code gives greater rights to women and decreases the legal control of male kin over them. With respect to the kinship structure, the code weakens the extended patrilineal kin group while strengthening the conjugal unit.

In contrast, in the model of the family contained in the Moroccan Code, women remain in a subordinate status. The law sanctions the extended kin group. It allows kin to control marriages, the marital bond is easily breakable, and inheritance rules maintain male privileges.

The legislation in effect in Algeria is ambiguous. There is slight encouragement for the development of the conjugal unit, but on the whole Algerian law continues to sanction the male-based extended kinship structure.

The Moroccan and Tunisian reforms occurred very soon after independence: within a year in Morocco and within six months in Tunisia. In both countries, they came from above rather than as a response to pressure from below. They were formulated by the government, the result of political choices on the part of the social groups in power. In both countries, individuals, mostly intellectuals or prominent figures in the nationalist movement, raised the issue of women's rights and family law. In Algeria, women were active in obstructing the most conservative plans to make Algerian law even more faithful to Maleki law. But nowhere was there an organized, sustained movement with this issue at the core of its platform.

Why has the political leadership in each country made the choices it has? The three countries reached independence with a different balance of power between the national state and local, kin-based communities and this, in turn, shaped state policy on family law and women's rights. By leaving intact the integrative mechanism of kin-based communities, the Moroccan policy can only help maintain the "republics of cousins." In Algeria, there has been a partial attempt to confront these communities. In Tunisia, the legal policy directly threatens them.

STRATEGIES OF STATE FORMATION

Even though Maghribi societies had developed some state institutions in the pre-colonial period, they lacked a state apparatus able to control effectively the whole territory. In the absence of bureaucratized states in the pre-colonial period (which was not chronologically the same for the three countries), tribal communities were major actors in the regulation of economic production and political conflict. Some were involved in an ongoing antagonistic relationship with whatever state existed at the time, with the goal of evading state control. Depending on the area, local revolts occurred either occasionally or with great frequency, for the most part aimed at avoiding taxes.[9]

Tunisia appears in its pre-colonial period as the country where kin-based communities had retained the least political autonomy and where the trend toward the emergence of centralized institutions was most recognizable. The history of pre-colonial Morocco exhibits an antagonistic relationship between central authority and tribal communities, as the former struggled to extend its power either through the use of force or through tactical alliances with local groups living in relative independence and with minimal state interference.

Colonization altered the situation. In Tunisia, the colonizers exerted their rule in large part through the administrative machinery available. They increased administrative centralization and weakened kin-based communities even beyond the loss of political leverage that these communities had experienced before colonization. In Algeria, the French dismembered entire communities by transplanting parts of them to distant areas, took the best lands and imposed their network of officials onto the largely segmented Algerian social structure. Algerians retreated into what was most secure, namely the solidarity of their kin-based collectivities, whenever that refuge was available. The effect of colonial rule was to destroy some of the tribal communities while leaving others in place and unwillingly reinforcing their internal cohesion. In Morocco, the French took the place of central authority and relied largely on a method of indirect administration in which they manipulated the local power structure. The result was that colonial rule affected tribal communities less than in either Algeria or Tunisia. At the end of the colonial period, the state was most highly bureaucratized in Tunisia, least bureaucratized in Morocco, and the Algerian state was somewhere in the middle.

Occurring in different structural settings, the struggle for national liberation and the transfer of power at independence took different forms in the three countries. In Tunisia, the nationalist strategy was to operate through a powerful party extending throughout the whole country. This was made possible by the relative integration of Tunisian society. State formation proceeded in large part without the reliance of the political leadership on kin-based communities.

In the Algerian war of national liberation, factions appeared not only on the basis of ideological differences but also among groups finding their support in different localities. Several post-independence insurrections in local areas demonstrated the revival of kinship and tribal ties. Segments of the leadership had at their disposal linkages with local, kin-based communities which they could mobilize when necessary in the struggle for power at the central level.

In Morocco, a party somewhat similar to its Tunisian counterpart found support predominantly in urban centers, but could not penetrate rural areas. There it lost out to the monarchy, which relied precisely on tribal communities in rural areas. In the period following independence, kin-based communities continued to be significant in Moroccan politics in that they served as bases of political support for power struggles played out at the national level. The strategy of the monarchy has been to establish systems of patronage, to act as arbiter among competing groups, and to orchestrate a complex web of factions.

National integration has been accomplished throughout most of the Maghrib, thus excluding competition as the predominant form of interaction between the state and kin-based groups. We are not witnessing secessionist movements in which tribal communities demand separation from the state or the creation of entirely independent political units. In Morocco and Algeria, however, these communities remain relevant to national politics.

For these reasons, the three Maghribi states have not been equally interested in bringing about changes in the relationship between the state and kin-based communities and, therefore, in reforming family law. In Tunisia, it was in the best interest of the government to break kin-based solidarities, and it was possible to do so because tribal groups had already lost much of their political leverage. In Algeria, it was also in the best interest of some leaders to foster a rearrangement of kinship by weakening kinship groupings, but other segments of the leadership depended in part on the continued availability of kin-based solidarities for political mobilization. In Morocco, the monarchy derived much of its power from its ability to maintain a balance among kin-based communities. It thus had a strong incentive to avoid any disruption of kinship organization.

Family law has been used as an instrument of change in Tunisia. It has served the status quo in Morocco. It has been held hostage to political cleavages in Algeria. Political elites have tended to make different choices in regard to family law and women's rights.

Notes

1. Charles Tilly (ed.), *The Formation of National States in Western Europe* (Princeton, NJ: Princeton University Press, 1975); Theda Skopol, *States and Social Revolutions: A Comparative Analysis of France, Russia and China* (New York: Cambridge University Press, 1985).

2. As in the title of Clifford Geertz's *Old Societies and New States: The Quest for Modernity in Asia and Africa (New York: Free Press, 1963).*

3. See several of the articles in Ghassan Salame, ed.

4. Germaine Tillion, *Le Harem et les cousins* (Paris: Editions de Seuil, 1966), translated by Q. Hoare as *The Republic of Cousins: Women's Oppression in Mediterranian Society* (London: Saqi, 1983).

5. See, for example, Jean Cuisenier, *Economie et parenté* (Paris: Moutin, 1975); and Hildred Geertz, "The Meaning of Family Ties," in C. Geertz, H. Geertz, and L. Rosen (eds.), *Meaning and Order in Moroccan Society* (Cambridge: Cambridge University Press, 1979).

6. The analysis in this paper focuses on the doctrine of the law. In everyday life, legal regulations are usually mitigated by social practices. What matters here is how the legal doctrine defines gender and kinship relations for the collectivity as a whole.

7. For a detailed analysis of legal reforms in each country, see Maurice Borrmans, *Statut personnel et famille au maghreb de 1940 à nos jours* (Paris and The Hague: Mouton, 1977).

8. More drastic reforms of inheritance laws were contemplated at various times, but rejected for fear of widespread opposition.

9. There is a growing literature on the social and political history of the Maghrib. A few examples are Lisa Anderson, *The State and Social Transformations in Tunisia and Libya, 1830-1980* (Princeton, NJ: Princeton University Press, 1986); Elbaki Hermassi, *Leadership and National Development in North Africa* (Berkeley: University of California Press, 1972); Allan Christelow, *Muslim Law Courts and the French Colonial State in Algeria* (Princeton, NJ: Princeton University Press, 1985).

28

Women in Kuwait

Taghreed Alqudsi-Ghabra

In the period before oil was discovered in Kuwait, men were away from the home for most of the year, either to trade or to dive for pearls in the Gulf waters. In their absence, women were left to take care of the family and all domestic issues. The discovery of the oil resources and their development brought about some serious social changes. In the 1950s, a group of Kuwaiti women publicly removed their *abbays* (black cloaks) as a form of protest against covering women's bodies, perhaps following the example of Huda Sha'arawi in Egypt who unveiled also as a form of protest against traditions that held back women's emancipation.

In a country of relatively generous economic welfare and prosperity, Kuwaiti women's exposure to the outside world through travel has influenced their perception of their role in society. Development for Kuwaiti women was also influenced by Kuwait's per capita income, which is considered the highest in the world. Further, Kuwait gained independence in 1961, prior to other countries in the Gulf, and was, therefore, a pioneer in building social and economic development programs that have transformed the lives of women.

Generally, the oil-rich countries' expenditure on education is high, and Kuwait is no exception. By 1985, its Ministry of Education was allocated 7.9 percent of the total budget, an amount equal to 4.2 percent of Kuwait's GNP. With the state's introduction of modern education, Kuwaiti women's skills and capabilities were enhanced. Education in the state of Kuwait is now compulsory through the eighth grade; in 1988, 49.6 percent of students enrolled in public elementary schooling were females. Through education, Kuwaiti women have achieved many advances, and have gained positions in government, business, academia, and other professions.

With the establishment of Kuwait University in 1966, the pace of development was accelerated for women. A number of women who did not have the chance to go abroad for higher education were able to pursue their education in Kuwait so that in the past decade the number of female university graduates has often exceeded that of males. Presently, 41 percent of Kuwait University degree holders are female.

Even though Kuwaiti women constituted only 3.7 percent of the total labor force in Kuwait for the year 1985 (Kuwaiti males comprised 15.2 percent; the rest were foreign workers), yet it is important to note that their participation in the labor force is increasing and their presence is important because it sets positive role models, an important step for women's emancipation in traditional societies. By the mid-1980s the board of the University of Kuwait had appointed Dr. Badriyya Al'awadi as the first Arab woman Dean of a College of Law and Shari'a. In 1993, Dr. Fayza Alkhorafi was appointed Rector of Kuwait University. These appointments are significant because they signal a change in women's status, setting a precedent that will determine the future participation of women in similar key positions.

When the Iraqi occupation took Kuwaiti citizens by surprise in August 1990, Kuwaiti women organized immediately and formed demonstrations. The first women's demonstration protesting the occupation and calling for the return of the legitimate Kuwaiti government was organized two days after occupation, followed by several others. Kuwaiti women's participation in different associations and professional groups has gained them visibility, recognition, and experience in the democratic processes. In addition to welfare type work, the Women's Cultural and Social Society seeks to advance the democratic representation of women in future parliaments. After the liberation of Kuwait in 1991, the country undertook limited steps toward democracy. Free parliamentary elections for men were held for the first time since the suspension of the Kuwaiti parliament in 1986. Even though different opposition groups gained representation, women are still deprived of the right to vote and to be elected for office. Kuwaiti women are currently working through organizations on two fronts; they are seeking more personal freedoms and rights, while at the same time they are paving the way for future political rights and representation in government.

Some basic issues that need to be addressed in the women's movement include issues related to marriage and divorce laws (personal status laws). There is a need to provide day-care and other family services for women who work outside the home, if modern society is to function effectively and cope with issues of modernization.[1]

Notes

1. Editor's Note: Although Kuwait has a democratically elected legislature, yet in Kuwait today women have not been granted the right to vote. This has been a controversial issue for Kuwaiti society and for the government since 1962, and each election year (the last elections took place on October 5, 1993) women voice their dissent to this law. However, Kuwait is a conservative country and the issue of whether the *shari'a* grants women the right to vote generally dominates the debate over this issue. In the last elections Kuwaiti women challenged the decision to exclude them from voting, basing their argument on their active role in the resistance movement against Iraqi occupation of their country. They are expected to raise this issue again in the next round of elections.

PART NINE

Women and Literature

29

Arab Women and Literature: An Overview

Bouthaina Sha'aban[*]

To introduce Arab women writers or Arab women novelists in such a brief presentation is understandably an impossible task, for the bulk of Arab women's literature from the sixth century until today is immense. Al-Khansa (575-664), the first Arab woman poet of repute, was not only a poet but also a literary critic. She used to stand in that world's fair of Arabic poetry, the Okaz Market, in present-day Saudi Arabia, scrutinizing the work of her fellow poets, and pointing out to them the merits and demerits of their poems. For fourteen centuries Arab women have been writing poetry and prose and running salons where poets meet regularly and recite their recent compositions with the hostess (who is always a woman) as the ultimate literary judge; and yet Arab women's literary contributions are neither properly recorded nor fairly acknowledged in history.

Even before the recording of Arabic literature began, it was women who conveyed oral traditions from one generation to another, keeping the heritage of Arabic storytelling alive. Poetry was for generations the most important genre in Arabic literature, while the short story and the novel as literary genres were quite late to appear in their modern forms — though traditional forms such as *Al-Hikayya* and *Makamah* were widely practiced.

In my latest research I have discovered that the first novel in Arabic literature was written by a woman, rather than by a man as previously assumed. Although it has been the general consensus in the Arab world that the first modern novel in Arabic literature is *Zainab*

* A similar article by Sha'aban appeared in the *Washington Report on Middle East Affairs,* February 1993.

(1914), by Egyptian writer Hussayn Haykal, this is only true if we exclude women writers. Afifa Karam, a Lebanese woman, wrote the first novel in Arabic in 1906, *Badi'a wa Fouad,* published by *Al-Huda* newspaper (New York). Since then Arab women writers have been writing novels and short stories, but without claiming the amount of attention accorded to male writers.

Most Arab women writers began by exploring the intricacies of their lives as women, of their families, and of family relations. Until the 1950s, the concept of women's literature, as expressed by Syrian novelist Widad Sakkakini, was "the literature in which a woman writer expresses her inner feelings and subtle sensitivity in female spheres which are out of men's reach. Women's literature describes female habits and modes of thinking which no man writer, however talented he might be, could reach."[1]

Yet the writer who coined this limiting definition exceeded it in her own literary productions. In a style that included sharp satire and shrewd humor, Widad Sakkakini's first story collection, *The People's Mirrors,*[2] sensitively portrayed the social and psychological environment confining her sisters, and tacitly incited them to rebel against prevailing prejudices and stereotypes. The description of women's grievances is quickly channeled to a form of rebellion that finds its best expressions in her novel *Arwa Bint al-Khutub (Arwa, the Daughter of Upheavals),* and her biography *Rabia al-Adawiyya (First Among Sufis).* In these two works, the author addresses injustices inflicted on women by a man-made system.

More subtle, though no less painful, injustices are depicted by Latifa Ziat, an Egyptian woman, who discovers at an advanced age that her lifetime spent tending and mothering other people's feelings and thoughts has allowed no time to register her own. The theme of her short story collection, *Al-Shaykhukha wa Kissas Aukhra (Old Age and Other Stories),* is that women's obsession with living up to the social image of themselves as faithful lovers, caring wives, and selfless mothers precludes any opportunity for self-realization or self-fulfillment. Her stories are a passionate call to women to question prevailing concepts of women's happiness, success, and achievement, and to redefine them according to their own personal goals and interests in life.

Since the 1960s, the number of Arab women writers has increased dramatically in various parts of the Arab world, among all social classes, and they have reached out to embrace ever broader social and political issues. In the late 1950s and early 1960s, novels and short stories written by Arab women also entered a more feminist phase.

During this new phase, feminist visions, aspirations, and outlooks were expressed in the works of Collet Khoury and Ghada Saaman in Syria, Nawal el-Sa'adawi in Egypt, Khanata Banuna in Morocco, Assia Djebar in Algeria, Sahar Khalifeh and Samira Azzam from Palestine, Layla Othman from Kuwait, and many more rising novelists and short story writers.

In their works, such Arab women writers have highlighted boldly the evils of political systems which, by being detrimental to women, have consequently operated to the detriment of men and of society at large. In her novel *Beirut '75*, for example, Ghada Saaman highlights the alienation visited upon both men and women by the social and political systems in Lebanon. Her message, however, is that amidst such unfathomable chaos women are, by far, the worst afflicted. They suffer from the double subjection of society and men.

This new generation of feminist writers has illuminated women's strengths and dispelled deeply entrenched taboos about their weaknesses. The new woman that emerges in Sahar Khalifeh's two-part novel, *Al-Saabar* (*Wild Thorns,* Interlink, 1989) and *Abad al-Shams*, defies and dissociates herself totally from two traditional conceptions of women: first, that women are weak and unable to maintain a family after the disappearance of its male provider, and second, the entrenched view of women's honor, which had disastrous repercussions on the fate of the Palestinian people in 1948.[3] From the author's brilliantly interwoven depiction of the social matrix of Palestinian society under occupation emerges a new confident and creative Arab woman who breaks the stereotype of women's weakness and inferiority. These Arab women authors are not only recording changes in challenged societies, but are the catalyst for this century's dynamic response.

Notes

1. *Insaf Al Maraa (Doing Women Justice)* (Damascus, 1959), pp. 63-64.
2. Cairo: The Library of Egypt's Publications, 1994.
3. In 1948, Palestinian men, including those in responsible positions, were obsessed with protecting their honor (their women from rape) from the Israelis. Even when they fought they did so to protect their women more than their land.

30

An interview with Iraq's Lami'a Abbass Ammara

Samer M. Reno

The renowned Iraqi woman poet Lami'a Abbass Ammara was born and raised in Baghdad. She emigrated to the United States in 1986 and currently resides in San Diego, California, where she continues to write poetry and to publish in the Arabic press. To date, she has published seven volumes of poetry in Arabic on such issues as Arab women's position in society — the titles of two volumes are *Ashtar* and *Iraqi Woman* — political events in the Arab world, and on Arab culture and civilization. In 1978, when Ammara lived in Baghdad, she was recognized by women's organizations for her struggle on behalf of women's emancipation. In Iraq, Ammara served as a board member of the Iraqi Writers Union, which was established by the famous Iraqi poet, Al-Jawahiri.

During the Lebanese civil war and during Israel's invasion of Lebanon in 1982, Ammara lived in Lebanon where she received several awards for poems written that reflect the struggle and suffering of the people — especially the impact of war on women. In the United States she continues to be active on several fronts.

What are your recent accomplishments in the U.S.?

In the U.S., I have been working in many fields, in addition to writing and reciting poetry on different occasions. I am currently editing a magazine entitled *Al-Mandaee,* which means "Knowledge" or "Knowledgeable" in Aramaic.

I was also honored by the Arab-American Journalists Association in a conference on poetry which was held in Los Angeles on August 20,

238

1993, where I recited my new poem "Leila al-Attar" (name of an Iraqi woman poet) and several other poems. I was recognized for the quality of my poetry and for my articles.

However, I intend to move away from poetry for a while, and I will devote a greater part of my time to writing and researching the role of women in our ancient history and civilization. I hope to write many books on this subject.

Do you define yourself as a woman poet?

All my life I sought to be a good poet and I saw myself in relation to other poets both male and female; and not only in relation to women poets. The important thing is to be a good poet; and I think that women should compete with men and excel rather than seclude themselves and think of their work strictly in terms of other women.

You had a long and illustrious career as a poet: can you give us a synopsis of the topics that you address in your poems?

I have used my poems to address unconventional topics in our culture. I have tried to introduce the public to new ways of looking at conventional issues through my poetry. And, of course, issues of Arab women were high on the agenda since I have attempted to address the Arab woman in the majority of my poems. Politics are an important element in my poetry, since my poems reflect the sufferings of the Arab peoples across this century in many crises beginning with the Palestinian crisis and ending with the devastations of the Gulf War on Iraq.

Throughout ancient history, the women of the Fertile Crescent played an important role, and their status was reflected in the fame and power of goddesses, such as A'shtar, and queen-rulers of kingdoms, such as Alisar, Balk'is, and Zanubia. To what do you attribute the change in status of the Arab woman in today's world compared to her role in history?

It is unfortunate that modern Arab history does not document or celebrate the names of Arab women whose contributions to their society and nations in the twentieth century can be compared to that of A'shtar or Alisar. Women in ancient Arab civilizations used to acquire their fair share of fame in society in accordance with their personal achievements and abilities, and their contributions to the progress of their society.

During the emergence of Islam in the seventh century, civilization in the Fertile Crescent, which includes present-day Iraq, was more advanced socially than its counterparts in the Arabian Peninsula. Women in the Fertile Crescent gained prominence and took their places in society, as rulers and educators and divine beings; however, the role that women in the Arabian Peninsula played before the advent of Islam was submissive and inferior to the position of men. In many cases female infants were interred alive after their birth in the patriarchal structure of the pre-Islamic world.

When Islam came, some of its teachings were aimed at restructuring the social fabric of society in the Arabian Peninsula, and one has to understand the position of women in the Quran against the status of women in the Arabian Peninsula at the time when Islam first appeared. In this context, I think the Quran sought to give women the basic minimum to guarantee them basic rights. It put an end to the burial of female infants considered less desirable than male infants; it sought to give women the right to have a say in accepting or rejecting their parents' choice of a spouse; it provided for some basic laws to guarantee women's inheritance. One can only assume that local traditions treated women rather badly, and the new Islamic laws restored their rights. The situation for women was therefore a lot worse prior to the advent of Islam.

However, in the Fertile Crescent before the advent of Islam the Sumarians had formed the cradle of civilization. Women's position was well advanced and there were women rulers like Zanubia. The Sumarians were among the first civilizations to invent the alphabet, and women had a degree of autonomy and control over their resources. In giving women their basic rights, Islam did not in any way bring them progress. Women then were free not to cover their heads, and they were free to engage in trade.

What is your view of the current revival of religious laws for women?

This movement seeks to apply what was right for women in the seventh century to the lives of women today. One cannot turn back the clock like this without causing some dire consequences to women's lives. What justification can there be for saying that women need not continue their education beyond primary school in a world which is as technologically advanced as ours?

These rules, intended to control women, are imposing restrictions and control not just on women but on the population as a whole. When religion is used to fortify those who are opposing oppression it can be a great source of strength — for example during the Algerian revolution religion was a source of strength for those who resisted occupation. But when religion is imposed from above, through the channels of authority and government, it becomes a method of control. People should be free to practice their religion and in such a free atmosphere they will worship out of their free will. When religion is used as a force against the self, when the state takes on the power to force the population to pray, people will soon begin to resent this control and their love for their religion and their devotion will soon dissipate.

What kind of childhood did you have in Iraq?

Up to age 14 I had to wear a *hijab* much like the black *chador.* But even as a child I resented it and I wrote an article then that was published in a local newspaper and made a big noise. I could not understand why when we had no money to buy shoes, far more utilitarian than the *hijab*, we had to spend money on this useless piece of clothing. In high school I took the *hijab* off and never wore it again.

In my country, Iraq, religious fanaticism was not enforced from above, most of the recent leaders had been tolerant of women's rights and were never religiously conservative. But religious tradition is something else and it is deeply entrenched in the population. Religious fanaticism is also imported for a variety of political reasons that vary from region to region.

How would you describe the status of women in the Fertile Crescent over the last few decades?

Women have advanced in most fields, but they rarely reach the top position of minister. Women can become the heads of their divisions or top executive government officers, but the glass ceiling prevents them from attaining ministerial jobs. There are no written laws against it, of course; based on my experience men's jealousy is enough of a deterrent and it is the real hidden reason that stands in the way of the advancement of women. The culture has taught men that women are not equal, and when they find that this unequal creature has reached a top level position they feel perhaps that this must somehow diminish their own worth. This happens in Western countries as well, although it is not so pronounced.

In my culture men accuse women of being the jealous sex. I think that it is the other way around, in fact, because most men have a hard time seeing a woman achieve a top position. Men in my country are fully aware of the capabilities of women, because when they look around they see highly qualified women, hard-working women in every field. They fear for their own share of the pie; the availability of jobs is not infinite. Still, women are very strong in all fields of teaching and education: this is a profession that is almost entirely female on all levels.

Where did you work after you left high school?

I chose the education field; I taught at the university, and felt most comfortable because my colleagues were mostly women. There was not this negative sense of jealousy, we all cooperated and understood our own limits and responsibilities. I also worked representing my country in the UNESCO in Paris, which is where I developed most of my views on male-female work relations. My director and country-man represented the typical jealous male colleague, and I finally left the job and returned to Iraq.

What is your personal view of the Iraqi woman both before and after the Gulf War?

The Iraqi woman before the Gulf War combined beauty and intellect. That is to say, she was brought up in a way that cultivated her spirit and her sense of individuality. And this was evidenced through the numerous women's associations that were formed and, on a more personal level, through the personality and style of women in their interaction with society.

The devastation of the war destroyed among other things this vibrant self-image of Iraqi women and women's laughter turned to a solemn cry. Iraqi women changed their vibrant attire to black garments to symbolize their grief and sense of loss for the loved ones killed during the war.

I believe that women are the face representing all civilizations; when they starve and go without adornment, all nations are to blame.

Women's lot would be improved if and when the economic sanctions against Iraq are removed. I understand that these sanctions are also self-defeating, since they impact negatively on American and European agriculture and industry, since they prevent Iraq from buying sufficient materials from abroad for the reconstruction and revival of the country. I fail to see the gains that might result from these sanctions that cause great suffering to many Iraqis, especially women.

How do you compare the role that Arab-American women play in the U.S., with their counterparts in the Arab World?

I think that this question may be divided into two parts: the individual and the institutional levels. On the institutional level, I think that Palestinian woman, because of their politicization, tend to be very active in forming productive and successful women's organizations in this country. They tend to be at this historical juncture an energizing force in American society as well as in their struggle for a homeland. There are always women's organizations in which Palestinian women play a productive role, through convening symposiums or conventions that address the problems facing Palestinians. I consider the Iraqi women's role to be more restricted in the middle of Arab-American women's activism. Their role, which is modified and restricted here, is merely a reflection of the national divisions within Iraq at the present time.

On the personal level, Arab families who reside in the United States should be prepared to face a serious generational gap with their daughters. The first generation of Arab women immigrants to the U.S. carry with them the remaining touches of Arab tradition, while the young generation looks at women's liberation from an American point of view. They see the need to assimilate completely in their new society. Some traditional families may object to the new Westernized role that some of their daughters may choose to play; however, the American legal system protects the rights of the daughter and this may become the cause for a serious generational problem.

31

An Interview with Syria's Kamar Keilany

Suha Sabbagh

Kamar Keilany is a well-known Syrian writer who has written eight novels and seven short stories, which have been translated into Russian, Dutch, French, Spanish, and English. Her literary style fluctuates between political symbolism and realism. Her deep appreciation for the word renders her prose more like poetry. For the last 40 years, she has published a weekly newspaper column about the issues that touch the lives of her devoted readership. Kamar in Arabic means "moon," and Kamar Keilany's readers compare her unorthodox views to the moon that is sure to shine over the city of Damascus, which is her spiritual base as she travels all over the world recording her views. I had the opportunity to meet with her on a trip to Washington, D.C., and to interview her about her life, her work, and her views on women's issues.

What was your experience like as a woman writer who sought to depart from the traditional role of women in the 1940s?

I come from an old conservative Damascene family with great respect for tradition. My father did not believe in educating the women in the family, both because he saw no need for it and because of the exorbitant price of higher eduction. My father's family was of the landed gentry and toward the end of the 1940s, when I was of school age, this class was not earning a good income. My sisters did not receive a higher eduction; however, my father was convinced that I had a gift and was highly talented. So, when I insisted on going on with my education, he did not put up a fight, because he thought that I would be

worth the financial sacrifice. I passed my Brevet exams in French at
the end of high school. Local schools were under the French system
of education, since Syria was under French Mandatory rule until
1945. Following that I received my B.A. degree in Arabic and I went
to teachers college.

What stands out in your memory of those days?

Memories mean a lot to me. I agree with Marcel Proust — memories
transpose me to those early days of growing up in Damascus. The
smell of Damascene jasmine, a particular kind, almost always evokes
in me the memories of my childhood and my youth.

I remember being controversial in a positive way. I first published
in the school journal articles that demanded the integration of
women in all university faculties. At that time, articles were mostly
ideological; articles about gender equality were still rare. I took my
new-found freedom very seriously and sought to be a perfect example
of what women are capable of achieving. I was nicknamed the rebel-
lious blonde, after I published a series of articles about the need for
women to wear dresses made of local cheap cottons to put across the
point that women must focus on their minds rather than become
identified through their looks. I made big news showing up at parties
wrapped up in local cottons generally worn by peasants.

After my graduation I taught until the end of the 1970s. Between
1967 and 1970, I was very active in the Women's Union, where I became the founder of the women's journal called *Al-Mara al-Arabia*.
The journal continues to be published to the present day. However, I
have found that I prefer working in areas where women are not separated from society on the basis of gender and are integrated in professional organizations, like the Union of Syrian Writers, where I
continue to be an active member and the only woman elected to the
executive committee. Following that, I worked with UNESCO and
with the League of Arab States in Syria.

In the 1950s I was married for a brief period of one and a half years.
I was one of a few women to initiate divorce in Syria and my family
respected my wishes. I had a daughter from this marriage but I refused to accept alimony or any form of financial compensation, because I believed that a woman can earn her own living. My daughter
is now 30 years old. She received several degrees including a master's
degree in Agro-Economics from the American University in Beirut. Yet
she has given up working in her field and chose to become a writer of
children's stories. I would not have chosen this path for her, since be-

ing a writer is always difficult and a financially insecure field. But she is excellent as a writer and she now owns a small publishing house.

What are some of the issues that you deal with in your novels and how do you see the role of women in these novels?

In my novels and short stories, I deal with the way in which historical events affect the individual. I deal with the way in which political events affect the personal side of life. Women have suffered a lot in your part of the world as a result of political events and their role is central to my work. As for political events, I was inspired to write by the Moroccan struggle for independence, by the loss of Palestine, and by the Lebanese civil war.

Bustan al-Karaz (The Cherry Orchard) is about the Lebanese civil war. A Christian girl named Camellia is happily married to a Muslim man, and until the eruption of the civil war the children are not aware of any problems resulting from their parents' mixed marriage. During the war, Camellia opts to go back with her children to her parents' house on the Christian side of the city for greater protection. Her numerous sisters represent the multiplicity of the problems in Lebanon. Nadia is Westernized and seeks comfort in becoming more assimilated into Western culture. Sonia is in love with a Palestinian and her relationship represents the early admiration that the Lebanese population had for the Palestinians and their cause. In the final scene, which takes place in the orchard during the cherry season, Sonia saves the life of a baby from a car crash. The baby lives, but is unable to sustain himself on his feet without the help of a second party. The symbolism of this scene to the position of Lebanon as a country is obvious.

I have written a book of short stories called *Alam Bila Hudoud (A World Without Borders)*, which is a collection of stories about the Palestine issue. One story in particular predicted the Palestinian intifada. It is about a group of Palestinian children who employ mischievous acts to annoy and subsequently get rid of Israeli soldiers and of the occupation. They use soap in the alleyways to make the soldiers slip or they throw stones at them. The children of the intifada carried out similar acts.

In another story in the same collection I deal with the United Nations resolution 242 in a symbolic way. A woman falls in love with, and is willing to marry, a Palestinian fighter, although he owns nothing and refuses to bring children into a world where they have no country. In spite of his objections, their son is born in a UN car. But the car crashes and the child is killed. Although the UN has recognized the rights of Palestinians in resolution 242, yet this recognition has not led to the recovery of Palestinian land.

What are the topics with which you deal in your weekly column?

In my weekly column I write on what strikes my fancy. I am very moody when it comes to writing and I do hate deadlines, although in 40 years I never missed writing a single column. Before coming to the U.S. I left behind five articles for my publishers and on this trip I see everything from the position of what I am going to write back home. Historically, Arabs have been travelers and explorers and I think of myself along the same lines.

My visit to Spain resulted in a series of articles about the history of Arabs in Spain during the Middle Ages. I tried to relive the days when Arab civilization flourished there and to imagine the contributions of the Arabs to Europe at that time. Spanish poetry was influenced by Arabic poetry. The word "troubadour" (poems put to music) comes from the Arabic words *tarab al-dour,* meaning musical enjoyment within the home. Islamic texts influenced many European writers, such as the Italian poet Dante Alighieri. Finally, flamenco music has its roots in the music of the *oud,* a stringed instrument which the Arabs brought to Spain.

I wrote on the Gulf War. I was touched by the plight of the women in Baghdad looking for milk to feed their children. I wrote about the south of Lebanon during the 1982 invasion by Israel because I was worried about Um Kassem, a very ordinary peasant woman who invited me into her house in Nabatiya.

I write about the use and misuses of the Arabic language. I also write about the old city of Damascus that is being destroyed as new buildings come up. And I will write about this trip to the United States where I came to see a world that is technologically more advanced than our world. In Syria people read Ghada al-Saaman for women's issues and women's rights and equality. For romance, they read Collet Khoury. I like to think that I am read for political depth and for my unique point of view.

What in your assessment are the problems facing Syrian women today?

Like women all over the Arab world, the modern Syrian woman is suffering from the double burden. Many need to work outside the home, but the services and the marketplace have not yet minimized the burden of household chores. There are no cut frozen vegetables ready in the supermarket at a reasonable price. There are no cheap family restaurants or prepared foods on the market. Child-care is still a problem. Consequently, working outside the home presents a real problem to women. Few women have the time to read and it is questionable to what extent working outside the home is in fact the process of self-realization that it is supposed to be. Although I raised my daughter as a single parent a woman's lot was a lot easier in my day because we lived with the extended family and the women in the family helped each other.

What in your opinion are women looking for in the current fundamentalist movement in Syria?

Women are seeking out religious movements because of their disappointment in their current situation and the state of affairs in the Arab world in general. We had an idealistic upbringing and we believed in nationalistic goals. Women are disappointed in the discrepancy between the ideal and the reality. There is also no possibility to fulfil more material dreams or career aspirations. It seems to me that women today are left with one of two choices: either they follow a very permissive path that alienates them from their cultural roots or they join the fundamentalist movement. In my day we still believed in the promise of modernization. We believed that education and modernization would automatically result in prosperity — we were naive in this respect.

I think women should have the right to be in a position to really make a choice; and if they choose religion, then it is their prerogative to do so. My main concern is that religion should not be imposed on women.

What book are you currently working on?

I am working on the memoirs of a young Damascene woman, based on my own experience of living in one of the oldest quarters of Damascus. It is called *The Star and the Big House.* The star sparkles in all directions and in Arabic the word puts across the idea of a body that is mobile. The house is at first the house which I grew up in, and then the city of Damascus, and then Syria, and finally the world as a whole. It is about my personal experience in this world.

What do you wish to see happen as far as the role of women in the Arab world?

I am concerned with women's issues but I do not share all the views of my colleague Nawal el-Sa'adawi, although I do appreciate her desire to remove the veil from women's oppression. I believe that women should become integrated in any profession they choose, and that is why I chose to work through the writers union as opposed to placing all my efforts into the women's organization. I think that women should not always seek to isolate themselves in groups that are exclusively for women. At the same time, I have great faith in the resilience of Arab women and I hope that they will use their abilities to become integrated in the various professions.

32

The Hidden History of Arab Feminism

Bouthaina Sha'aban*

The clear dividing line between a journalist and a writer in the West has always been blurred in the Arab world. Many Arab journals and papers were launched by writers and educators who considered journalism an extension of other forms of writing and who felt that they had an urgent social and political mission.

Between 1892 and 1940, Arab women writers concentrated their efforts on printing their own journals, in which they published poetry, fiction, and criticism, as well as essays aimed at promoting women's role in society. Any assessment of Arab (or, for that matter, global) women's literature cannot be done without evaluating the Arab women's press, which was for half a century the major platform for Arab women writers.

In 1892, the Syrian, Hind Nawfal, started her first journal, *Al-Fatat* (*Young Girl*), in Alexandria, Egypt, ushering in a flourishing era: there were more than 25 Arab feminist journals owned, edited, and published by women — all before the First World War. These editors stated in their editorials that their most important concern was women: women's literature, women's rights, and women's future. In her editorial to the first issue (November 20, 1892) of *Al-Fatat*, Hind Nawfal wrote: "*Al-Fatat* is the only journal for women in the East; it expresses their thoughts, discloses their inner minds, fights for their rights, searches for their literature and science, and takes pride in publishing the products of their pens." Editors of other journals urged women who are "attentive to the future and betterment of their

* This article first appeared in *Ms.* magazine, May/June 1993. Reprinted by permission.

sex to write so that their works may be read and become, in the meantime, a part of the literary heritage." These journals appeared in Cairo, Beirut, Damascus, and, to a lesser extent, Baghdad. The editors displayed profound political knowledge, sensitivity to the sources of social problems, reliable economic sense, and sophisticated professional skills in the domains of publishing, marketing, and financial viability. To name just a few: *Anis al-Galis*, owned, edited, and published by Alexandra Afernuh (Alexandria, 1898); *Shajarat al-Durr*, by Sa'dya Sa'd al-Din (Alexandria, 1901); *Al-Mara'a*, by Anisa Attallah (Egypt, 1901); *Al-Sa'ada*, by Rujina A'wad (Egypt, 1902); *Al-A'rus*, by Mary A'jami (Damascus, 1910); *Al-Khadir*, by Afifa Sa'ab (Lebanon, 1912); *Fatat al-Niyl*, by Sara al-Mihaya (Cairo, 1913); and *Fatat Lubnan*, by Salima Abu Rashid (Lebanon, 1914).

Although regular coverage was given to the experience and achievements of Western women, all these journals stressed the necessity to learn from women's movements in the West *without* giving up what is positive in Arab culture and Muslim religion. (As far as women and Islam are concerned, studies often confirmed that there is literally nothing in the Quran that makes "the veil" a required Islamic study, and that polygyny is against the spirit and the actual wording of the Quran.)

A stream of articles that appeared in a number of these journals established an interesting link between the emergence of political movements for national independence and the awakening of a feminist consciousness in the Arab world, arguing that no country can be truly free so long as its women remain shackled (an important connection that Arab women in the next generation failed to stress). The point that feminist issues are national issues was made not only by women, but also by such prominent men as Adil Jamil Bayham and George Niqula Baz. Women writers expressed real interest in national affairs and political issues, and gave no indication whatsoever that they were living on the periphery of political life. Suffice it to mention, perhaps, that the Arab Women's Union, with its clear pan-Arab vision, was formed in 1928, 17 years before the League of Arab States.

Some nationalists even started to see the feminist writings of this era as a key for national reform. The well-known nationalist lawyer Habib Faris wrote to Fatat Lubnan in 1914: "National reform could be achieved once the government decides to support women writers who are best qualified to sow the seeds of just and righteous principles among the people. The writings of women in newspapers and journals are more compelling and more effective in bringing about reform than any other force."

Yet some women writers dealt with feminists issues that we are still, almost a century later, trying to resolve. Labiba Shamu'n wrote in 1898: "I can't see how a woman writer or poet could be of any harm to her husband and children. In fact, I see the exact opposite: her knowledge and education will reflect positively on her family and children ... Neither male art nor creativity has ever been considered as a misfortune to the family, or an impediment to the love and care a father may bestow upon his children. The man who sees in a learned woman his rival is incompetent: he who believes that his knowledge is sufficient is mean, and the man who believes that women's creativity harms him or her is ignorant."

In another 1898 article, exploring the social and psychological evils of granting men unlimited power to divorce, *Shajarat al-Durr* strikes an unusual chord: "Fear of divorce may distort a woman's character and mind, drive her to conspire against her husband, and treat him as she would treat a wicked enemy rather than a love companion. Women in reality may find it necessary to use tricks and games to satisfy her husband at all costs, because she fears him and she would fear a totally untrustworthy person. She tries to be a shrewd enemy to an adversary who is, forever, hanging the threat of divorce over her head."

Articles about the position of European, U.S., Chinese, Indonesian, and Indian women appeared regularly in these journals, as well as biographies of great women, both European and Arab. The accounts of non-Arab women, in general, never conveyed the slightest feeling of prejudice against Western women or against their style of life. Most of these articles stressed the necessity to benefit from the experience of other women without losing sight of Arab history, culture, and religion. In addition, the journals published accurate social studies about the status of women, of employed women, of educated women, and of housewives. These studies often pointed to the source of social ills that kept women on the margin of life, and called for true reform. Quite a few of these articles stressed that if differences between the sexes were to be examined accurately, we would find that the results are in women's favor. They argue that women surpass men in sensitivity, kindness, sympathy, and deep thought, because women are the source of life and origin of everything valuable in it. But most of the articles stressed that the point is not to prove the superiority of women over men (and by so doing commit the same mistake men have committed for centuries): rather, such arguments try to prove that what others used to call weakness in women's character is in fact, true strength and a solid basis for social structure.

The journals also reported on the feminist societies that began to appear in all quarters of the Arab world, and on news of international women's conferences.

In addition to feminist networks that were set up in Cairo, Alexandria, Damascus, Beirut, and Baghdad, women journalists corresponded with the organization Women and Peace, which called upon women in all corners of the globe to use their powers against the escalation of tension and the production of weapons. They argued that women are the first, and the worst, hurt by war. These journals exerted a real effort to win Arab women to the cause of peace.

It is clear from letters of readers and correspondents that the women's press during that time constituted a central element in the Arab press. But the important role these journals played during the first half of this century is not yet acknowledged. It is unfortunate that no proper archives exist in the Arab world of this rich heritage, and no studies have appeared about it. It deserves introduction to Arab and Western readers alike.

Introductory Reading List

Abbott, Nadia, *Aisha: The Beloved of Mohammad* (London: Saqi Books, 1986).

Abbott, Nadia, *Two Queens of Baghdad* (London: Saqi Books, 1986).

Abu Lughod, Lila, *Veiled Sentiments: Honor and Poetry in a Bedouin Society* (Berkeley: University of California Press, 1987).

Abu Nassr, Julinda (ed.), *Women, Employment and Development in the Arab World* (Berlin and New York: Mouton, 1985).

Accad, Evelyne, *Sexuality and War* (New York: NYU Press, 1990).

Ahmad, Leila, *Women and Gender in Islam: Historical Roots of a Modern Debate* (New Haven, CT: Yale University Press, 1992).

al-Khayyat, Sana, *Honour and Shame: Women in Modern Iraq* (London: Saqi Books, 1990).

al-Qazzaz, Ayad, *Women in the Arab World: An Annotated Bibliography* (Washington, D.C.: Association of Arab-American University Graduates, 1975).

Altorki, Soraya and el-Sohl, Camilla F., *Arab Women in the Field: Studying Your Own Society* (Syracuse, NY: Syracuse University Press, 1988).

Altorki, Soraya, *Women in Saudi Arabia: Ideology and Behavior Among the Elite* (New York: Columbia University Press, 1988).

Amrouch, Fadham, *My Life Story: The Autobiography of a Berber Woman* (New Brunswick, NJ: Rutgers University Press, 1989).

Atiya, Nayra, *Khul Khaal: Five Egyptian Women Tell Their Stories* (Syracuse, NY: Syracuse University Press, 1982).

Augustin, Ebba (ed.), *Palestinian Women: Identity and Experience* (London: Zed Books, 1993).

Badran, Margo (ed.), *Huda Sharawi's Harem Years: Memoirs of An Egyptian Feminist* (London: Virago Press, 1986).

Badran, Margo and Cooke, Miriam (eds.), *Opening the Gates: A Century of Arab Feminist Writing* (Bloomington, IN: Indiana University Press, 1990).

Buonaventura, Wendy, *Serpent of the Nile: Women and Dance in the Arab World* (New York: Interlink, 1989).

Caspi, Mishael Maswari (trans.), *Daughters of Yemen* (Berkeley: University of California Press, 1985).

Cooke, Miriam, *War's Other Voices: Women Writers on the Lebanese Civil War* (New York: Cambridge University Press, 1988).

el-Sa'adawi, Nawal, *Memoirs from the Women's Prison* (London: The Women's Press, 1983).

el-Sa'adawi, Nawal, *Memoirs of a Woman Doctor* (Berkeley: City Lights Books, 1989).

el-Sa'adawi, Nawal, *The Hidden Face of Eve: Women in the Arab World* (London: Zed Books, 1980).

el-Sanabary, Nagat, *Determinants of Women's Education in the Middle East and North Africa: Illustrations from Seven Countries* (World Bank, 1989).

el-Sanabary, Nagat, *Women and Work in the Third World: Impact of Industrialization and Global Economic Interdependence* (Berkeley: Center for the Study of Education and Advancement of Women, 1983).

Esposito, John L., *Women in Muslim Family Law* (Syracuse, NY: Syracuse University Press, 1992).

Fakhiro, Munira A., *Women at Work in the Gulf: A Case Study of Bahrain* (New York: Routledge, 1990).

Fernea, Elizabeth Warnock, *Guests of the Sheik: An Ethnography of an Iraqi Village* (New York: Anchor Books/Doubleday, 1965).

Fernea, Elizabeth Warnock (ed.), *Women and the Family in the Middle East: New Voices of Change* (Austin, TX: University of Texas Press, 1985).

Fernea, Elizabeth Warnock and Bezirgan, Basima (eds.), *Middle Eastern Muslim Women Speak* (Austin, TX: University of Texas Press, 1980).

Gadant, Monique (ed.), *Women of the Mediterranean* (London: Zed Books, 1986).

Hijab, Nadia, *Womanpower: The Arab Debate on Women at Work* (New York: Cambridge University Press, 1988).

Joekes, Susan, *Women in the World Economy* (New York: Oxford University Press, 1990).

Kandiyoti, Deniz (ed.), *Women, Islam and the State* (Philadelphia: Temple University Press, 1991).

Keddie, N. and Baron, B. (eds.), *Women in Middle East History: Shifting Boundaries of Sex and Gender* (New Haven, CT: Yale University Press, 1992).

Kudat, Ayse and Abadzi, Helen, *Participation of Women in Higher Education in Arab States* (World Bank, 1989).

Makdisi, Jean Said, *Beirut Fragments: A War Memoir* (New York: Persea Books, 1990).

Malti-Douglas, Fedwa, *Women's Body, Women's World: Gender and Discourse in Arabo-Islamic Writing* (Princeton, NJ: Princeton University Press, 1992).

Meghdessian, Samira R., *The Status of the Arab Woman: A Select Bibliography* (New York: Greenwood Press, 1980).

Mernissi, Fatima, *Beyond the Veil: Male-Female Dynamics in Modern Muslim Society* (Bloomington, IN: Indiana University Press, 1987).

Mernissi, Fatima, *Doing Daily Battle* (New Brunswick, NJ: Rutgers University Press, 1989).

Mernissi, Fatima, *The Forgotten Queens of Islam* (Minneapolis: University of Minnesota Press, 1990).

Mernissi, Fatima, *The Veil and the Male Elite: A Feminist Interpretation of Women's Rights in Islam* (New York: Addison-Welsey, 1991).

Mikhail, Mona, *Images of Arab Women: Fact and Fiction* (Washington, D.C.: Three Continents Press, 1978).

Najjar, Orayb Aref, *Portraits of Palestinian Women* (Salt Lake City: Utah University Press, 1992).

Peteet, Julie, *Gender in Crisis: Women and the Palestinian Resistance Movement* (New York: Columbia University Press, 1982).

Raccagni, Michelle, *The Modern Arab Woman: A Bibliography* (Metuchen, NJ: Scarecrow Press, 1978).

Rugh, Andrea B., *Family in Contemporary Egypt* (Syracuse, NY: Syracuse University Press, 1987).

Sabbagh, Suha and Talhami, Ghada (eds.), *Images and Reality: Palestinian Women Under Occupation and in the Diaspora* (Washington, D.C.: Institute for Arab Women's Studies, 1989).

Sabbah, Fatna A., *Woman in the Muslim Unconscious* (Oxford: Pergamon Press, 1984).

Sha'aban, Bouthaina, *Both Right and Left Handed* (Bloomington, IN: Indiana University Press, 1988).

Sharawi, Huda, *Harem Years* (New York: Feminist Press, 1987).

Strum, Philippa, *The Women are Marching: The Second Sex and the Palestinian Revolution.* (New York: Lawrence Hill Books, 1992).

Tawil, Raymonda, *My Home, My Prison* (London: Zed Books, 1986).

Tillion, Germaine, *The Republic of Cousins: Women's Oppression in Mediterranean Society* (London: Saqi Books, 1986).

Toubia, Nahid, *Women of the Arab World* (London: Zed Books, 1988).

Tucker, Judith E. (ed.), *Old Boundaries, New Frontiers* (Bloomington, IN: Indiana University Press, 1993).

Tucker, Judith E., *Women in Nineteenth-Century Egypt* (New York: Cambridge University Press, 1984).

Tuqan, Fadwa, *A Mountainous Journey: An Autobiography* (London: The Women's Press, 1990).

Warnock, Kitty, *Land Before Honor: Palestinian Women in the Occupied Territories* (New York: Monthly Review Press, 1990).

Wikan, Unni, *Behind the Veil in Arabia* (Chicago: University of Chicago Press, 1982).

Young, Elise, *Keepers of Our History: Women and the Israeli-Palestinian Conflict* (New York: Teachers College Press, 1992).

Zenie-Zeigler, Wedad, *In Search of Shadows* (London: Zed Books, 1988).

Appendix A

General Union of Palestinian Women, Jerusalem-Palestine: Draft Document of Principles of Women's Rights (Third Draft)

PREAMBLE:

Based on the Declaration of Independence which was the outcome of the Nineteenth Session of the Palestine National Council in 1988, which reads: "The State of Palestine is the state for all Palestinians wherever they may be. It is the state for them in which they enjoy their collective national and cultural identity, and to pursue a complete equality of rights. In it will be safeguarded their political and religious convictions and their human dignity by means of a parliamentary democratic system of governance, itself based on freedom of expression and freedom to form parties. The rights of minorities will duly be respected by the majority, as minorities abide by decisions of the majority. Governance will be based on principles of social justice, equality, and non-discrimination in public rights of men or women, on the grounds of race, religion, color, or sex under the aegis of a constitution which ensures the rule of law and an independent judiciary";

Based on the United Nations Conventions, Universal Declaration of Human Rights and other international documents and conventions pertaining to political, civil, economic, social, and cultural rights, specifically the Convention on the Elimination of All Forms of Discrimination Against Women;

For the purpose of building a democratic Palestinian society which believes in the equality and social justice of all its individuals;

We the women of Palestine declare the Document of Principles of Women's Legal Status to be ratified and incorporated into the constitution and the legislation of the future Palestinian State.

GENERAL PROVISIONS:

We the women of Palestine, from all social categories and the various faiths, including workers, farmers, housewives, students, professionals, and politicians, promulgate our determination to proceed without struggle to abolish all forms of discrimination and inequality against women, which were propagated by the different forms of colonialism on our land, ending with the Israeli Occupation, and which were reinforced by the conglomeration of customs and traditions prejudiced against women, embodied in a number of existing laws and legislation. In order to build a democratic society which ensures equal opportunities for women in rights and obligations within the following principles:

The future Palestinian State and the National Authority must be committed, regardless of its jurisdiction, to the Declaration of Independence and to all international declarations and conventions pertaining to human rights, particularly the 1979 Convention on the Elimination of All Forms of Discrimination Against Women.

Enhance the principle of equality between women and men in all spheres of life, and declare so in the constitution, as well as in legislation of the National Authority, clearly and unequivocally. This is in addition to guaranteeing the practical implementation of this principle by taking legislative and administrative procedures to prohibit all forms of discrimination against women and repealing the status of inequality against them by endorsing legal protection for women similar to men and in all aspects.

The commitment to women's right to hold public posts whether through elections or appointment, women in judicial, legislative, or executive posts should be on an equal footing with men, and this should be ensured in a law that is compelling, functional, and implementable.

From the vision of the Palestinian women for a society of justice and equality, the general provisions stated above are basic guidelines from which we acquire support in order to:

Preserve a cohesive Palestinian society: We the women of Palestine comprise half of Palestine. We are an integral part of this society. We also believe that the issue of women's liberation and equality with men is the task of the society as a whole. Thus, we believe in the necessity in working hand in hand with men to establish a Palestinian society permeated with social justice and equality for all.

Enhance Palestinian culture and uniqueness: We the women of Palestine join all democratic forces in our vision which affirms that the level of human development is measured by the implementation of women's rights and the availability of equal opportunities for women in all spheres. Palestinian heritage embodies different visions of the role and positions of women in society. Therefore, we see that enhancing women's equality and respect of her rights requires from us the promoting of the positive side in our Palestinian and Arab heritage and culture.

Reinforce the national and social struggle of Palestinian women: The Palestinian women's struggle has been depicted over the decades of the Palestinian national struggle as an immeasurable contribution in all spheres; women were martyred and thousands were imprisoned. Palestinian women also played a vital role in the preservation of the unity of the Palestinian family as a social base to support individuals in the absence of a Palestinian national authority. Palestinian women were forced to delay many tasks associated with their social position and instead focus all their attention towards the issue of the national and political struggle. It is now the time to affirm that the issue of women's legal rights in all aspects is a cornerstone for building a democratic Palestinian society.

Achieve equality: We, the women of Palestine, see equal rights between men and women in all spheres as a basic principle for the emancipation of women and men. This requires a clear statement which unambiguously guarantees the equality of women and men in all Palestinian legislation. This also requires having legislative and administrative procedures to ensure its implementation. This demands that we unite our efforts to remove those social norms which prohibit women from success in society, in order to guarantee the respect of human rights and the principle of rule of law. From this juncture, we demand equality in the following:

Political Rights: To guarantee the right of women in voting, running for office, involvement in public referendums, and the ability to hold political and public judicial posts on all levels. This is in addition to equal opportunity with men in political parties, non-governmental organizations concerned with political and public life in Palestine, and the representation of the state in international and regional organizations as well as in diplomatic corps.

Civil Rights: To grant the woman her right to acquire, preserves or change her nationality. Legislation must also guarantee that her marriage to a non-Palestinian, or a change of her husband's nationality, while married, will not necessarily change the citizenship of the wife. This includes her freedom from the imposition of her husband's citizenship. Women should also be granted the right to give citizenship to her husband and children, be guaranteed the full freedom to move, travel, and choose her place of residency, and have guaranteed her right to adequate housing. Motherhood should be looked upon as a social post. House chores should be regarded as a task of social and economic value. The law should stand next to the woman to protect her from family violence and practices that infringe on any of her guaranteed rights, including her right to express herself, her right to join any activity, assembly, or association, by guaranteeing her right to go to court as a citizen with full rights.

Economic, Social, and Cultural Rights: The Constitution and Palestinian legislation must guarantee the equality of women at work, ensuring equal pay with men working in the same work, providing equal opportunities in promotion, training, compensation, rewards, health insurance, and maternity rights. Equality in making contracts, administering property, obtaining banking contracts and property mortgage in all procedures practiced in courts and judicial bodies. We also affirm the importance of equality in social welfare, health benefits, education, and training services, and the guarantee of her full equality regarding issues pertaining to personal status.

The efforts of women as well as all democratic forces in Palestinian society must unite to remove all obstacles hindering the equality of women with men. We must work hand in hand towards a democratic society which fulfills a comprehensive national independence, social justice, and equality.

This draft was signed by numerous women's groups in the West Bank who participated in rewriting the PLO's draft that came from Tunis.

Appendix B

STATISTICAL PROFILES

	Total population (millions) 1992	Population under 16 (millions) 1992	Annual no. of births (thousands) 1992	Annual no. of under-5 deaths (thousands) 1992	Under-5 mortality rate 1992	GNP per capita ($) 1992	% of under-5 children under-weight	% of children reaching grade 5	Total fertility rate 1992	Maternal mortality rate
Algeria	26.3	11.9	901	65	72	1830	9	95	4.9	140
Egypt	54.8	22.5	1732	95	55	630	9	91	4.2	270
Iraq	19.3	8.9	753	60	80	1500	12	72	5.7	120
Jordan	4.3	2.0	171	5	30	1120	6	91	5.7	48
Kuwait	2.0	0.8	54	1	17	16150	6	83	3.7	6
Lebanon	2.8	1.0	78	3	44	2150	—	—	3.1	—
Libya	4.9	2.3	206	21	104	5310	—	69	6.4	70
Morocco	26.3	11.1	854	52	61	1040	9	93	4.4	300
Oman	1.6	0.8	67	2	31	6490	23	63	6.8	—
Saudi Arabia	15.9	7.1	574	23	40	7940	—	43	6.4	41
Sudan	26.7	12.6	1128	187	166	420	35	92	6.1	550
Syria	13.3	6.7	569	23	40	1160	—	88	6.2	140
Tunisia	8.4	3.3	230	9	38	1740	10	89	3.5	50
United Arab Emirates	1.7	0.5	35	1	22	22220	—	78	4.5	—
Yemen	12.5	6.5	611	108	177	520	30	—	7.2	—

From The Progress of Nations 1994 UNICEF Report

NATIONAL PERFORMANCE GAPS

	GNP per capita 1992	Under-five mortality rate 1992			% of children reaching grade 5			% of under-five children underweight		
		Actual	Expected	Difference	Actual	Expected	Difference	Actual	Expected	Difference
Algeria	1830	72	43	-29	95	82	+13	9	13	+4
Egypt	630	55	97	+42	91	59	+32	9	22	+13
Iraq	1500	80	49	-31	72	78	-6	12	15	+3
Jordan	1120	30	60	+30	91	72	+19	6	17	+11
Kuwait	16150	17	12	-5	83	96	-13	6	3	-3
Lebanon	2150	—	—	—	—	—	—	—	—	—
Libya	5310	—	—	—	—	—	—	—	—	—
Morocco	1040	61	63	+2	69	70	-1	9	18	+9
Oman	6490	31	20	-11	93	92	+1	—	—	—
Saudi Arabia	7940	40	18	-22	63	92	-29	—	—	—
Sudan	420	166	125	-41	43	50	-7	35	26	-9
Syria	1160	40	59	+19	92	72	+20	—	—	—
Tunisia	1740	38	45	+7	88	81	+7	10	15	+5
United Arab Emirates	22220	22	10	-12	89	97	-8	—	—	—
Yemen	520	—	—	—	78	55	+23	30	24	-6

The national performance gap is the difference between a country's actual level of progress and the expected level for its per capital GNP.

From the Progress of Nations 1994 UNICEF Report

Percentage of girl children who reach at least grade 5 of primary school

Oman	93
Algeria	92
Syria	92
Jordan	90
United Arab Emirates	90
Tunisia	87
Kuwait	83
Egypt	80
Regional average	79
Yemen	66
Iraq	63
Morocco	59
Saudi Arabia	56
Sudan	40

Percentage of married women of child-bearing age who use family planning

Oman	9
Algeria	51
Syria	52
Jordan	35
United Arab Emirates	No data
Tunisia	50
Kuwait	35
Egypt	47
Regional average	44
Yemen	7
Iraq	18
Morocco	42
Saudi Arabia	No data
Sudan	9
Lebanon	Old data
Libya	No data

The female literacy rate as a percentage of the male literacy rate

Oman	No data
Algeria	66
Syria	65
Jordan	79
United Arab Emirates	Old data
Tunisia	76
Kuwait	87
Egypt	54
Regional average	67
Yemen	49
Iraq	70
Morocco	62
Saudi Arabia	66
Sudan	28
Lebanon	83
Libya	67

	% women literate 1970	% women literate 1990	% pt. rise
Saudi Arabia	2	48	46
Jordan	29	70	41
Tunisia	17	56	39
Libya	13	50	37
Algeria	11	46	35
Iraq	18	49	31
Syria	20	51	31

From the Progress of Nations 1994 UNICEF Report

Index